TWELVE CAMELS FOR YOUR WIFE

*An Englishman's Lifelong
Love Affair With Turkey*

By
GEORGE DEARSLEY

Copyright © 2021 George Dearsley
All rights reserved.

FOREWORD

Turkey has given me so many happy memories and the Turkish people have shown me untold kindnesses so I hope this book can in part repay them. I must thank my friend Peter Sands for his meticulous checking of the manuscript for errors and for his sound advice on how I might improve my storytelling. Thanks, too, to friend and author Jacky Hyams for re-reading the text for typographical mistakes. The book is dedicated to my wife Carolyn, daughters Charlotte and Sophie, to my extended family and also to my friend Jamie Philp, one of the funniest people I have ever known, who took his own life aged 48 in 2016 after a long battle against depression.

CONTENTS

Foreword	ii
Chapter One: Three Men In A Van	1
Chapter Two: First Impressions	16
Chapter Three: Held At Gunpoint	44
Chapter Four: Linked With An Assassin	54
Chapter Five: Danny And The Cockroach Hotel	75
Chapter Six: The Mongolian Circus	89
Chapter Seven: Earthquake	101
Chapter Eight: Mad About The Köy	124
Chapter Nine: Talking Turklish	145
Chapter Ten: The Red Crabs	162
Chapter Eleven: Arms Length From Death	170
Chapter Twelve: Paws For Thought	187
Chapter Thirteen: Food Glorious Food	200
Chapter Fourteen: Summer House	213
Chapter Fifteen: It Came From Chy-Nah	220
Chapter Sixteen: Mens Sana Corpore Sano	230
Chapter Seventeen: Very Superstitious	241

Chapter Eighteen: Kids And Camels 250

Chapter Nineteen: Annoying Habits 259

Chapter Twenty: Kind Hearts And Hospitality 275

Chapter Twenty One: Fate 288

Chapter Twenty Two: Moving On 296

CHAPTER ONE

THREE MEN IN A VAN

The man in the horn-rimmed glasses and black sweater sucked his teeth and stroked imaginary stubble on his chin. He seemed quite taken with the idea that I wanted to buy his royal blue Bedford fifteen hundredweight van to drive part way on the "trip of a lifetime" to Japan. But sentiment would play no part in this transaction. In 1971 money was tight and like every private seller he wanted as much as he could get.

"OK, you can have it for £150," he said.

"I really cannot go any lower."

My father Len, an ex-lorry driver turned postman, had already checked the vehicle over for obvious faults and found none. I looked in his direction and perceived the slightest of affirmative winks.

"It's a deal," I said. I handed over a bundle of notes I had sweated to earn in two student holiday jobs, delivering furniture and later pop records and turntables around London, and we shook hands. The man gave me the log book. I was twenty-one and now officially the proud owner of my first vehicle, licence number ARK 603.

Rain began to patter on the roof as we drove home to Hackney from Enfield, down the A10, passing the ground of my favourite football team Tottenham Hotspur, where I had learned to handle Rudyard Kipling's "twin impostors" Triumph and Disaster since I was nine years old. We would doubtless be meeting again in the future. I felt elated but also a little fearful. What began as a rather crazy fantasy was now becoming alarmingly real. The van was parked outside our semi-detached house at 71 Albion Drive, bought in the early Sixties for £1,000 from the son of our long-term Jewish landlord Mr Solomon, after he died. Over the next four months I divided my time between earning money for the adventure and kitting the van out as a mobile home. Other chores included organising an international driving licence, arranging insurance and obtaining a comprehensive series of road maps from the Automobile Association.

The idea for the trip had been conceived over a few beers among the dreaming spires of Oxford University, where this working-class lad had just spent three exhilarating years. My route to Oxford started from my tiny East London primary school, St Paul's, when I won a place to an all-boys boarding school Christ's Hospital, Sussex. On the day of the exam, I had German measles and had to sit at a desk fifteen feet in front of the three hundred other applicants. The school, a charity for pupils of less well-off parents, was to change my life and led to me winning an exhibition (a type of scholarship) to Oxford. I was the first ever pupil from St Paul's to go to that university. Chris Ball, my friend and fellow student at Oriel College, Oxford, was to be my co-traveller on the trip East. He had an uncle working for the customs authority in Kuwait who said if we could reach the Persian Gulf kingdom he would find us a berth on a cargo ship to Japan, via Singapore and Hong Kong.

Meanwhile, another Oxford student, Kate Johnson, had generously invited us to stay at her father's house in Tokyo, where he worked as an executive for a major oil company. Such offers don't come along too often and Liverpudlian Chris, a big Everton fan, and I both jumped at the chance to see something of the world before we started our careers. I had secured a job as a trainee reporter on a weekly newspaper in Whitley Bay, near Newcastle upon Tyne, so had to be back in England by late September 1972. Chris was more fluid. Over six feet tall, slim, with curly brown hair and thin avian nose, Chris had aspirations to become an actor and had already taken leading roles in productions by the Oxford University Dramatic Society.

The weeks leading up to our departure date of Friday March 24 dragged. I bought some thick foam for us to sleep on in the back of the van and cut it to size. I also built a cupboard with sliding doors inside the vehicle and stocked it with food, including twenty-four tins of meat balls in heavy onion gravy. We would cook on a collapsible camping stove fired by butane gas. I purchased and installed an array of kitchen utensils and cutlery and a five-gallon water tank.

Finally, the big day arrived and two carefully detonated alarm clocks woke me at 6.45am. My girlfriend Sue had arrived the night before to see me off. But our mood was sombre as she helped me load the final few items into the Bedford. The words of Harry Nilsson's song Without You jangled around my head.

No, I can't forget this evening

Or your face as you were leaving

But I guess that's just the way the story goes

You always smile but in your eyes your sorrow shows

Yes, it shows

There was to be a third passenger, or Arkonaut as we laughingly called ourselves, at least for part of the journey.

Another Oxford pal Jeremy Ward was intent on travelling to Iran and wanted to hitch a ride, possibly to Istanbul. He wasn't sure. With his long hair and round, metal-framed glasses, classics scholar Jeremy resembled John Lennon, to the slightly myopic. His three passions in life were music, football and smoking dope. I recall going into his university room one day and seeing him tearing pages from an expensive English-Greek dictionary to make joints. We were still loading the van when his unmistakable bounding gait came into view. His first words produced a logistical bombshell.

"George, sorry but I have lost my driving licence," he said. Chris had not yet passed his driving test and the hope was that Jeremy would share the driving duties.

"Never mind," I said. "We can't do much about it now."

We left home at 8am with 28,358 miles on the clock and drove to Bethnal Green tube station to pick up Chris. Then we detoured to Waterloo railway station to drop off Sue who was heading back to her flat in Guildford. There was a sense of nervous tension in the air. Chris pointed out the Moscow Narodny Bank in Moorgate where he had worked as a cleaner.

"You should have cleaned out the vault," I joked.

Producing an immaculate James Mason accent, thespian Chris looked into the back of the van.

"Did anybody die in this plane crash?" Within minutes he had changed to Michael Caine in the film Get Carter.

"You're a big man, but you're in bad shape. With me it's a full-time job. Now behave yourself."

On the journey to Dover the mood lurched from ebullient to pensive. Jeremy revealed a hitherto unknown phobia of gas containers.

"What if there's an explosion?" he posed.

"Our ashes will be found among a small lake of meatballs in gravy." Chris responded. Finally, we reached Dover and joined the queue to board the Roi Baudouin ferry at 11.30pm. We arrived at Ostend at 4.20am and motored straight to Brussels. Poor signposting meant we initially failed to find the road we needed to the town of Namur but we eventually located it and just after 8pm decided to pitch camp. Despite a great deal of scepticism, we enjoyed a hearty meal of Oxtail soup followed by meatballs.

Quite how we managed to sleep three people in a Bedford van I cannot recall. All I know is that a diary I kept said breakfast was brief, just a cup of tea and some biscuits. We headed to Luxembourg. We were low on petrol when we entered the town of Bande, only to find that everyone was attending a funeral. Every shop and garage were closed. With the needle on zero we managed to reach the town of Barniere de Champion and at last filled up. We crossed into Germany, following the Mosel river to Mülheim an der Ruhr and on to Coblenz. The city exploded on our right side with an apparently endless array of lights. Here the Mosel meets the Rhine and the street lamps weaved their own special light show on the shimmering water.

That night we camped outside Mainz. Jeremy's fear of a gas explosion was all but assuaged and we ate curried steak and kidney and rice. Now a new phobia emerged. Jeremy reckoned we were nearing the time of the year when vampires lurked. I went to bed with the wheel brace as a weapon and a crucifix, just in case. We awoke with no puncture marks in our necks. But Jeremy now complained of being dehydrated. We looked along the wonderful Rhine with its cargo boats and barges idle, then passed a series of hamlets that would have made wonderful Christmas cards. Every so often we would stare up at a medieval castle built high into the rocks.

We drove South, stopping briefly at a shop to buy three oranges for two Deutsch Marks (about 22p). A bunch of grapes was more than six DM (around 80 pence) which we thought was very expensive. So much for the Common Market which the UK would join in January. Luckily wine was exceptionally cheap but, as it was Sunday, shops were forbidden to sell it. I was struggling to remember any of my Grade Four O-level German. I recalled the word *schwer* (heavy). Chris had mastered *schönen tag* (good day) and Jerry said he knew the word for shit (*scheisse*).

"Well you're all set for bartering for hash then," Chris told Jerry. "You can say 'good day, heavy shit'."

We drove on through heavily wooded countryside to Karlsruhe. I rested in the van while Jeremy and Chris went to explore the town but they returned disillusioned that it had "no soul". We voted to hit the road to Basel, with a heavy rainstorm starting. The rain was so depressing however that we turned off the road between Ettingen and Rastatt and decided to camp.

Day four saw us reach Switzerland. We wanted to find a public bath. We felt grubby and needed a good wash. But the one we were directed to by a beautiful blonde-haired girl in an information office was closed on Mondays. Back on the road our route led us to Lucerne, then on to Göschenen. There we caught a train through the mountains to Airolo. At the end of a long tunnel we emerged from total darkness to a stunning plateau bathed in bright sunlight and walls of snow sloping away on either side of us.

We pushed on to Lugano, a lakeside town, which was like I imagined Monte Carlo to be. There were hotels and restaurants with tables down to the roadside, palm trees, fountains, steep cobbled roads meandering to squares and churches. We wandered the town for two hours before taking the Chiasso road and pitching camp. A phone call at a local post office brought good news. One of Chris's friends, Susie, was working as an au pair in Milan and had arranged for us to spend a night or two at a flat belonging to one of her pals, Maria. Susie's employer was a famous record producer called Lucio Salvini who had worked with top orchestra conductor Herbert von Karajan. He was away on business so we were able to relax in his luxury apartment on the Via Santa Agnese, with an original painting by the Spanish artist Joan Miro on the wall. Italian elections were due and Susie warned us the city was dangerous. A left-wing multi-millionaire publisher called Giangiacomo Feltrenelli, who had financed a group of militants called *Gruppi di Azione Partigiana* (Partisan Action Groups, GAP) had been blown to pieces in an explosion at the foot of a power pylon near Milan. He had feared a right-wing coup and the speculation was that he had been killed by his own explosives while trying to sabotage the city's electricity supply.

Despite the concerns we joined Susie as she took her charges Simone and Valentina, both under ten, to the park. It was the Milan rush hour and we enjoyed seeing commuters dashing to work as we relaxed sitting on a bench. Nearby a few teenagers were kicking a faded leather football around and an elderly couple were feeding the birds. That evening the record producer's wife Wilma had invited us to dinner. The door was opened by a very attractive thirty-year-old woman with blonde ringlets, like Lee Remick in the film Loot. She handed us two bottles of Martini and a jug of ice. She spoke good English, but with a heavy Italian accent.

"If I entertain you, I cannot get on and prepare this most wonderful meal," she said. Around forty-five minutes later we sat down to a delicious Tortellini in guscio di pane (pasta in bread shells) as a starter, followed by veal and salad. We drank wine, brandy with our coffee and champagne as a nightcap.

How the other half live. We left at two in the morning to go to Maria's flat. Despite our late arrival and the fact that she had work that morning, Maria, like Wilma, was a warm and generous host. She showed us to our room and we crashed out.

We had arranged to receive several phone calls at noon from loved ones and also from people who had promised to help us on our journey. But before that we visited the Santa Maria delle Grazie to view Leonardo's The Last Supper, Chris and I getting in free on our international student cards. What a privilege it was to view that wonderful work of art. The colours may have faded over time but the painting generated a special kind of aura. The church was bombed in 1943 but the masterpiece survived and the workmen who rebuilt the structure had to work carefully around it. We also visited the Duomo, Milan Cathedral, and snuck a look inside La Scala Opera House, where they were preparing for a performance of Elektra, a one-act opera by Richard Strauss. The auditorium was bathed in dark shadows and although the stage was filled only by workmen and scenery-builders I closed my eyes and tried to imagine Napoleon or Mussolini in the Royal Box. In the foyer was a collection of bric-a-brac including old violins, programmes, sheet music, death masks, and plaster cast hands of Chopin. On the way back to Maria's flat we were accosted by a svelte, black-haired, twenty-something gypsy girl.

"You want fun?" She said. We hurried on.

Next stop was Trento where more extravagant Italian hospitality awaited. We set off in the early evening using the autostrada, driving mile after colourless mile with hardly any distance markers. Eventually we reached the valley town with its twisting, narrow one-way streets and headed into the hills to find Pergine, where Maria's aunt lived. She had kindly agreed to entertain us. One of Maria's cousins came to meet us and led us in her car through the cobbled, dusty streets, illuminated by a full moon. On the road we saw dozens of hilltop fires. Susie had told us they were lit by prostitutes signalling to their customers.

Pergine was the kind of place that every frustrated and stressed city-dweller would love to find. "Simpatico" I believe the Italians say. We stayed in a very old house, which was made into two flats, on the edge of town. Maria's father-in-law lived upstairs and her aunt and cousins, Lucia, Renata and Jonny lived downstairs. The following morning Lucia drove us to an old castle and later Renato showed off his new five hundred cc motorbike and convinced me to ride pillion. I had never been on a motorcycle and was more than a little nervous. But I soon got the hang of it. I clung on to Renato's leather jacket learning to sway left and right when he did. After exploring the countryside for an hour, we went back for lunch.

Lucia's mum said it was simple, peasant food. But it was a gorgeous array of spaghetti mixed with oil and grated cheese, followed by liver, cold potatoes and tomatoes and, of course, half a dozen glasses of red wine. Despite bloated stomachs we had arranged to play football in the afternoon, a five-a-side match against local youths. We fell badly behind at first but by full-time the score was 6-6 and honours were even. We returned to Maria's home to clean up and Lucia's mother gave us more wine and a light fruit cake which you had to dip in wine and suck dry before swallowing. Before dinner we drove into Trento to buy some flowers for our generous host. When we returned, she had prepared yet another sumptuous meal, minestrone soup, followed by eggs and salad and cheese and, of course, more wine.

As if the day had not been exciting enough, we then drove high into the hills to a disco where we danced and drank until the early hours. When they totted up the bill it came to five hundred lira each, about 32p. We drove home over bone-shaking roads and stopped at a pizza shop bustling with life at 1am. I presume Italy had some drink-driving laws but nobody seemed to take any notice. Maybe the police didn't patrol the small towns and villages much. We shared a pizza and drank more wine as the whole shop broke into a sing-song. We matched the Italians' songs with some Beatles' hits. It was half past three in the morning before we crawled into bed.

The van had been leaking oil for a few days. I had been topping it up but someone suggested taking it to Il Mechanico, who ran a small repair shop on the outskirts of the town. After a thorough inspection he found three nuts missing from the gearbox. As Italian sizes were different from the UK it was going to be nearly impossible to find replacements. Also, it was Easter Sunday and all shops were closed. But Lucia seemed to know everyone in the area and an hour later we took a handful of nuts and bolts back to Il Mechanico. In a few minutes the problem was fixed.

It was time for us to resume our journey and after fulsome embraces, handshakes, kisses and smiles we drove off into the sunset, heading to Verona, then Padua and on to Venice. It was Day thirteen of our trip and the excitement of seeing the city of canals was tempered by waking to what sounded like thousands of ball bearings hammering on the roof. It was raining hard. But our mood was lightened when Jeremy confessed that he had not brought any rain wear with him. Instead he decided to cut three holes in a huge black bin-liner and wear that to tour the city. Chris and I were doubled up shedding tears of laughter as Jeremy "tested" his invention in a car park. However, fearing public ridicule, he instead opted for a colourful Indian blanket which he wrapped around himself, like an actor in a Spaghetti Western.

Venice is a "must see" destination and we spent eight hours soaking up its incredible treasures. The Piazza San Marco, once described by Napoleon as "the most beautiful drawing room in Europe", is a stupendous centrepiece. But everywhere we looked we saw jaw-dropping sights such as St Mark's Church, founded in 828, and embellished up until the sixteenth century, a striking mixture of Greek, medieval, Byzantine, Tuscan, Lombard and Venetian art. The rain had eased to a light drizzle but the light was good, showing off the city's natural colours. We stood on the Rialto, toured the Academia Galleries and the Peggy Guggenheim building, housing a fabulous collection of paintings by Picasso, Dali, Bacon, Pollock and others and walked leaden-footed back to the van in the early evening underneath a blazing sunset, a real Tiepolo sky.

We headed South, seeing the Adriatic for the first time. At Mesola we crossed a rickety bridge, the lorry in front causing the warped planks to buckle and ride up ominously.

"It's the troubled bridge over water," sang Chris to the Simon & Garfunkel tune. Day sixteen saw us reach Florence, which was teeming with tourists, choking and sweating in the hot sunshine. The Uffizi Gallery was like Oxford Street in the January sales but we were able to admire great works of art such as Giotto's Madonna and Child, Rembrandt's self-portrait and other masterpieces by Michaelangelo, Albrecht Dürer, Caravaggio, da Vinci, Rubens and many more.

We set off for Rome, arriving in time to catch the Pope's noon address before heading to the Colosseum and the Circus Maximus. Maybe tourist fatigue was setting in but after only three hours in the capital we plotted a course for Naples, following the coast road in the warm afternoon sunshine. Day eighteen was a Monday and while millions of commuters back home were trudging off to work, we awoke to breakfast on the Mediterranean. We washed our grubby clothing and bodies and spent a day relaxing by the sea.

The following day Jeremy kept repeating "See Naples and Die" a phrase made famous by Johann Wolfgang von Goethe. But as the bay of Naples came into view it seemed diseased with scores of industrial complexes and thick black billowing smoke. As we neared the city, we passed the debris of a student riot. Stones and pieces of brick littered the road and heavily armed police and soldiers stood around looking threatening. Parking was impossible. Every second Neapolitan seemed to have a white hat and a bunch of tickets. When we eventually found a space, a group of shifty-looking youths straight out of Fagin's crime school, crowded around the van trying to buy English pounds for two thousand lira, about five hundred more than the normal bank rate. Whether their notes were real or fake we never found out. Others offered to sell a variety of goods, clothes, rings, watches, at a "special price". The atmosphere was oppressive and menacing so we drove off to Pompeii.

Not that driving was any less fraught. Italians either hogged the narrow roads, meandering slowly without a care in the world, like Sunday drivers, or else came up behind you at speed honking their horns and overtaking through the narrowest of gaps. As one car passed, I spotted a sign in the back window which read: "Attention, winner in twelve crashes." Pompeii, by contrast, was an oasis of calm. An elderly curator took us around a very old house and later the public brothel where we saw a sign saying: "Ten different ways to make love." We were intrigued.

"Very nice," said the guide in an accent similar to the one Borat would make famous years later.

Next stop was Brindisi where we asked about taking a ferry to Greece. Unlike the North, the South of Italy was mired in abject poverty, slum housing and depressing architecture and we felt no urge to explore. We reached the port and caught the 10.30pm ferry, driving on to the ship two hours before departure, making ourselves as comfortable as possible in blue aeroplane seats. I slept fitfully and awoke at 7am with the ship in choppy waters to the sound of retching from several mainly pasty-faced Greek passengers. By 10am we had arrived at Igoumenitsa on the Greek mainland. As we waited to pass through customs, we saw stony faced officials meticulously search the three cars ahead of us. But the officer who came to look at our vehicle took a perfunctory glance and waved us through.

We were low on water and I stopped to ask an old woman, who was scrubbing clothes on her front doorstep, where we could buy some. She gestured to a field and under an aluminium cover we found an old well. We covered more than one hundred miles, stopping at Agrinio to buy provisions. The following day Jerry was planning to part company, seeking to reach Istanbul quicker than our more leisurely route allowed. We took another ferry across the Gulf of Patras to Rio and on reaching Patras we drove to the bus station to check on buses Jerry might take to the Greek capital. They left every hour but the next six were fully booked. So instead he caught a train to Athens. Depending on connections, it would not take him more than a day to reach Istanbul I didn't hear from him until I was back in England. In a letter he wrote: "I'm in Tehran selling hash to survive."

"Do they like corned beef out there, then?" my innocent mother asked.

Chris and I hit the coast road to Corinth and, after exploring the once famous city-state we journeyed through Argos and

Napflion to Tolo. Here on a previous visit Chris had sold a belt to a Greek waiter. It was a long-shot but we found him still serving in the same bar. To celebrate the reunion, he produced a bottle of ouzo and refused any payment for it. An hour later we were all dancing like Anthony Quinn in the 1964 film Zorba the Greek. The next day we detoured to visit the Ancient Theatre of the Asklepieion at Epidaurus. The incredible amphitheatre could hold fourteen thousand people and the acoustics were so good you could hear footsteps on the stage from the backmost row eighty yards away. Day twenty-seven saw us in Athens. I was expecting mail from home at the central post office but there was none. I felt the same gnawing emptiness that I had experienced years before at boarding school on days when the post monitor laid out the letters after breakfast and my name was missing. We made our way to the Acropolis, nudging our way past throngs of Americans. I saw an elderly Yank, Nikon slung round his neck, wearing cream cotton slacks and a straw Fedora

"The Parthenon? Do you mean that pile of stones on top of the Acropolis?" he asked his wife.

That evening we went out for dinner. Chris bought himself a natty, navy blue sailor's cap that made him look like the man from the St. Bruno tobacco advert. I bought an English newspaper to find Tottenham had drawn 1-1 against AC Milan in Italy to reach the UEFA Cup Final. The news made up for the earlier disappointment at the post office.

On the following two days we clocked up more than four hundred miles, travelling via Delphi to Thessaloniki. Day thirty-two, Monday April 24, saw us arrive at the Turkish border at Edirne. I knew nothing about Turkey and was quite unprepared for the excitement and wonder that awaited us. I had no idea I was about to set foot in a country that was to captivate me and shape the rest of my life.

CHAPTER TWO

FIRST IMPRESSIONS

A guard looked at my passport and then fixed me with an icy stare. His olive-green shirt had sweat stains around the armpits and his jaw displayed dark stubble even though it was just after 11am. His cubicle was drab and badly in need of an air freshener. I gave a weak, half smile as he looked downwards again. Then as if trying to break the bench he was sitting behind he brought the metal stamp down with an almighty thud.

"Next," he said, with the dispassionate air of a man whose shift still had several hours to run. Chris had got out to stretch his legs.

"Come on, let's go," I said and he clambered back into the van's passenger seat. Sniffer dogs had already given our vehicle their blessing, their bored handlers chatting and having a smoke.

Ipsala, the nearest town to the border crossing, was unremarkable and certainly not worth exploring. Even today it merits only sixteen lines in Wikipedia. My diary read: "We drove into Turkey crossing the river Evros at 11am and passing through customs at Ipsala without incident. We pulled off the road at Malkara and, for the first time since we left England, I felt a genuine fear of the strangely-clad people with their weird stares and glinting eyes. Turkey was already beginning to create an atmosphere which raised the hairs on the back of my neck." That fear was soon to change to intrigue and then to warm affection. Our future plans depended on what we could do with the van. We knew from research done previously that it was illegal to sell it in Turkey. So, to progress to Kuwait and possibly Japan we would have to garage it somewhere. If that proved impossible, Chris would have to go on alone and I would spend time in Turkey before returning to the UK.

As we drove along the E80 I spotted a dog in the distance standing motionless in the middle of the road. I slowed down and as I drew nearer, I sounded my horn, hoping it would run to safety. But at that moment a coal lorry overtook me at 40 mph and its right wheel arch smashed into the petrified creature's hind quarters with a sickening thud. I swerved to avoid bloody remains. I would have stopped but there was no chance the dog could have survived. The dog was a *kangal* used for guarding sheep. In the mirror I spotted a young shepherd boy anxiously running to the scene and sheep scattered nearby. We detoured off the main road and camped on a beach near Tekirdag. A local gave us some fresh vegetables and a drink of *rakı*, Turkey's famous anise-flavoured alcoholic drink.

In the morning we took the road to Silivri. To our left was verdant farmland and to our right beaches with waves crashing on to the shore. A shopkeeper sold us a hot, doughy loaf for the equivalent of 2p in English money, some oranges and cheese. By nightfall we had reached Yeşilköy on the outskirts of Istanbul. We settled down in a secluded factory car park and were almost ready to sleep when a group of night watchmen appeared with truncheons and torches. We were fearful they might become aggressive. But they quickly realised we were foreigners and, despite no common language, they seemed happy for us to stay. After smiles and handshakes, they continued with their rounds. The following morning, however, we were rudely awakened by two police officers banging on the roof of the van with batons. They weren't so conciliatory. So, we dressed hurriedly and drove off.

By 8.30am we were walking in the courtyard of the Blue Mosque. Everywhere we went we were accosted by small boys trying to sell us postcards, souvenirs or sheets of photographic slides.

"Mister, Mister, Mister," they screamed. We passed a group of hippies playing Frisbee in the park and headed to Taksim to check out the Syrian and Iraqi consulates, only to find they were closed due to a special holiday. Instead we detoured to the British consulate where an official advised us that we could garage the vehicle at most customs depots.

After further inquiries at a Turkish government office we were told we could leave the van at Nusaybin on the Southern border and travel by train to Baghdad and from there by bus to Kuwait. At Istanbul's main post office, we collected a letter from Kate Johnson's mother in Tokyo confirming the arrangements of our stay. So far so good. All that remained was to work out our route to Nusaybin. We wandered Istanbul on foot, crossing the Galata Bridge with its floating causeway wobbling in the choppy sea. Then we retraced our steps and headed to the Grand Bazaar, a sprawling collection of labyrinthine streets, passageways and corridors making up one of the oldest markets in the world. Most things were quite cheap but the Afghan coats we had set our hearts on buying were quite expensive at between £15 and £20.

We returned to the van and drove along the European side of the Bosphorus to the affluent quarter of Bebek, where film stars and top footballers lived. We stopped to make tea and were approached by five young Turkish lads. They spoke little English but invited us to play football with them near their home in Beşiktaş, three miles South. They piled into the back of the van and we drove back along the famous waterway dividing Europe and Asia, parking up in a side street. The "pitch" was a tiny patch of grass on the side of a busy dual carriageway but it served its purpose. Afterwards, we were joined by another of the gang, a fourteen-year-old boy called Levent, who spoke far more English. The questions came thick and fast.

"Where are you from?"

"Where are you going?"

"How long will you stay in Turkey?"

"Do you like Turkey?"

Soon Levent's mother Suzan appeared with tea and a tray of sandwiches. We sat around the van while Levent wrote out a list of useful Turkish phrases which included "how much does it cost?".

"Turkish people will stare at you. If you feel uncomfortable just say this. *Siz neden bize bakıyorsunuz?* Why are you looking at us?" he said. That evening the boys took us to a house where university students lived. We played music and talked until about 11am. Levent's friend Mahmut wrote in my diary in Turkish. It translated: "I am pleased to meet you. I guess you like Turkey. Thanks for the hours that we spent together." I didn't know it at the time but Levent would become a lifelong friend. My love affair with the country had begun.

Day thirty-five was an important one. We rose ludicrously early because I had set an alarm clock wrongly and drove to Taksim Square. We parked up and scurried through the rain to the Iraqi consulate where an astonished workman was whitening the shiny stone steps. My stupidity with the clock now became clear. Two yawning policemen pointed to their watches. It was only 6.30am. Shame-faced we trudged back to the van for shelter, returning at 9am to fill out a dozen forms and leaving our passports to be appropriately stamped so we could take our visas. We were told to come back at 1.30pm so went off sightseeing, climbing to the top of the Galata Tower and exploring the archaeological museum, including the magnificent tomb of Alexander the Great. At the central post office, we collected a letter from Chris's uncle Alan confirming the arrangements to find us two berths on a freighter to Japan. The timings meant I would be able to spend three to four weeks in Japan before returning.

We drove back to Beşiktaş to meet Levent and his mates and play another game of football. But when we arrived, we discovered there were at least two hundred schoolboys crowded around a different football area to the one we had used the day before, all chanting our names. After the match they followed us back to the van peering through the windows as if we were Hollywood superstars. The university students invited us to dinner again and over a meal of fish and salad, washed down with beer, we chatted about the kind of things students discussed in those days, mainly politics. Our hosts talked about Turkey's left-wing revolutionary movements and the state's iron grip on the country via the police and the military. Changing the subject, Levent said that, if the law allowed - which sadly it didn't - we could sell our van for around £900.

The following day the lads knocked on our van windows on their way to school. Soon we were heading to the Syrian consulate to repeat the form filling and to secure further visas. We needed passport photographs so we stopped at a shop called Foto Selvi in Sıraselviler Caddesi, near Taksim. The portly, moustache-wearing owner led me to a wooden stool and I sat while he organised spotlights and then stood next to an ancient wooden plate camera. It had no controls other than a lens cap, which the man removed with a flourish, judging the exposure by the time it took his arm to make one extravagant circle before replacing it. Little did he know that in England his expertise had been overtaken in every train and bus station by a small electronic booth. The resulting black and white photographs were perfect, albeit my pose was a little aggressive. More than twenty-five years later I found myself in Istanbul again needing passport photographs and called into the same shop.

"You won't remember me, but I came here in 1972," I told the same man.

"I'll look in my files and make you some copies," he replied.

"No, that's ok. You can do a new set," I replied. Last of the big spenders. He was still using the old plate camera.

We went off to tour Topkapi Palace. Sultan Mehmed the Conqueror ordered its construction in 1459, six years after the conquest of Constantinople. Atatürk turned it into a museum. Its treasures included the Spoonmaker's Diamond as well as Ottoman clothing, weapons, armour, religious relics, illuminated manuscripts and much more. The palace was made famous by the 1964 crime film Topkapi starring Peter Ustinov. That afternoon, back in Beşiktaş, Mahmut showed us a shop where we could buy provisions for our onward journey. But after making our selection, he refused to let us pay and handed over some lira notes. We learned later than his family was quite wealthy but he was only about fifteen and we felt really guilty. I would later arrange to bring him a pair of Adidas football boots which in those days only Turkish professional players wore. He became the envy of his neighbourhood.

In the evening we walked with Levent, Mahmut and two other friends to the side of the Bosphorus and drank tea. The cafe was full of old men smoking shisha pipes. Chris was keen to try one but because the lads refused to let us pay for anything, we decided just to drink tea. The following day we crossed the Bosphorus to watch Fenerbahçe beat Karşikaş 2-0. One or two players might have got into English second division teams but overall the standard was poor. Two years earlier Fenerbahçe had amazingly beaten Manchester City 2-1 in Istanbul in the second leg of a European Cup tie, having drawn 0-0 in Manchester. All the locals were keen to remind any foreigner they met, probably in the same way Americans celebrated the 1-0 win over England in the 1950 World Cup. That night was very cold and Levent brought us a pot of tea from his house because our butane gas canister had expired.

"Two blankets, tonight," Chris cautioned. The next morning Levent again brought us tea in bed.

"We need haircuts," we told him.

"Don't worry. I have a relative who is a barber. I'll take you to his shop." He explained there were four styles, numbered one, two, three and four. Number four, we learned was a short back and sides and number one like Yul Brynner. At 11am Mahmut arrived with bread and salami for breakfast and an English newspaper showing England had lost 3-1 to Germany at Wembley. We couldn't believe it. This was the first time any German side had beaten England on British soil and they had knocked England out of the European Championships. Revenge indeed for 1966, with Uli Hoeness, Gunter Netzer and Gerd Müller scoring for the enemy.

That afternoon we drove to Sariyer on the Bosphorus and drank more tea. Mahmut disappeared and came back with cakes and bread sticks. In the evening we drove back to Taksim to go to a cinema to watch a cowboy film called in Turkish *At, Kadın, ve Şikayet* translated as A Horse a Woman and a Grievance. "Based on Hamlet," screamed the poster, implausibly.

The following day, after a visit to Levent's barber relative it was time to say our goodbyes or at least *yakında görüşürüz* - see you soon. We took Levent, Mahmut and two friends with us as far as Kabitaş where, after a final set of photographs, we shook hands and drove on to the car ferry across the Bosphorus.

Day forty saw us reach Ankara, the capital, but sadly lacking the dynamism of Istanbul. After some perfunctory sightseeing we left the city at 4pm and headed towards Adana. The countryside in the fading sunlight was stunning. On one side were honeycomb hills and on the other a huge Salt Lake. We camped just off the road midway between Şereflikoçhisar and Aksaray, in a side road of brick-red baked mud, praying the rain would hold off. Overnight there had been a shower and the mud stuck to our shoes but fortunately we were able to pull back on to the main road. We were approaching the Anatolian plateau and the landscape grew ever more barren. Houses were mainly constructed with mud and the people had faces like dried figs from a tough life in the fields. Between Aksaray and Nevşehir we passed three ruined caravansaries, the old roadside inns where travellers could rest and recover from the day's journey.

Next stop was Göreme, now a massive tourist centre, but back in1972 relatively undiscovered. The strange volcanic fairy chimneys came into view as we meandered down a twisting road to the valley below. We spent hours touring the fresco-filled churches and adjacent homes built into the rocks. Nearly fifty years later my daughter Charlotte would rise above this incredible, fairytale location in a hot air balloon.

Our route took us to Kayseri and later Malatya. That evening we parked up in the middle of nowhere about thirty-five miles from the nearest town or village. We woke the following morning to find three men peering in through the windscreen. They were like extras from the film Lawrence of Arabia, swathed in headscarves and armed with museum exhibit rifles and bandoliers of bullets. We learned later that they were probably Yörüks, a tribe that has criss-crossed Anatolia for centuries. The name comes from the Turkish verb *yürümek*, to walk. They live in woollen tents, usually head for the mountains in summer and return to the plains in winter. In the midthirteenth century there were more than two hundred thousand in the Aegean area alone. Nowadays there are only a few hundred, surviving by breeding animals. According to documentary film-maker İffet Eren Danışman Boz, during migration nomads walk approximately four hundred kilometres (around two hundred and fifty miles) with camels and goats, their only source of livelihood.

The faces of our visitors had more cracks than an ancient leather sofa and enough gold teeth to buy a top of the range antique hand-woven carpet. Behind them stood two horses and a camel, looking bored and swatting flies with their heads. We climbed out of the back of the van in trepidation, wondering whether this would be our final moments on Earth. One of the men began jabbering in an accent I couldn't detect. But their body language seemed friendly and soon we were shaking hands. We showed them photographs of loved ones and smiled a lot as they circled the vehicle. They looked admiringly as if our battered van was a brand-new Lamborghini. Maybe they wanted to make us an offer to buy it. Finally, I had an idea. I rummaged in the back of the van and pulled out two tins of meatballs in onion flavoured gravy, offering them as a gift. The men seemed delighted. After more smiles and handshakes, we went our separate ways. Chris and I never stopped to wonder whether the tribesmen possessed a tin opener.

We were now just four hundred miles from Nusaybin and the van was behaving itself, except for a slight misfiring, especially in low gear or on a steep hill. My knowledge of car maintenance was rudimentary to say the least but the best guess was dirt in the carburettor. After a short comfort break the van wouldn't start. I checked the spark plugs and they seemed very oily and black. I pulled out the manual and began working my way through the likely possibilities. This was the moment we had dreaded. We were stuck in the middle of nowhere. No telephone. No language. And we hadn't seen a car all day. How long would we be isolated here? I had just finished cleaning the plugs when we spotted a vehicle in the distance. Minutes later a battered Land Rover pulled up and a bald Turk with a huge black handlebar moustache got out. He could speak no English but realised we were in trouble.

"Ah, Bedford," he beamed. He motioned for me to start the ignition. The sound he heard prompted him to pull an electrical screwdriver from an inside pocket. He then dismantled the distributor and tightened something inside. After five minutes of poking around he put everything back together and asked me to try the ignition again. Now it fired up first time and idled smoothly. Our prayers had somehow been answered. I offered him some money but he refused it. However, he spotted some sandpaper we had brought from England and we gladly gave him a couple of sheets. He couldn't have looked any happier if we had given him next week's winning national lottery numbers.

We pushed on to Elazığ where we ran into a series of police road blocks. There had been a plane hijacking a day earlier and police were hunting suspects. Just outside the town we camped for the night. Completing the final two hundred miles or so to Nusaybin seemed like a fairly simple task. But at Mardin, around fifty miles from our target, the road disintegrated into a dirt track with potholes the size of basins. Rain had fallen steadily all day and speed was impossible. Mud and dirt sprayed up from the wheels coating both sides of the vehicle with a thick red grime. Nusaybin was a scruffy town of grey-black ramshackle shops, disconsolate farmworkers with weather-beaten faces and shuffling animals. At last we reached the customs depot and darted through a heavy downpour into a shabby office. The bored official inside spoke a few words of English. But his answers to our questions were not what we wanted to hear.

"There are no facilities here for garaging your vehicle," he said. "The nearest place you can do this is Kilis." When we looked at the map, we realised Kilis was about three hundred miles due West. We were crestfallen. The advice we had been given in Istanbul was totally wrong. In future years I would learn always to check information, especially directions, many times over. Most Turks are so willing to help they will say anything rather than admit they don't know. Best to ask three or four different people and see if you get the same answer more than once. I gave Chris the option of catching the Baghdad train alone but he insisted on staying with me. It was a gut-wrenching task to follow the road that ran parallel with the Syrian border.

We set off at 6pm, stopped for food after about an hour and then drove on into the night, despite already having covered nearly three hundred miles that day over treacherous terrain. According to our map the road was meant to be unsurfaced. But after passing Kiziltepe it proved to be the best since we had left Ankara. Every few miles we would spot two border guards crouched over leaning against their rifles with their hands deep into their pockets desperately trying to keep warm. Some ninety minutes further on the road began to break up again. We climbed into desolate hills and camped fifty miles from Şanlıurfa. That night our sleep was broken by two lorry drivers peering in through the front window. We waved angrily at them and they melted away into the darkness. We were back underway by 6.30am and hadn't gone far when the heavily cracked asphalt disintegrated into red mud. We crawled along at around fifteen mph until after 9am when the surface improved and speeds of forty mph were possible. We reached Kilis at noon.

At the customs depot an officer looked at us as if aliens had landed. He summoned a teacher from the local school to interpret and, to our delight, told us we could garage the van there for as long as we wished at three Turkish lira a day, (about 10p), the price of packet of cigarettes. The teacher kindly offered to store all the movables from the van at his house, which we respectfully declined. We were slightly suspicious of his intentions and decided the stuff was safer at the police compound. A car appeared and the driver, a stunt double for Oliver Hardy, took Chris, me and the teacher to the Syrian border about seven miles away. We assumed this was a goodwill gesture but once on the road we heard the driver mumble as he rubbed his thumb and forefinger together. We were informed we were in a taxi and the fare was sixty-five lira. We bartered Hardy down to fifty (about £1.30).

On the Syrian side another taxi was waiting and after more negotiating we were on our way to A'zaz for five Syrian pounds (about 45p). From there we took a far cheaper taxi, four times the distance for half the earlier price and arrived in Aleppo. At an information office we learned there were no buses to Baghdad and only two trains a week, the next one leaving two days later at 11pm, cost thirty Syrian pounds for a third-class ticket (about £2.70). The frustrating thing was that the rail line ran all along the border and right past Nusaybin. We had no option but to find a hotel and the one we chose quickly proved to double as a popular brothel. But we had a bed each and a cold tap for seven Syrian pounds in total, (about 63p). We went for a meal of meat and vegetable stew with rice, the only thing we had eaten in twenty-four hours, except for two oranges.

That night at the hotel there was a screaming altercation between an Arab woman and the proprietor, plus drunken carousing in the street outside until 3am. Car horns also blared and when we finally nodded off a muezzin woke us up with his call to prayer. The next day, Sunday May 7, our plans changed again. We discovered we could catch a bus to Damascus and then another bus to Baghdad or Basra. We were assured the bus service was good and we could avoid another night in the hotel. As we sat in a park awaiting the bus's departure a group of men and schoolboys surrounded us. Some of the school pupils spoke English and described the explosive political situation in the Middle East. Little did they know what horrors future decades would bring.

The bus left at 5.30pm and was built like a tank, with hard leather seats and huge tyres. The driver's hooter was like a tug-boat horn and was worked by pulling a cord dangling through a hole in the roof, where our bags were stored. We surveyed our fellow passengers, mostly soldiers returning to camp from leave. At one stop most of the soldiers disembarked to buy lettuces which they washed under a tap inside the bus. A mechanic, who must have weighed at least twenty-five stones, flung out a flabby arm and offered a lettuce to Chris and me. With an hour to go we started talking to the soldiers and began to sing them English pop songs. Their faces broke into smiles to reveal their gold reserves embedded in their gums.

We arrived at Damascus at midnight, found a hotel and slept the moment our heads hit the straw-filled pillows. We were wandering around a market the following day when a man approached us.

"American? German? English?" he asked.

"English," was said in unison.

"Come, let's drink tea," he replied. I was immediately suspicious because I had read stories about police informants befriending foreigners and then deliberately dropping drugs into their luggage when they weren't looking in order to claim a large reward. The stranger said his name was Hassan and he had fought for Britain in the Second World War before being captured at Tobruk, spending four years in a prisoner of war camp. In 1946, for reasons unclear, he claimed he had been repatriated to Liverpool. It all sounded like bullshit but we gave him the benefit of the doubt. We sat outside a cafe as Hassan began to outline a plan that would earn us "good money".

"Kuwait is a wonderful city," he opined. "But the one thing it doesn't have is damask. You can buy the fabric from my cousin's shop and sell it for twice the price in Kuwait. No problem." Our budget was very tight and any way to augment our meagre funds seemed like a good idea. After finishing our tea, we walked a couple of blocks to his relative's emporium. All manner of cloth was stacked high in bundles. We chose a bale of pink and silver damask, thanked our new friend and headed off to find the bus station, satisfied with our pioneering entry into the Arabic rag trade.

"I will even contact you in Kuwait and help you to sell it," Hassan assured us.

The bus left at 2pm and the journey to Kuwait was an unforgettable experience, forty-four hours across the desert with very few roads, navigating by compass and sharing the bus with a motley assortment of passengers, caged birds, chickens and a goat. Stupidly we completely forgot to bring any food with us. As we took our seats two young boys got on carrying a tin bath. They placed it in the aisle. A few minutes later a swarthy man with body odour issues and a vivid scar on his face emerged with a large, black plastic bin. He tipped it up and dropped a three-foot long block of ice into the bath. This would be our refreshment for the road trip. As it melted, we reached in with paper cups for a drink. After ninety minutes we crossed the border into Iraq. The horizon seemed to merge into one expanse of sand and brush grass. We had our passports checked four times, three times at outposts and once at a central customs depot where we were forced to wait for nearly two hours. A customs officer made a list of every passenger and their baggage. Some signed their names against the inventory, others simply left an inky thumb print.

Back on the road the driver and co-driver passed a whisky bottle between them. At 1.30am we stopped for tea at a shabby, bare-stone, roadside shack. We reached Baghdad at dawn and four hours later we were loaded on to a second bus. This one had a pink plastic pipe circling the inside of the vehicle and disappearing through the roof. I have no idea what it was for. Maybe decoration, who knows? There was also a horizontal wardrobe mirror in the aisle and a plastic life-size model of a parrot hanging upside down from its perch. As the driver pulled away the co-driver playfully pinched a thick wad of flesh at the back of his neck. The air inside grew fetid from body odour and putrid food waste, trodden into the floor. We passed villages with mud houses and women carrying huge weights on their heads, reaching Basra at 8.30pm and the customs depot by 11pm. There was plenty of shouting from aggrieved Arabs who were accused of having the wrong paperwork. But eventually we entered Kuwait and at 3am made a final stop at a cafe about twenty miles from Kuwait City. Our Iraqi money had run out but the cafe's cheery owner bought us tea. I had quite forgotten it was my twenty-second birthday. We thought the sun was coming up. But quickly realised it was the red and orange glow of thousands of burning fires from the oil fields.

When we finally existed the bus, we had scarcely slept in forty-eight hours. We had no Kuwaiti money and our sweat stained clothes were making our skin itch. We managed to tempt a bus inspector with an English fifty pence coin to let us ride in a local bus to Ahmadi, the suburb where Chris's uncle Alan lived. We were dropped off at a stop without any idea where we were. But within minutes a car pulled up and an attractive Arab woman who spoke good English asked where we were going. We showed her the address we needed and she laughed.

"I live very close nearby. Get in."

"You must be very tired and hungry," said Chris's uncle when we arrived. Alan, from Liverpool, was in his late forties and had been working in Kuwait for about fifteen years. He gained his master's ticket and captained his first ship in his mid-twenties which was something of a record.

"Come on, we'll soon get you cleaned up, fed and watered." He helped us with our luggage. "What the hell's this?" He was pointing to my bale of damask.

"Yeah, I'm going to sell it to make some money. We bought it in Damascus." Alan's face broke into a wry smile.

"You'll be lucky. That stuff is everywhere here. You might not even be able to give it away."

"Hassan, you ****." I cursed.

Life in Kuwait was total hedonism. Temporary membership at two private beach clubs was swiftly arranged and, after gorging ourselves on food and drink, we would flop around midnight like obese seals into an illuminated swimming pool. There was a series of invitations to picnics and parties. We were introduced to a pretty air hostess called Andrea Teale and later her father invited us for dinner. He had Polish ancestry but had been born in Hull and spoke with a thick Yorkshire accent. He had a tractor tyre for a waist, a bald patch and ping pong ball eyes. But he was a very happy man. He had been working in Kuwait for twenty years and, although he seemed to dislike the place intensely, the inflated salary kept him there. No matter how subservient he was required to be by the oil company that employed him he was laughing all the way to the bank. On one shift over Christmas, he boasted that he earned £180 on top of his normal pay. He had already purchased a house back in the UK and was hoping to retire in a few years when he reached forty-five.

"So much for the little runt they said would run home to his mum from naval school," he boomed like fellow Yorkshireman Brian Blessed.

The oil company provided him with free gas and electricity and a servant and saw to his every need, even the colour of his toilet. He was only in it "for t'brass", he assured us.

"If they say fart, I fart," he roared. It was no surprise when his charming and charismatic wife served up roast beef and Yorkshire pudding.

After spending a fortnight in Kuwait and selling a pint of blood for £14 at a hospital, we were on our way again. Alan had negotiated a berth on a sixteen thousand tonne cargo ship which would take us to our next destination, Japan. The vessel was called the Al Rumathiah and the officers would sing a song to the tune of the Beach Boys' hit Sloop John B. "We sailed on the Rumathiah, the ship that ran on beer." And it did. The ship's cargo was mainly scrap metals. The officers were all English, neatly dressed in white shirts and shorts and white shoes like cricket boots without the studs. The crew was Indian. Having two long-haired students aboard must have been a bit of a novelty to the sea-hardened mariners. Most of them took us into their confidence and pretty soon, over enough cans of beer to start an aluminium recycling plant, we soon had their intimate life stories. One engineer said he had three ex-wives and had to stay at sea twelve months a year to pay off the alimony.

"I'm thirty-two, I've been at this game since I was fifteen. I know we're all piss heads, sailors like a beer. But don't you worry. We'll get you where you want to go."

They entertained us with seafaring stories including the myth of the so-called "golden rivet". There is a tale that every ship is built containing a single, commemorative golden rivet usually at the front of the vessel. The story seems to have links to the golden spike that was temporarily hammered into the tracks at the completion of the US transcontinental railroad in 1869. The rivet's location is allegedly different for each ship and undisclosed, known only to the crew. In reality gold is too malleable a material to be used in shipbuilding. If a golden rivet was made, it would be impossible to hammer it in without destroying it in the process. Nowadays the golden rivet story is used as a practical joke or fool's errand played on junior sailors, exploiting their naivete, like sending an apprentice for a "long stand", a tin of "tartan paint" or a "bucket of steam". After scouring the entire ship without success, it eventually dawns on the hapless recruit that he has been duped. None of the officers appeared to like the captain, Mr Parry, from Wales and new to the ship. He was a bit aloof and a stickler for protocol.

"That bugger sleeps at attention with his thumbs down the sides of his pyjamas," said one of the engineers.

One night we were told there was to be a movie show. At various ports the officers were able to swap tea chests full of films. This was the very pinnacle of at-sea entertainment.

"We're going to watch the film about the attack on Pearl Harbour. Tora! Tora! Tora!" said John the ship's senior electrician or in merchant navy parlance the "sparks". The dustbin lid size reels of film were unloaded and the projector set up in the dining room. Tables were moved aside, chairs organised in rows, the lights were dimmed and the opening credits rolled. The 1971 epic war movie, directed by Richard Fleischer and starring Martin Balsam, Joseph Cotten and Jason Robards, cost twenty-five million dollars to make but achieved a handsome profit. The *tora* of the title, incidentally, is the two-syllable Japanese codeword used to indicate that complete surprise had been achieved. The film is also notable for its revisionist view of history. For decades the common narrative had been that the commanders in Hawaii, General Short and Admiral Kimmel had been negligent. But the film's producers argued that they had been scapegoated. In the film-makers' eyes the top brass had provided adequate defensive measures for the apparent threats, including relocation of the fighter aircraft at Pearl Harbour to the middle of the base, in response to fears of sabotage from local Japanese. Sadly, they had been undone by woefully limited warning of the increasing risk of aerial attack.

The exciting movie was as well-received by the ship's officers as it had been around the world. But as the Japanese suicide pilots began their deadly mission, I became acutely aware of another drama unfolding. The ship was rolling heavily from side to side in a fearsome storm that had whipped up from nowhere. As on-screen bits of battleships and aircraft carriers were flying skywards amid deafening explosions, in our own ship's dining room cups and saucers were sliding off tables and smashing on the floor.

"It's brewing up outside," I heard one officer say to a colleague.

I looked behind me to see the projectionist, a Geordie called Colin, hanging on to his equipment for dear life as it swayed to and fro.

"Shall we stop the film," he shouted.

"No! Fuck off!" came the chorus of replies from the engrossed audience. I'm no seafarer but the roll seemed very pronounced.

"How far can we go over to one side before we simply overturn?" I shouted to one officer, amid the din of kamikaze aircraft.

"I think we have one or two degrees left before that happens," he stoically replied.

Now, at the height of the battle scene, and with more smashed crockery than at a Greek wedding, the projectionist finally decided to pull the plug.

"That's it. I'm done," shouted Colin. "The show's over boys."

"You twat," shouted one unhappy customer. Amid universal groans the lights went up and the disgruntled cinemagoers gingerly swayed their way back to their cabins, picking a route through a jigsaw of porcelain.

"Don't worry," joked Danny, another engineer from Liverpool. "We know who won. The bloody Japs."

The voyage to Japan took nearly four weeks, with stops at Singapore and Hong Kong. We disembarked at Kobe and took the bullet train to Tokyo to link up with Kate Johnson and her parents. The Johnson family's generosity was fulsome. They lived in a beautiful apartment in Roppongi in the centre of the city. It boasted a popular night club scene and a few foreign embassies were located there. That evening we dined at an expensive restaurant called The Terrace Rooms, our food cooked in front of us by our own private chef. The meal's price on the menu, which I assumed was for four people, was actually per head.

We toured the Ginza shopping area and then swam in the American Club. After four days the Johnsons' daughter Kate arrived from England, full of Oxford stories. The whirlwind tourist itinerary gathered pace. We visited Kamakura, a seaside Japanese city just south of Tokyo, and walked in the belly of a thirteen-metre high bronze Buddha. We took a trip to Hakone, part of the Fuji-Hakone-Izu National Park, less than one hundred kilometres from Tokyo. From here you can usually see Mount Fuji but mist and haze denied us. We were taken to Noh plays and Kabuki theatre to watch the classical Japanese dance dramas, to sushi bars and more smart restaurants. We visited Kyoto, considered the cultural capital of Japan and home to numerous Buddhist temples, Shinto shrines, exotic palaces and beautiful gardens.

After four weeks of incessantly absorbing Japanese culture, it was time for me to head back. The Al Rumathiah was due back in the Gulf. Chris decided to stay in Tokyo and found part-time jobs marking English scripts and appearing on English language television programmes. My plan was to get back to Turkey, pick up the van, drive to Istanbul and reach England in time to start my first job, as a junior reporter. In what now seems an incredibly foolhardy idea, I had convinced my girlfriend Sue to fly to Istanbul to join me on the return leg. "You can stay with my Turkish friend Levent," I blithely wrote. Incredibly, she agreed. But what I had not bargained for was that the freighter's return voyage from Japan would be beset by delays and Sue ended up living with Levent and his mother, complete strangers, for nearly two weeks before I reached Istanbul.

When I got to the docks the ship was being repainted. It was the most comical affair. Three teams of Indian crewmen, acting as painters, were positioned on separate cradles dangling on ropes secured to the side of the vessel. But the cradles were almost directly beneath each other so that paint dripping from the cans of the workers above dropped on to the heads of the men below. One of the crew was nicknamed Puck Match, after a popular brand of matches, because his hair was bleached bright red, a sign that he had completed the pilgrimage to Mecca. However, Puck's locks were now almost completely battleship grey.

Back in Kuwait Uncle Alan, anxious for me to avoid the long bus journey through the desert, generously paid for a plane ticket to Damascus. A wonderful kindness. When I eventually returned to Turkey to retrieve the van it was still there in the police compound but one tyre was flat. I changed it for the spare and set off for Istanbul to link up with Sue, bid Levent and his family farewell and then to drive back to Blighty. At Aksaray in Central Anatolia I picked up a Turkish hitch hiker, a man in his late twenties. He asked if he could drive the van for a few minutes but he had no sooner taken the wheel than we were flagged down by a police car. The man was arrested and taken away for driving without the proper documents but they allowed me to continue without sanction.

Back in Istanbul, Sue was pleased to see me. She had settled in well to life with a working-class Turkish family. There were scores of questions.

"How was life aboard ship? How was Tokyo? What was Chris doing?" She was a survivor. I really admired the way she had made a life for herself after her parents divorced, leaving home in her late teens, gaining qualifications in microbiology and renting a flat in Guildford, Surrey, a long way from her roots in Bridgend, South Wales. Petite, with long brown hair and a cherubic face with pink cheeks, we had met at a Halloween party in South London a year before and saw each other as often as we could, usually at weekends. We had no telephone at home so to call her I would walk two hundred yards to a red phone box at the end of the street. Sometimes I would drive to Guildford, sometimes she would take the train to London to stay at my parents' house. She was even persuaded to stand in freezing weather watching me play amateur football on Hackney Marshes.

I knew that in one month I was due to start my job. But first I wanted to show Sue something of the country that had so captivated me. After spending two days with Levent and the boys we headed South again, this time to the Aegean coast. We drove via Bursa and Balıkesir towards Izmir. That night I came down with a fever and when I awoke, I felt clammy and dizzy. I asked Sue to drive the van and when we reached Izmir I called in at a doctor's. The middle finger of my right hand was badly swollen. The doctor's best guess was that I had put my hand on a poisonous sea urchin while swimming. He gave me some antibiotics, vitamin pills and an ointment and we drove out of Izmir to a picture postcard fishing village, Inciraltı. For several days Sue took over writing my diary. The medicine clearly wasn't working and I began to feel very unwell. I sensed poison was travelling to my head and I became quite woozy. A Turk called Erol, who had befriended us at a café, took me into Izmir to hospital. As ever money was tight, so I opted against going to the private hospital and chose the local state hospital instead.

I joined a long queue on a threadbare carpet waiting to enter the dingy Accident and Emergency unit. The man in front of me had a makeshift bandage wrapped around his hand which he cradled against his chest. The white cloth was vivid red with blood and he winced with pain. His wife stood alongside him, her arm wrapped around his waist. The queue was reducing very slowly and I had been waiting for at least thirty minutes when I heard a commotion behind me. Two orderlies pushed their way past, carrying a wooden stretcher. It was impossible to see the patient but the white sheet that covered him or her was bloodstained in at least half a dozen places. They disappeared through swinging doors at the end of the corridor.

A further hour passed before I finally entered the ER. I was taken into a cubicle and told to sit on a primitive wooden bed, covered with a tarpaulin and an unironed sheet and wait. A few minutes later a male doctor appeared and began to examine my finger. I had spent the waiting time looking up some relevant words in my yellow pocket Turkish dictionary. The doctor gently squeezed my finger and nodded as I explained what had happened in broken Turkish.

"You like Turkey?" he said in equally broken English.

"Of course," I nodded.

"It's a beautiful country, isn't it?" he responded. Then he gestured for two security guards to come and tightly hold my arms. The doctor produced a piece of leather, inserted it between my teeth, and told me to bite hard, gesturing what I needed to do by inserting a finger between his own teeth. After splashing the finger with liquid nitrogen, which produced an immediate freezing sensation, he took a scalpel and gutted it like a large sardine. I didn't feel any pain but automatically winced anyway. Puss oozed out as the doctor squeezed hard. I felt a bit faint but managed to stay upright.

"There, that's your problem," said the doctor, smiling. He told a nurse to bandage my finger, gave me some pills and a bill for the Turkish equivalent of £2 and sent me on my way. In two days, I made a full recovery but still have a faint two-inch scar as a souvenir.

My strength returned and we continued with our sightseeing tour, taking in Ephesus and Meryemana, reputed to be the Virgin Mary's last resting place. Today it's a huge tourist and spiritual complex but in 1972 just a tiny stone building. Ephesus, then as now, was astounding. The library is the most spectacular building. But the highlight, for me, was and still is the public latrines. What better way to promote social integration than to have people emptying their bowels in open rows, with all bodily fluids and solids properly flushed away. Incredible to think that public sanitation only came to London with the Victorians but the Romans had it almost two millennia ago.

We drove North to Bergama and on to Truva (Troy). As someone who had been enchanted by Homer's The Iliad and The Odyssey, Troy was a massive disappointment, a symbol of how in those days Turkey often failed to care for its greatest archaeological treasures. On Tuesday August 29 we crossed the border into Greece. Our route home took in Thessaloniki and Skopje. Near Pec, in what was then still communist Yugoslavia, Sue and I parked up by the side of the road to go to sleep. In the middle of the night the Bedford's sliding driver's side door was jemmied open and a thief grabbed two bags in the footwell. Wearing only underpants I leapt from the van and gave chase.

In the moonlight I could make out the outline of the man. I drew closer to him and he grunted something and threw a rucksack at me. Then he turned again and threw something else, which clattered to the ground. I looked down to see an eight-inch carving knife. By now the man was out of sight. I picked up the blade and the rucksack, which appeared to belong to an English hiker, and returned to the van. My feet were cut and bleeding but, through anger and adrenaline, I felt no pain. I threw on some clothes, started up the van's engine and drove slowly up and down the stretch of road.

Suddenly I saw a light in the bushes and pulled alongside. Whether through contrition or for some other reason the thief did us a favour by leaving our bags on the pavement. The only thing missing was my camera. It wasn't expensive but annoyingly I was near the end of a roll of film. Priceless memories captured on Kodak of Tokyo and the return voyage on the Al Rumathiah were lost forever. In darkness we drove on towards Pec and spotted a car with an English number plate parked up and a tent nearby. We woke the occupants, two lads in their late teens. Their car had been broken into and the rucksack was theirs.

As the miles to England ticked by, bits of bodywork began to fall off the van and the tyres had scarcely any tread left. But miraculously it made it home with 37,645 miles on the clock. The van had travelled 9,287 miles. I sold it for scrap but in hindsight I should have kept the registration plate ARK 603 which at today's prices is worth around £4,000, more than twenty-five times what I paid for the original vehicle.

My love affair with Turkey had begun. It was like having a distant girlfriend and I wanted desperately to get back there. Like any romance it's hard to explain what had captured my emotions. Maybe the kindness of Levent and his friends. Maybe the sense of danger and intrigue. I knew there was a heck of a lot more of the country to see. And I was eager to absorb more of its culture.

First, I needed to begin my career in journalism. I travelled from my father's house in Hackney to Victoria coach station. It was September 25 and a slate grey sky and biting wind announced winter was coming. My employer Westminster Press had generously agreed to pay for a train ticket to the North-East. But I figured I would get an overnight bus instead and pocket the difference.

"Where to, sir?" said the chipper ticket man from behind his grill.

"A single to Whitley Bay please," I requested.

"Blimey, no one buys a single to Whitley Bay in September," he scoffed.

I slept fitfully on the journey, my emotions lurching from excitement to trepidation. As the coach approached its destination, I saw huge waves breaking against the promenade, showering water on to the pavement. In my first week as a junior reporter the editor, a tall, grumpy but meticulous man called Dougie Blackhall, invited me to write an article about my foreign travels by way of introducing myself to the town's readership.

"Remember, the three most important things in journalism are accuracy, accuracy and accuracy," he warned.

I was very proud of my first ever piece in print and my first byline until a few days later a letter arrived from a busybody local councillor called Freda Rosner, the town's equivalent of Mary Whitehouse. She scolded me for driving on the UK's highways in what was clearly an unroadworthy vehicle.

"How irresponsible of your newspaper to encourage such dereliction of health and safety regulations," she wrote. There's always one, isn't there?

CHAPTER THREE

HELD AT GUNPOINT

I rented a two-room flat in a road called Ocean View in Whitley Bay and a fortnight later girlfriend Sue joined me. Keen to find an amateur football team, I kept myself fit by going for morning runs along the shore to the famous St Mary's lighthouse and back. Another couple had a similar flat in the house and we shared a bathroom, kitchen and the electricity bill. The man scolded me once for filling an electric kettle to the brim to make a single mug of coffee. I was wasting kilowatts apparently.

It had always been my ambition to become a football writer. But on a small local newspaper you get to cover everything: courts, council meetings, church fetes, theatres, night clubs. I quickly realised that life in general was far more interesting than twenty-two men booting a ball about. The pay was pitiful, £14 a week, around forty per cent of the money I had earned in my student holiday job in London driving a delivery van. But the perks were free entry to the local cinema and theatre and enough pub and restaurant openings needing publicity to keep me well fed and watered. In addition, Sue, a trained microbiologist, had secured a temporary job as a cook in a burger bar called the Big Fry Diner where I could go for the odd subsidised lunch.

Reporting gave me a buzz. I interviewed stars such as The Platters, Jimmy Ruffin and Gene Pitney. I satisfied my football writing urges by following the town's team in the Northern League, home and away, to strange places including Tow Law, Shildon and Billingham. There were emotional, character-building moments like when I had to interview a couple whose five-year-old daughter had drowned four hours earlier in their garden pond. The so-called "Death Knock" is something no journalist enjoys.

They invited me in, gave me tea and cake and spoke fulsomely about their lovely girl. They even provided a photograph.

In the little spare-time I had, after working twelve-hour days, I researched places to visit in Turkey. To sustain my obsession, I also began giving free lectures on Turkey to Women's Institute groups and the like. A friendly Press officer in the Turkish embassy in London sent me a whole series of colour slides on Turkish culture and famous buildings.

Throughout the Seventies I made several trips. Going to Turkey, and certainly flying back from Istanbul, was always an adventure. The check-in process was chaotic and would often take two hours as passengers had to have their tickets and passports photocopied before receiving a boarding pass. Once aboard, travellers sometimes found flights were overbooked. We were never bumped off. But on one trip a Turkish Airlines stewardess asked me to have a woman's baby sit on my lap as she was already looking after another infant. Most people who could afford a foreign holiday in those days headed for Spain, Greece or France. But for young people who had put careers on hold, the hippy trail to the East was now in full swing. Afghan coats were in fashion. The Beatles had travelled to India for yoga, meditation and to play the sitar and tambura. Backpackers regularly stopped off in Turkey. In Istanbul they headed to The Pudding Shop in Divan Yolu, where they could share experiences with like-minded travellers and leave messages for friends to collect days, sometimes weeks or even months later.

A few hippies who were happy to stay in Turkey, rather than head further East, formed a commune on a farm near Mt Olympos, or as the Turks call it Tahtalı Dağı, also known as Lycian Olympus, near Kemer, a seaside resort in Antalya Province. They adapted a few old stone buildings set in a citrus grove, with a winding path leading down to a beautiful cove. An English guy called Ray ran the farm. He had a wife and kids in the UK and was battling between dropping out and leading a conventional life. The commune comprised Americans, English and Germans, many wanderings about naked. Local kids would creep through undergrowth to gawp at the nude hippies undertaking their farming chores.

The Turkish tourism industry was virtually non-existent and guidebooks a rarity. I managed to buy a Nagel's guide from Foyles bookshop in London. But up to date information was at a premium. One modern-day blogger who recalled a trip to Selçuk in 1970 wrote: "There were no hotels, carpet shops, outdoor cafes or other tourist infrastructure. When we were there the only other visitors to the ruins at Ephesus was one Turkish family. There were no guide books. I do not even remember a gate or admission being charged. Goats roamed through the ruins of the Temple of Diana, hidden behind some houses. There was a well at the top of the hill that the village women came to and from which they took water in a vase balanced on their head back to their homes."

If anything, my feeling of excitement in 1973 about being back in Turkey for the third time was more intense than my initial two visits with the van. Simply walking around was like being in a giant, living museum. It was fascinating to see the porters (hamal), bent double, carrying gigantic loads on their backs through the narrow streets around the covered bazaar or the colourfully dressed water sellers.

In Eminönü you could see men feeding fishy titbits to giant pelicans or buy a delicious grilled fish sandwich, made using half a loaf, from a replica Ottoman sultan's boat, bobbing in the water of the Bosphorus. Along the side of that waterway were thousands of tiny fishing boats, used by locals to help feed themselves, alongside larger vessels with men repairing their nets. You might spend a few minutes watching a shoeshine man bringing a gloss to a businessman's footwear. Decades before the car would bring gridlock to the roads along the Bosphorus, people would travel to and fro by horse-drawn cart.

The old wooden houses were also wondrous to explore and admire. From the sixteenth century, skilled craftsmen had built town houses using wood. Most were two or three levels with a ground floor storage area. Toilets were outside, and an upstairs multi-purpose room was where residents ate and slept. Unfortunately, despite laws to protect the beautiful but vulnerable structures, escalating property prices would soon lead to a spate of arson incidents which would clear the way for more lucrative brick and cement-built structures. From 1999 to 2004 UNESCO, alongside official Turkish organisations, undertook a restoration programme. In 2006 Turkey set up KUDEB, an organisation specialising in traditional building techniques, which continued the work. A number of wooden houses still survive. Some, like those along the Bosphorus, are worth many millions of pounds.

In the seventies you would turn a corner in Istanbul to be confronted by a man escorting a huge dancing bear on a chain, a practice now thankfully outlawed due to animal rights legislation. The streets were full of old American cars, Chevrolets, Buicks, Oldsmobiles, Cadıllacs, Studebakers, DeSotos and Pontiacs, many used as taxis and kept running by the ingenuity of thousands of back street mechanics. The large and flashy vehicles had once been significant status symbols for rich Turks during the 1950s, a decade when the country's economy boomed. They were imported from the USA and Europe, where General Motors and Chrysler had factories. But the imports were banned when Turkey began its own car production in 1960, assembling Britain's Ford Consul. Further trade restrictions followed to protect the domestic automobile industry. As the private cars got older, their owners sold them off for taxis. They graced Istanbul's streets for years until new safety laws eventually deemed them unroadworthy.

In 1974, I organised a "road trip" holiday with girlfriend Sue and two male friends, journalist Martin Tasker and his chartered surveyor pal Steve Wilcox in a Citroen Dyane. Unfortunately, Turkey decided to invade Cyprus. The Mediterranean island became a British protectorate in 1912. By 1922, it was a crown colony before gaining independence in 1960, on the proviso that Britain maintained its military territories. A Greek-inspired coup triggered a Turkish invasion and the subsequent separation of Cyprus's two largest ethnic groups.

The Citroen's engine size was only four hundred and twenty-five cc and I vividly remember two farmhands in Austria laughing as we inched our way up a long, steep hill. They waved their arms in a cranking motion as if turning some kind of invisible wheel. Their grins were mirrored by the driver of a gold-coloured Mercedes which swept effortlessly past.

Martin and Steve were so worried the Citroen wouldn't make it to the top that they got out and began to walk. But when we eventually reached the top, we had the satisfaction of seeing the Merc that had passed us a few minutes earlier broken down at the side of the road, steam puffing out of its radiator. Car-ma.

Shortly after crossing the Turkish border at Edirne at sunset we were stopped by men dressed in ordinary workmen's clothes.

"Where are you going? Show us your passports," one man barked. As they checked our identities two of the makeshift Home Guard began painting out our headlights with blue paint as a black-out (or should I say blue-out) precaution against possible Greek bombing raids. Wow, they were taking this war seriously. Finally, they waved us on. I had to squint my way to Istanbul, rarely venturing above fifteen mph. We passed a number of what looked like haystacks until we drew closer and spotted anti-aircraft guns pointing out between the bales.

Before reaching Istanbul we checked into a campsite run by a Polish man. After settling in, the owner beckoned us to his accommodation and emerged with a large wooden box. He opened the top and pulled out an eighteen-inch-long live snake. As we stared wide-eyed, he put the snake's head in his mouth and proceeded to perform a kind of sword-swallowing act. He cranked back his head and the reptile slipped down his throat until it had all but disappeared. Then with the panache of a circus showman the Pole whipped it out again.

"Have you ever seen anything like that?" he proudly asked. I wonder what Simon Cowell would have made of him had he auditioned for Britain's Got Talent.

Three days later Sue and I, friends Martin and Steve were joined by Levent. We went to a student party and enjoyed an evening of chatting, music and drinking beer, which ended well after midnight. We were heading home when a voice cried out.

"Stop." Looking around we saw two men pointing pistols at us. The hastily recruited over-zealous defenders of the Turkish nation, who had been given guns, armbands and whistles, said we were all arrested as "spies".

"You are coming with us," one said sternly. In still stifling heat, they marched us to a police station twenty minutes away and proudly delivered their prey to a portly, blue-shirted officer sitting in a rocking chair at the front of the building

"Captain, these people are suspicious," one said. "I think you should interrogate them." The officer fiddled with his bushy black moustache, rocked forward and narrowed his eyes.

"Thank you, Mehmet. You have done your duty. You can go now," he responded. He looked us over for a few seconds.

"Where are you from?" he inquired. Levent, in a manner a little too belligerent for my liking, explained. The police chief then gestured with his right hand as if batting away an imaginary wasp.

"Go on, go home," he said. We were very tired and when Levent inquired if the police might stump up the price of a taxi fare, he uttered an inaudible curse. Then he made a clucking sound and threw his head back, the classic Turkish way of saying "no"

Two years later on our annual trip we linked up with a couple of friends from England, Jackie Spreckley and husband Richard, who were travelling overland to Iran in a Volkswagen camper van. Martin and Steve from the 1974 trip flew out too. The six of us, plus another Turkish friend called Kadir, travelled as far as Van in the East of Turkey. Sue and I returned to Istanbul by bus and train. On the way we visited Derinkuyu, an undergound city in Nevşehir Province in Central Anatolia.

Derinkuyu is thought to have first been established around the seventh or eighth century BC. Later it grew to at least eighteen levels and sheltered up to twenty thousand people. There were rooms for stables, accommodation, churches, storage and even a winery. Doorways made of massive stone wheels could be rolled in front of an entrance, to make an impenetrable wall. Thousands of ventilation shafts and water courses provided fresh air and drinking water. It was a breathtaking site. But incredibly the entrance was an inconspicuous metal door about four feet square at ground level. It was like accessing the British Natural History Museum via a manhole cover.

A day later that experience was topped by a visit to Nemrut Dağı named by UNESCO in 1987 as a world heritage site. The two thousand-metre-high mountain lies twenty-five miles North of Kahta, near Adıyaman. In 62 BC King Antiochus I of Commagene built at the summit his own astonishing mausoleum flanked by huge statues eight to nine metres high of himself, two lions, two eagles and various Greek and Iranian gods. Either through severe temperature changes over the centuries or deliberate vandalism by rival armies the statue heads have all fallen off. But someone ensured they were propped up correctly and they now often feature in posters and videos from the summit, promoting Turkey. One resembles Elvis Presley.

My guidebook recommended climbing Nemrut in the early hours of the morning in order to see the sunrise. But it urged visitors to hire a Land Rover from the town below rather than attempt to drive to the top in a private vehicle. As we headed towards Kahta I was trying to read a Turkish newspaper using a dictionary. On page one there appeared to be a story about a group of Germans who had ignored the published advice and had been hijacked by bandits. As far as I could tell one of the tourists had been shot and killed and three others seriously wounded.

"Kadir, can you help me to translate this," I asked. Embarrassed, he declined. We hired a Land Rover as instructed, rising from a bed and breakfast place in the early hours to drive up the mountain. In the gloom we passed the stricken Volkswagen, similar to one taking us Eastwards. All four tyres were missing and the interior had been completely gutted. On one side we made out a series of bullet holes.

At a small village our Land Rover was stopped by a makeshift militia carrying ancient rifles and wearing bandoliers of bullets.

"Where are you going?" the leader asked our driver, who explained our mission.

"Be careful," replied the villager. "We think the bandits who did this have gone. But nobody can be sure." Near the top our driver parked up and we disembarked to finish the trek on donkeys. As the sun rose, the full splendour of the site was unveiled. The view was incredible. We posed for photographs with a rifle-toting nightwatchman and alongside the fallen heads.

When we finally reached Van, Kadir was reunited with his family. They threw a wonderful party for us, including a meal of rice and lentil soup and kebabs. To the amusement of neighbours, we erected three tents in their back garden, washing in giant blue plastic bowls. But the following day we saw a darker side of Turkey. We were walking along the street when a Turkish man strode up and grabbed our friend Jackie's breast. A European woman was obviously a rarity and it was probably like some Hollywood film star visiting. Before any of us could react one of Kadir's friends leapt on the man and dragged him to the floor. He then punched the molester several times in the face before allowing the man to run away.

CHAPTER FOUR

LINKED WITH AN ASSASSIN

Year by year Sue and I were working our way slowly but surely through Turkey's major tourist attractions. Next up was a trip to Alanya. I persuaded Sue to scramble more than two hundred and fifty meters up a steep hill to reach the old Selçuk citadel at the summit dating back to 1226. I was looking forward to the wonderful panoramic view which included Cleopatra's beach, a glorious stretch of sand, one of the best in Turkey, as well as the harbour and *Kızıl Kule* (Red Tower) a 108-foot-high brick landmark According to legend, Roman general Antony gave Alanya and its environs to Cleopatra, the Hellenistic queen of ancient Egypt, after she was captivated by the beach and its azure waters. Our tee-shirts were soaked in sweat as we panted our way to the top. I was so distracted that I failed to concentrate on where I was putting my feet and suddenly recoiled as I stepped on a snake. Fortunately, it slithered off without exacting revenge. Once at the peak I took plenty of photographs. Back at the hotel I began to rewind my film only to realise to my dismay that the sprockets had broken at the start and none of the thirty-six frames had been exposed.

"Well that's tomorrow sorted. We'll have to climb back up to the citadel and do it all again," I said. Sue wasn't amused.

That holiday had a sting in the tail. We were half-way back to Istanbul on a ten-hour coach journey.

"You did pick up my passport from the hotel reception, didn't you?" I asked Sue. Why it should have been her responsibility I'm uncertain.

"No, didn't you?" she replied. We were flying home in thirty-six hours and there was no time to go back. In the days before mobile phones - indeed most telephone communication was primitive - we couldn't even ring ahead to warn Levent. I went into a childish foul mood and hardly spoke for the rest of the bus journey.

When we reached Istanbul, Levent got a message to the hotel and they promised to send the passport by courier. But it was unlikely to arrive in time. We were going to have to go to the British Consulate in Istiklal Caddesi and procure an emergency passport. I envisaged having to wait in the traditional long queue. But the consular officials were sympathetic and the whole process took less than two hours.

Back in England, my career in newspapers was gathering momentum. After a year by the sea at Whitley Bay, I moved to The Northern Echo, in Darlington, County Durham, then the largest selling morning regional newspaper in England with a circulation of around one hundred and twelve thousand. Its reputation had been massively enhanced by editor Harold Evans, who had moved seven years before to edit The Sunday Times. Over the next few decades, he would become one of the country's greatest-ever journalists. I rented a flat sixteen miles away in picturesque Barnard Castle opposite one of the town's iconic landmarks, the Butter market, an octagonal Market Cross structure, a gift to the town from Thomas Breaks and built in

1747. I even found Levent a job at a local restaurant but he decided to stay in Turkey to look after his divorced mother Suzan. Sue and I married in the town, with Stephen Brenkley, later to become a famous cricket writer, as our best man.

When friends inquire what inspires my infatuation with Turkey the word "hospitality" invariably crops up. I was walking with Sue and Levent one day in Beşiktaş when I heard music coming from below the pavement. I asked Levent what it was and he said it was a wedding.

"Can we look in?" I inquired. "I've never seen a Turkish wedding."

"Sure," he replied. We walked down some steps to a basement and, sure enough, there was a huge wedding party. Guests were still arriving and the bride and groom were out front greeting them. We waited patiently in a queue. A man came up and asked who we were and Levent explained his friend from England was visiting Istanbul.

"Come, come," said the man. Barging past the waiting guests, he introduced us to the bride and groom.

"This young man and his girlfriend have travelled all the way from England," he gushed. The happy couple smiled broadly and embraced us like long lost relatives. Then the man ushered us away and sat us down at the top table.

"Sit here, enjoy yourselves. You are our honoured guests," he proclaimed. We ate a wonderful meal and then sat through the speeches. Formalities over a hugely overweight Turk in evening dress trousers and white open necked shirt started singing singing "Save Your Kisses for Me", the winning song of the 1976 Eurovision Song Contest, performed for the United Kingdom by Brotherhod of Man.

We joined in the dancing and even had our photograph taken. The next day our pictures were in one of the local newspapers! ENGLISH TOURISTS VISIT ISTANBUL WEDDING, was the headline. Unreal.

Back in the 1970s a journalist friend invited me to his leaving do in Manchester.

"We're going to a Greek restaurant. We'll have some great food and then smash a load of plates," he said. "It'll be a blast. The place is called Efes," he added.

"Hang on," I queried. "Are you certain it's a Greek restaurant? Efes is Ephesus in Turkey. I'm pretty sure it'll be a Turkish restaurant." He looked pained.

"Trust me," he said. "It's definitely Greek. Bring your bouzouki if you've got one. Kaliméra." Of course, I was right. The restaurant was Turkish-owned with traditional Turkish food. But the staff hadn't the heart to correct my misguided friend when he requested plate throwing. To fulfil his wishes, they went out and bought a load of extra crockery specially for the occasion and a good time was had by all.

This anecdote is a vivid example of the Turks' inherent desire to please. The list of similar experiences is a long one. Once in a Turkish eatery in London I asked for chips which weren't on the menu. The waiter apologised and promptly sent out to a nearby chippy to buy some. It's not just in restaurants. Go to a chemist in Turkey and, if they don't have the pills you want, they'll send a boy out to interrogate nearby shops.

One of the most obvious differences between England and Turkey in the 1970s was the newspapers. They were printed in full colour in Turkey while in England the power of the print unions meant the ancient hot metal process would condemn even national papers to print only in black and white until Rupert Murdoch's Wapping revolution in 1986. Turkish papers were also far more graphic. I remember one carried a front-page colour picture of a man who had been involved in a traffic accident which had torn off one of his arms. He was wandering in shock with a policeman running behind him carrying his severed arm. In January 1974 a scheduled domestic flight between Izmir and Istanbul ended in disaster. The aircraft became briefly airborne during take-off, but lost altitude, struck a drainage ditch, disintegrated, and caught fire. Four of the five crew members and all but six of the sixty-eight passengers were killed. The photographs, including body parts stuck in trees, would never have been allowed in a British newspaper.

Turkey was undeniably a dangerous place to visit in the 1970s. From 1968, a right-wing militia, the so-called "Grey Wolves" (*Bozkurtlar*) affiliated with the National Movement Party (MHP) were often seen on the streets of major cities, particularly Ankara and Istanbul. Their number was difficult to estimate. Historians say between several hundred and a few thousand. But their uniformed marches and demonstrations led to violent clashes with leftist groups and comparisons were drawn with the Hitler Youth and other Nazi groups.

On May 1, 1977, International Workers' Day, the Grey Wolves opened fire on left-wing demonstrators in Taksim Square. Most witnesses stated that the high-powered rifle shots came from the building of the water supply company (Sular İdaresi) and Intercontinental Hotel (now the Marmara Hotel), the tallest building in Istanbul at the time. Some reports put the death toll at forty-two with up to two hundred and twenty injured. None of the perpetrators was caught.

Between 1975 and 1978, deaths from political violence rose from thirty-five to nearly one thousand, and by 1980 the figure was three and a half thousand. People claimed they could tell the difference between right and left-wing activists by the shape of their moustaches.

Two days after returning from a holiday to Turkey in 1981, I was ordered to London by my news editor to help cover the glittering wedding of Prince Charles and Lady Diana Spencer on Wednesday July 29. My instructions were to be on the carriage route at 4am for a procession not due to pass until after 10am. Diligently obeying, I stood shivering on an empty pavement which gradually filled with happy onlookers many carrying Union Jack flags. My function was simply to watch in case something newsworthy happened: a carriage wheel falling off, a soldier fainting or, God forbid, someone trying to harm the happy couple or other dignitaries.

With about half an hour to go I was cold, hungry and miserable. My glum face obviously stood out in a sea of well-wishers. Suddenly, I felt a hand on my shoulder.

"Excuse me sir, can I have a word?" said a voice from behind me. I spun round to see a tall, clean shaven man in a sand-coloured trench coat. "I'm a police officer. Would you mind stepping this way and identifying yourself?"

Annoyingly, I was about to lose my place at the front of the crowd which was now six or seven rows deep. Nonplussed, I fished in my pocket for my Press card and explained my presence.

"Do you have any other form of identification," said the stranger, unimpressed. I was still carrying my passport from the holiday and confidently handed it over. As soon as he saw the Turkey stamps his mood changed. I had failed to remember that Turk Mehmet Ali Ağca, an alleged member of the fanatical Grey Wolves group, had tried to bump off Pope John Paul II only two months earlier. The Pope was shot four times and suffered severe blood loss. The cop, obviously Special Branch, pulled out a walkie-talkie and began talking to a colleague. Then he asked me a series of questions about where I lived, my family, my background. He asked for my father's telephone number and passed it on to HQ for a colleague to ring him at home. The whole process lasted about twenty-five minutes before I was released and allowed to resume my duties, which were now nigh on impossible because all I could see was the back of fifty flag-waving Royalists' heads. By the way, after spending nineteen years in prison in Italy and ten more in a Turkish jail, Mehmet Ali Ağca converted to Roman Catholicism. On December 27, 2014, thirty-three years after his crime, Ağca arrived at the Vatican to lay white roses on the recently canonized John Paul II's tomb. He wanted to meet Pope Francis, who prudently declined the request

I was on a solo holiday in Turkey, one year, and arrived in the seaside town of Marmaris, then quite undeveloped. I went to the tourist information office only to be told by the manager that there were "no beds available". He wanted to chat to practise his English and ordered two teas. About twenty minutes later a postman arrived to drop off some mail.

"Hey Mustafa," said the official, "take this guy home and find him a bed."

The postie, who I immediately noticed had three fingers missing from one hand, dutifully led me through some narrow streets and eventually we reached his modest home. He quickly instructed his wife to prepare their only bedroom for me as he searched for spare blankets for him and his missus to use on the sofa. The living room opened out on to a small, concreted patio which ran into the sea. Years later this would become Marmaris's impressive multi-million-euro promenade.

Mustafa and his wife spoke no English but his next-door neighbour was fluent. As the couple fussed about readying my room I stood on the patio, waves gently lapping over the stone edge and asked the man next door about the postie's missing digits.

"He used to work as a carpenter but had an accident with a mechanical saw," he ventured.

"I'm sorry I don't have much Turkish. Can you please explain to him how grateful I am to him and his wife for their kindness?" I asked. "And by the way how much should I pay him for bed and breakfast?" He said the equivalent of £2.50 would be quite enough.

"Mustafa doesn't chase the money. He is a contented soul as long as he has enough at the end of the year to buy his wife a new gold bangle," He added. Later, when I looked, I saw she had about fifteen rattling away on her wrist.

In September 1980 General Kenan Evren led a bloodless military coup, placing two political leaders under house arrest and dissolving parliament. Muslim fundamentalist leader Necmettin Erbakan was tried for political agitation and forty-three thousand people were arrested and, in some cases, tortured. A new constitution was drawn up insisting that political parties could attain seats in Parliament only if they could claim at least ten per cent of the vote. Martial law ended by 1983 with the election of the centre right Motherland Party (ANAP) and its leader Turgut Özal. Though economic reforms, free market principles and emphasis upon trade was promising at first, the decade's worldwide recession sent Turkey into a period of massive inflation, deficit, and unemployment.

Throughout the 1980s, security in eastern Turkey became increasingly precarious. Based in Syria and Iraq, the Kurdistan Workers' Party (PKK) increased its forces and directed a guerilla war against the Turkish state. Civilians were caught in the crossfire: Turkish troops razed villages suspected of helping the PKK, and the PKK razed villages suspected of being pro-

Twelve Camels for Your Wife

government. Meanwhile, the use of the Kurdish language in schools or in the media was banned, as was any expression of sympathy for the Kurds.

On one visit to Istanbul, I walked through a park near the Blue Mosque twenty-four hours before a PKK bomb exploded in a rubbish bin on my exact route. But the traditional Turkish hospitality remained undiminished. On a holiday with journalist friend Gordon Watts, we chanced upon the Istanbul offices of a major Turkish newspaper. We walked in, flashed our English Press cards, and were immediately introduced to a senior executive who gave us a full guided tour of the news gathering and production process. The hospitality thing even seemed to rub off on the UK's little piece of Istanbul. Gordon and I later pitched up at the British consulate, wafted our Press cards about and asked if we could meet the consul general Tim Gee. We were told by a flunky he was due to meet some foreign delegation but could we come back in a couple of hours. When we returned, we were ushered into the consul's office and enjoyed a wide ranging chin-wag for more than an hour, sustained by tea and biscuits at Her Majesty's expense. This was the building that, in 2003, was badly damaged by a bomb which killed the then consul.

Still in Istanbul, Gordon and I started a rather childish game whereby we gave points to the most shocking things we saw. Limbless beggars warranted a "four or five". Then, one day, in Istanbul's famous Grand Bazaar we heard a strange whirring noise. We turned around to see a man who had apparently lost the entire bottom half of his body. He was harnessed to a skateboard and was using pieces of wood grasped in each hand to propel himself along the crowded streets. "That has to be a nine," said Gordon. Would we ever see a "ten" we pondered? A few days later in another market we saw a man in a djellaba, a long, loose nightgown-type garment, being led with a rope around his waist by another man. Nightgown man had an eyeless hood over his head.

"I dare you to ask him to take it off," said Gordon. Could this have been Turkey's answer to the Elephant Man, Joseph Carey Merrick, whose disfigurement was made famous by John Hurt in the 1981 film, directed by David Lynch. Propriety got the better of us and we never did find out. The odd-looking couple drifted away in the crowd. But we gave him a "ten" anyway.

On that same trip Gordon and I went to a *hamam*, a Turkish bath. And not to just any old one. We went to Çemberlitaş, one of the most famous in all Turkey. It was constructed in 1584 by Mimar Sinan, one of the country's most famous architects. Most *hamams*, certainly in the big cities, have separate areas for men and women. But off the tourist trail you can find unisex ones. One of the most important people in the hamam is the *tellak* (scrubber), usually built like a heavyweight boxer and invariably boasting a huge black moustache. In olden times *tellaks* were often migrants without real homes in Istanbul. They often lived permanently in the *hamam* and sent a portion of their salary back to their family. Until the late eighteenth century, the majority of them were Albanian and the job was passed down through generations.

Customers are often surprised to find the rooms are not as hot as in a traditional European sauna. That's because traditionally they were used mainly as meeting rooms to sit and chat. To maintain your modesty, you are given a red gingham cloth, sometimes six feet long and two feet wide, sometimes the size of a large tea towel. In some places, however, they use saggy pairs of black disposable underwear. When you are acclimatised to the heat the *tellak* will enter armed with a square mitten called a *kese*. It's only marginally less painful than a Brillo Pad and is used to exfoliate. It can be quite embarrassing as he scrubs away more grime than Kim Woodburn and Aggie MacKenzie usually turn up. The action often takes place on the *Göbek taşı* (Belly Stone) so called because you normally lie on your belly, at least for part of the time. As the *tellak* rubs the *kese* in your face you pray he has changed it since exploring the nooks and crannies of his previous customer. If you are very unlucky the *tellak* will deliver, for no extra charge, some manoeuvres usually reserved only for a licensed chiropractor. Actor Ryan Gosling tells how once in a Turkish bath he ended up contorted on the stone with part of the scrubber's belly being accidentally forced into his mouth. There was a scandal a few years back where a "woman" who had worked in the women's section of a hamam for many years was revealed as a man. No such luck that the reverse might happen to Gordon and me. We were both pummelled and scrubbed, washed and rinsed until we were bright pink. Then we were given huge white towels to wrap ourselves in and led to a seating area to recover, with a glass of hot tea.

For many the *hamam* is a holiday ritual like a visit to the Turkish barber where a haircut can last an hour. There are regular stops for tea or to watch an exciting moment on television from a recent football match or camel wrestling event. After the initial cut you can choose whether to have your hair washed. Then there is more trimming and snipping. Towards the end of the procedure lighted cotton buds are wafted around your ears to burn off fluff. Your nostrils are trimmed and the back of your neck is shaved with a cut-throat razor. Then your gown is removed, your shoulders brushed and special perfume sprayed on your sternum. Recently I have noticed fellow customers having more elaborate treatments, including what looks like a mud pack applied to their faces, sometimes jet black, sometimes green. The bill for a normal haircut is usually around £2.

I even found a Turkish barber a few miles from my old home in England. Returning from Turkey once I decided to drop in for a trim. The barber was shocked when I gave him my requirements in Turkish. He asked me how I came to speak Turkish and we began chatting about our respective backgrounds. I asked him where he was from.

"Oh, you won't have heard of it. My home town is called Torbalı," he said.

"Really," I replied. "I drove through it yesterday on my way to the airport." His jaw dropped.

Gordon and I headed off to Izmir, checked into a cheap hotel and, exhausted from travelling, decided to have an early night. A few minutes later there was a knock at the door. I opened it to be confronted by two glamorous women looking as if they had just come from a high society ball. Not having very much of the language at the time, I simply wished them good evening and closed the door. But it was clear they were "working girls". Despite working on national newspapers for many years I had never needed to write those immortal words "I made my excuse and left." I had never visited a brothel. Well, not knowingly anyway. Once on a job in Spain, around 1983, a photographer colleague Peter Willcock and I found ourselves in a bar. I ordered an orange juice and was surprised when the barman charged me the equivalent of £8. I was about to remonstrate with him when a Miss World look-alike sidled up and pleasantly invaded my personal space. Soon afterwards Peter and I did indeed make our excuses and leave. Honest guv.

I had read a lot about brothels in Turkey and remembered seeing one in action in Yilmaz Guney's incredible movie Yol. Prostitution - male and female - is actually legal in Turkey. Some brothels are government run but the majority are controlled by shady mafia types. Once, while arriving at Istanbul's Atatürk airport, I found myself standing behind two Russian ladies in their early twenties. Both almost six feet tall, lithe and heavily made up, they were each wearing five-inch heels, diamanté encrusted hot pants and carrying no luggage except for tiny clutch bags.

"I don't think they're here to see the archaeological museum," I thought to myself. Maybe they were just a couple of rich men's girlfriends. Who knows? But the eyes of many nearby Turks in the queue for passport control were on stalks. There were complaints one year in Trabzon on the Black Sea coast that so many Russian prostitutes, dubbed Natashas, had commandeered hotel rooms that tourists and local businessmen couldn't find a bed. In Hopa, a town not too far away to the South, a woman formed a support group for local wives in protest at the temptation incoming Russian good time girls were posing to their menfolk.

While my career was flourishing with a move to Manchester and a job on the Daily Mail, my marriage sadly ran into trouble and Sue and I divorced. The breakdown of the relationship was something I will always regret. In 1980 I met a stunningly beautiful girl called Carolyn at a leaving party for a colleague. She was eighteen, lived in Bury, North Manchester and worked in the Mail's accounts department. Her father Jim had been a professional opera singer with The D'Oyly Carte but had given up his career to marry her mother Barbara. Carolyn, too, sometimes sang opera for money and also acted in amateur dramatic productions. Slim, fair haired and bubbly she had a magnetic personality. The relationship quickly became serious and we married in 1984.

She had holidayed in Greece a couple of times but had never been to Turkey. So, we booked a flight. One day in Istanbul we went to a night club (*gazino*). This is nothing to do with gambling. At a *gazino* you usually have a meal and watch cabaret, often a series of acts. The venue was in Arnavutköy just North of Beşiktaş along the Bosphorus on the European side. This particular evening there were about six or seven acts including singers and dancers. One belly dancer ended up jiggling about on our table. I still have the black and white photograph. Then the owner came over.

"Your wife is beautiful. Would you swap her for twelve camels?" I didn't know if he was serious or whether it was an expansive prank, he regularly played on foreigners coming to his establishment. Anyhow, I knew nothing about camel husbandry so I turned him down. My friend Peter Sands had a similar experience in Morocco. He was offered ten camels for his wife Pam.

"Sorry, I don't smoke." He jokingly replied. The buyer hadn't a clue what he was talking about but he and Pam thought it was very funny.

Our first daughter Charlotte was born in 1986. In 1989 we decided to book a last-minute package holiday to Turkey and by accident discovered Şile, a fishing village on the Black Sea. Back then, it was essentially a weekend getaway destination but later became a full-blown seaside resort. I can't remember exactly why we chose it. The chance to see Levent again was an obvious factor. The fourteen-year-old we had met all those years earlier was now grown up and had married Azime, the daughter of a wealthy widow, whose late husband had been a Turkish cabinet minister. Levent was living in Ankara, where he did various jobs including running a small shop.

Şile back in 1980s was a relatively small town. And the journey from Atatürk airport was long and arduous, at least three hours by taxi. The roads meandered through tiny villages and we often had to stop while a shepherd manoeuvred his cattle, goats or sheep to let vehicles pass. Along the road butchers would sell their cuts of meat hung from nails on what looked like artists' easels. Later the government would build a motorway which reduced the driving time to less than an hour. Except at weekends, of course, when the road is often gridlocked and police regularly have to turn cars back from entering the town. All that was way off in the future. I remember the Thomson holiday brochure said it was "the perfect place to write your first novel". That seemed like tourism-speak for "lacking amenities".

We stayed at a small guest house which featured a huge parrot called *Çapar* (mottled) sitting on a perch. There was no cage and the parrot had free run of the property. We asked the manager if he would pose for a photograph like a pirate with the parrot on his shoulder and an upturned broom under one arm. He happily obliged. Charlotte was then aged three. Our second child, Sophie was born a year later. We spent most of the time on the beach making sandcastles or reading.

At the end of the holiday, the guest house owner heard Carolyn and I talking about buying property in Turkey. He said he had recently separated from his wife and they had a flat to sell. On the very last day we went to see the flat and were blown away by the view, the best in town. It was on the top floor of a four-storey block and overlooked both the beach and the harbour. Although it was up eight flights of stairs with no lift we were captivated. It had three bedrooms, three balconies, herringbone parquet flooring in the lounge and the total footprint was 124 square metres. The asking price was £14,000.

There and then we said we would have it and the investment yielded many happy family memories from 1989 until we sold it in 2014. The purchase included one of the biggest acts of Turkish hospitality we have ever experienced. Having shaken hands with the owner's husband, the issue was how to send the money. Levent had come to visit us for a couple of days with his wife and mother-in-law. Seeing our predicament, she fished in her handbag, pulled out a chequebook and wrote out a cheque for the full amount. We wired her the money when we returned to the UK.

For simplicity we had put the deeds to our new holiday home in Levent's name. But when we tried to change the ownership details, we hit a snag.

"Sorry, foreigners cannot buy property in Şile. It is in a military zone," said an official. We knew there was an Army barracks in the town and every Tuesday jets would fly overhead and take part in shooting exercises. But we were hardly in a potential war zone. Why the sensitivity? We checked with Levent's uncle who, at the time, was the third highest ranking general in the Turkish Army.

"Nonsense," he said. "There is no impediment." We even prevailed on the general to write a letter to that effect to the local mayor. But on our next holiday I spent three hours in vain waiting to see the town hall official in charge. He was very busy, I was told. The following year, it was the same story. I waited patiently but he was never available.

By now I was on first name terms with the security guard in the foyer. But it was clear I was getting the run-around. This time I did at least get to meet the elusive clerk's female secretary.

"Ah, you are from England. Do you know, I would love a proper pair of sunglasses," she opined. For the following year's holiday, I arrived with a pair of Ray Bans. Back to the town hall and a cheery hello to Ahmet the guard. Finally, after handing over the glasses and another day's delay, a meeting with the boss was arranged. I entered the man's colourless and spartan office, the inevitable portrait of Atatürk on the wall behind him. A single strip fluorescent light beamed down harshly. He shuffled some papers in the folder in front of him.

"Ah, Mr George, this job has a thousand and one problems," he said wearily. Then he added: "Do you know how much a civil servant like me earns in a year?" Forewarned by my Turkish friends that a charitable donation might well be required to grease the complex mechanics of local government, I fished in my pocket and drew out a bundle of Turkish lira. To protect the official's reputation, I'm not going to say whether or not I left it on his desk. However, suddenly everything appeared to be "in order". A rubber stamp was found in a drawer and thumped down heavily on the relevant document, followed by a signature resembling an earthquake warning on a Richter machine and I was on my way to the title deed office. There a man opened a leather-bound book the size of large suitcase and wrote my details in ink. Levent's name was changed to mine and I was given a new title deed. The flat was officially ours.

Having a holiday home curtails the urge to explore new places. But there are advantages to becoming part of a community, albeit for only two or three weeks a year. We quickly became friends with most of the town's movers and shakers, including Ufuk, son of the owner of one of the biggest hotels. It boasted an adjoining swimming pool and bar called the Moondrop and we were regular customers. The kids would sleep in their buggies or in a hammock near the bar as we played darts, drank and chatted into the early hours.

Apart from the beach Şile's main attraction is its lighthouse, painted in distinctive black and white bands. You can buy salt cellar lighthouse souvenirs to remind you of your trip. Built by French engineers, it was commissioned by the Ottoman Sultan Abdulmecid 1, who died a year after it opened in 1860 from tuberculosis (like his father) at the age of 38. At nineteen metres tall is the largest active lighthouse in Turkey and the second largest in the world. It flashes four times a minute and we regularly used to go to sleep comforted, maybe slightly mesmerised, by its light which can be seen from thirty-five kilometres away. Originally lit by kerosene, then by gas, the light source, comprised of eight lenses, was eventually powered by electricity. It turns via an intricate weight-driven mechanism inside the tower using something called an "anchor escapement". A falling weight on a chain reaches the bottom of the tower in two hours. The lighthouse keeper has to pull it up by rewinding the chain. So basically, it's like a giant cuckoo clock, without the bellows. Nowadays it's a tourist attraction but back in 1989 it was simply a working lighthouse. However, we knocked on the door one day and a kindly man, who spoke no English, gave us a guided tour.

When the children were young, we naturally spent a lot of the time on the beach or in the nearby beach cafes. But later we also found a horse-riding activity centre at Imrendere not far away where Sophie, a keen rider in those days, could practice. Another potential trip out was to Ağva, the next resort due East along the Black Sea coast. It's a picturesque town with quaint hotels and cafes. The main feature is a beautiful river running right through it and a relaxing boat trip will take you to the mouth of the sea and back. If you are fitter and more adventurous you can hire one or two-person canoes and paddle yourself up and down the waterway. You can also cross the river on a slightly rickety rope powered pon toon.

Another local beauty spot destination is *Saklı Göl* (it means secret lake). There you can have a meal or just drink tea while feeding the ducks, watching cormorants swooping down and listening to the croaking of a thousand frogs. Or you can take a walk around the lake on woodland paths. So Şile is no Las Vegas. But it had its moments. To call family back in the UK we would often go to the post office (PTT) and queue up. Until an automatic central telephone system emerged in the mid-1990s operators would connect the local and the international calls, often eavesdropping on both ends of the conversation. The line was invariably crackly and you were usually allowed only three minutes.

One of the town's characters was a man we called Pyjama Mehmet. He earned the sobriquet because he always wore striking trousers with a navy blue and white pattern. Moustachioed Mehmet was a street photographer who would take pictures of tourists then go away to process the film and return to tour the beach cafes, bars and restaurants in the early evening hoping for a sale. Although he had never been outside Turkey, his English was excellent and was peppered with amusing colloquialisms and Cockney rhyming slang which he must have picked up either from tourists or from watching British TV soaps. If we bumped into him in the street, he would always greet us with "Hello my old China." He always called Sophie "miniature". His job was a thankless task and it would have eventually been made redundant by the advent of smart phones. But sadly, Mehmet had a heart attack and died in his thirties. Before that tragedy he had been involved in a drama at the British consulate in Istanbul. Denied a travel visa to visit the UK, he went away and returned with a can of petrol, doused himself with it, and threatened to do a Jan Palach. After a tense stand-off good sense prevailed and visa-less Mehmet was sent home without charge.

Another well-known character was a slightly simple man with a huge nose. We first saw him when he was in his late teens. Four older men had cruelly tied him to a chair for a joke and were whipping him with leafy branches. Another time we saw two lads spraying him with water from a hose pipe. He was clearly a source of amusement for some heartless people. Others were rather kinder and gave him food and tea. He lived with his mother behind the main street on the way to the post office. I'm not sure he had ever been to school and his speech was a little impaired. He also walked with a strange loping gait. But some days we would pass him and he would say hello in a range of foreign languages, English, French and Spanish. We walked into town once to find him at an intersection dressed in a full police uniform directing traffic. In his holster he had a toy gun.

Another summer we were in Şile when a female Swedish amateur football team hit town. They had been due to play in an international tournament in Istanbul but for reasons unclear it had been called off at the last minute. Showing a severe naivety to Turkish culture they began training topless on the beach. A crowd of several hundred people quickly gathered to watch the session before the police politely asked them to cover up. I imagine the officers took their time. However, the mayor invited the football squad to take part in the annual procession for the Şile festival, albeit in full kit. I still have photographs of that parade which included three beauty queens riding on camels and desperately trying to look dignified as their tiaras slipped off one way and another.

Our friend Ufuk hosted the Miss Şile Beauty Pageant in his family's hotel the Değirmen and for three years Carolyn and I sat on the jury. An announcer would welcome the crowd and the judges.

"First let me introduce so-and-so one of Turkey's most famous painters." Thunderous round of applause. "Next to her is such-a-body who is President of one of Turkey's biggest banks." Big round of applause. "To his right we have Mr XYZ the famous TV soap opera star." Big round of applause. "And finally, George and Carolyn who holiday here every year." Polite round of applause. We had found our own tiny slice of celebrity.

CHAPTER FIVE

DANNY AND THE COCKROACH HOTEL

The sun was hot and the beer was cold. Just like it should be on a family summer holiday. Daughter Charlotte was helping her younger sister Sophie to decorate a sandcastle with bits of broken shell. Carolyn was on a sun lounger trying to find the point of equilibrium between the perfect tan and risk of melanoma. And me? I was sitting in our favourite beachside cafe. I had my head in a book, James Cameron's Point of Departure, the collection of mercurial essays that first persuaded me to become a journalist. We were back in the holiday resort of Şile near Istanbul. Shoeless waiters flitted at breakneck speed between large umbrellas, delivering platefuls of meatballs and chips, as tempting as any potion Circe, of Greek mythology, ever produced.

My concentration was momentarily broken by the sound of an English accent. A stranger was in conversation with Charlotte, who had temporarily abandoned her sand sculpture. I looked up to see a small, tanned Jewish looking man and I immediately suspected that this was a guy whose vicissitudes I had followed for several years in newsprint. I folded the corner of the page in my paperback and sauntered over.

"Are you Danny de Souza?" I asked proffering a hand.

"Yes," he said. And so, began an adventure that would last nearly twenty years, richly embroidered with humour and ultimately heartbreak.

Danny de Souza, or Danny Koplowitz (his real name), was one of those people who seem to live four lives in one. Born in a refugee camp in Wiltshire on October 4,1945, he became a schoolteacher. Then in the Sixties he dropped out, travelled abroad and ended up being sentenced to death in Turkey for possessing 5.5 kilos of cannabis, despite claiming it was just for himself and a few friends. The sentence was later commuted to thirty-six years in jail. He ended up doing twelve. Well, it was the era of the Hippy Trail to Samarkand, the magazine Oz, Woodstock and the philosophy of "turn on, tune in, drop out" the phrase popularised by American psychologist and writer Timothy Leary.

As my interest in all things Turkish grew after my initial road trip I followed Danny's case closely, usually through the pages of the Guardian. Danny served time in three prisons in Istanbul, Antakya and Izmir, locked up with murderers, rapists and gangsters. There were frequent stabbings and several riots. He was behind bars for a time with the American Billy Hayes, whose story was told in Turkey's most vilified film ever Midnight Express. There are still protests when the movie is shown. The prison warders are portrayed as sadistic, lazy and corrupt. The Turkish legal system also comes out of the movie very badly. The film was made almost entirely at Fort Saint Elmo in Valletta, Malta, after permission to shoot in Istanbul was denied. When it first appeared, Turkish commentators claimed it had destroyed the country's tourism industry and poisoned relations with the West. Later, both Oliver Stone, who wrote the screenplay, and Hayes expressed their regret about how Turkish people were portrayed. When Hayes later visited the places where he had been incarcerated, he had to be accompanied by plain clothes Turkish policemen for his own protection. Sally Sussman, who subsequently made a documentary about the film, concluded that it was made with "no malice" and no intention to offend the Turks. But that's not how Turks saw it, then or now. It was banned for many years in Turkey and not shown on television until the 1990s. Danny always scoffed at the movie's denouement where Hayes escapes by impaling the head of his sadistic guard, intent on raping him, on a wooden hat peg. "He actually bribed his way out," insisted Danny.

Later Danny established a school for orphaned or abandoned children in jail who, in those days, were often banged up with criminals to clear them from the streets. When the classroom was destroyed in a riot Danny, despite dire warnings of retribution from fearsome co-prisoners, helped rebuild it. Later he wrote a captivating book on his experiences called Under a Crescent Moon. Pete Townshend, of the rock band The Who, had also been following Danny's case through English newspaper reports. He wrote a complimentary note on the cover.

In one passage Danny wrote: "If I had to sum up the wretched conditions in one word it would be 'RATS'. Hundreds of them. Swarming out from drains and cracks at night, scampering around the courtyard, flitting under bunks and crawling through pipes to enter the cells. Grey, greasy and ugly, some were as big as cats, others were so tiny they could squeeze through keyholes to reach edibles. There was no way to fight them. Sometimes the children trapped a real monster and burned it alive. But that hardly diminished their numbers.

Because of the overcrowding, many children slept on the floor. We were woken frequently in the night by their terrified screams when the rats nipped their fingers or toes."

He quickly became something of a celebrity and was featured in Turkish and international magazines and newspapers. Eventually, I suspect, he became a bit of an embarrassment to the authorities who probably realised that he was more of a public relations asset to them outside rather than inside the prison walls. Incredibly, Danny went on to date the daughter of the trial judge who sentenced him and when you didn't think his life could become any stranger, he discovered that his father, Jan, had been a high-ranking officer in East Germany's secret police the Stasi.

I had pondered the idea of visiting him in jail but then got cold feet. What if the authorities thought I was a possible drug dealing associate? Maybe they would refuse me entry to Turkey in the future, I mused. To meet him on the beach seemed like fate. And we immediately became firm friends. At that time, he lived in Moda, Kadıköy, a fashionable district of Istanbul. One evening he picked me up at Atatürk airport as I arrived from England. He was driving a battered, red convertible Ford Capri.

"Do you mind driving?" he asked.

"Me?" I replied, remembering the dodgems-like free-for-all back in 1972. It was going to be far worse twenty-odd years later.

"You'll have to. I'm colour blind at night," confessed Danny.

Another time Danny was stopped by the police for driving erratically. He was clearly under the influence of drink or drugs and, in the days before breathalysers, was ordered to take a roadside sobriety test. He tried every trick.

"Aw come on. I play backgammon with your boss every Tuesday," he lied. Finally, Danny went into a song and dance routine. The streetwise traffic cops had never seen anything like it. Here was a foreigner, speaking perfect Turkish, pirouetting in front of them like Fred Astaire. Thoroughly amused, one eventually turned to the other and said: *Boşver*. The Turkish for "sod it". They let him go without penalty. Incidentally, according to an hilarious blog I once read called Arse About Fez, Turkish girls often carry Viagra to bribe traffic police if they get caught over the alcohol limit. Bona fide pills, you might say.

During one holiday Danny tried to convince me to buy into, or even possibly take over, an English teaching language business in Istanbul. We looked it over but decided against. Danny was briefly married to a beautiful Turkish girl called Sevgi but it didn't last. Later he bought a hen coop in the rather upmarket seaside resort of Gümüşlük near Bodrum - we bumped into Jeremy Irons there once (the resort not the hen coop) - and turned it into a one-room flat. It contained a bed, a computer, a printer and an electric hob for cooking. It was cluttered but, compared to his Turkish prison cell, it was luxury indeed.

Around this time, I was freelancing for national newspapers in England and asked Danny to send me translated Turkish newspaper cuttings to re-cycle in the British Press. The Turkish print media was always full of oddball and bizarre tales and, although they often made no more than a paragraph or two in Fleet Street, payment was around £30 a pop. Good money back then. Danny and I shared the spoils. One snippet involved a police officer who had gone into a tailor's shop while on duty to try on a new pair of slacks. His uniform trousers fell off the changing booth's clothes peg and as his service revolver hit the ground it discharged a round which wounded the officer, not fatally, in the leg. "What a Turn Up," was the ingenious headline on the two-paragraph story, known in the trade as a NIB, which stands for news in brief. Another tale involved a girl who promised to sleep with her local football club's entire first team if they won promotion. It proved a powerful incentive and when the championship was finally secured the promiscuous fan apparently kept her promise. Well, it makes a change from an open top bus parade.

Yet another daft story told of two brothers who fell out over a plan to knock down the small house where they lived and build a lucrative block of flats. After years of deadlock one brother waited for his sibling to be out of town, destroyed half the house and built a very slim eight-storey structure on the footprint. His brother was furious but continued to live next door in the remaining half of the old house. The photograph accompanying the tale was insane and its beggar's belief how planning permission was ever obtained.

Danny also earned money by translating Atatürk's speeches and other historical documents into English. However, because he didn't trust his excellent Turkish or maybe because he was just a bit lazy, he once confessed to me that he sub-contracted the work to a local Turk at a much lower rate of pay and merely put a modern English "gloss" on the resulting scripts. He took great delight in relieving the Turkish government of money, feeling it was some kind of payback for his years behind bars.

Everyone in the area knew the "crazy Englishman" and his podiatrically challenged dog Six Toes (*Altı Parmak*). They called him *Köyün delisi*, (mad villager). But somehow it changed to *Köyün Dannysi*. A friendly local muezzin would climb to the top of the mosque's tower and use the public address system, usually reserved for the call to prayer, to tell Danny he had a letter waiting at the post office. By now Danny owned a small, ancient, saloon car that looked like something a clown might use in a circus. The front passenger side window would not wind up and on the floor was a layer of sand and dust thicker than in a Bedouin's tent. The thing regularly broke down. Danny, completely unskilled in anything mechanical, would simply sit behind the wheel of the stationary vehicle until one of the locals came across from a tea garden or shop to diagnose the fault and repair it.

When Danny's ex-policeman father died in East Germany in 2002 it was big news. A TV company wanted to make a documentary on his dad's life and Danny asked me if he could use our holiday flat to do some of the filming. I readily agreed and when we next arrived, we found, by way of payment, a huge plastic water tank tied on to the roof. Danny knew the water pressure to our flat was often poor and ensured we now had a permanent cure. Well not quite. The plastic tank should really have been situated in the loft space above the flat, under the roof, not on top. We came home one day to find it had blown off and was lying fatally and irreparably holed a hundred metres down the street. That was certainly an ill wind that blew nobody any good, except possibly for a neighbour who chopped up the tank for some kind of animal feeder.

Danny then set about sorting out his dad's affairs in Berlin. He had to change his name by deed poll in London to Koplowitz to prove he was the old man's genuine heir. He found nothing of note in his father's home and was about to leave when a final search revealed a huge amount of cash hidden behind a partition. There was more in several bank accounts too, around 100,000 US dollars in all. He went back to the former owner of the hen coop in Gümüşlük and bought an adjacent rectangular metal cow shed.

"You'll never get planning permission," I told him. But Danny proved me wrong. He claimed to have spent hours in the vaults of the local council offices checking the tortuous building regulations. Or maybe he just left a bundle of Turkish lira in someone's in-tray. Who knows? Whatever happened, the next time we visited, Danny had turned the animal shelter into a four-bedroomed hostelry called the Karafatma (Cockroach) Hotel. A small army of close friends had come together to build it and Danny proudly showed me a photograph album charting every stage of construction.

Guests, he insisted, had to be students, artists, musicians or close friends. As boss, Danny's duties extended only to supplying marijuana. Evidence of anything but the most rudimentary cleaning regime was non-existent. One day we turned up to be told by Danny to drive immediately to town.

"Buy flea powder," he ordered. We usually spent the first few hours of any visit scrubbing the place clean, buying food for the guests and often cooking it too. The residents invariably had exotic stories to tell, like the beautiful Russian concert pianist Benya, who had been forced by economic circumstances to play Gershwin in hotels and cocktail bars in Istanbul's trendy Beyoğlu district.

But nothing prepared us for the time around 2009 that we dropped in to meet a newly arrived Brooklyn Jew called Gary Berlind and his incredible string instrument the viola da gamba. Gary, in his sixties, thinning on top and carrying a few surplus kilos told us he was the only man in Turkey who could play the centuries old instrument mentioned in Shakespeare's play Twelfth Night. It differs from the cello in having six strings instead of four and is tuned more like a lute or guitar. It came to prominence in England after 1600 and among other things is featured in four paintings by the Dutch artist Vermeer. Danny's eyes lit up.

"I have a Turkish pal who owns a top open-air restaurant. He'll love this. I'll tell him about Gary, promote him as the cabaret on Saturday and we'll all get free food and rakı," he said rubbing his hands like Del Boy Trotter. A quick phone call confirmed the restaurant, called *Limon*, would be only too delighted to feature Gary as their star turn. Gary sometimes dressed in full pirate's costume with a tricorn hat and thigh-length leather boots when performing. But for this gig he wore a more prosaic black slacks and black tee-shirt. Danny donned an all-white suit and dark sunglasses like the man from Del Monte. He, Gary, Carolyn and I headed off to the eatery.

Elton John would not have received a more rapturous welcome by the owner. There were kisses on both cheeks, hugs, handshakes. We were greeted like long-lost relatives. Dozens of diners were already tucking into their expensive mezes in the open-air restaurant, as Gary took his seat on a small stage built on large rocks. The balmy evening was unusually windy and the clothes pegs Gary had brought to hold his music on to the flimsy black metal stand would not suffice. I offered my services to keep the pages in order and turn them as required. Finally, Gary began to play. Now I am no expert when it comes to centuries-old musical instruments. But the sound that emerged seemed more like the soundtrack of the Saw film franchise. Anyone who has ever sat in a school auditorium listening to an eager eleven-year-old scratching out a tune on a violin or cello will be able to visualise the look I was seeing on the faces of the up-market restaurant's clientele. Gary, brow furrowed, and concentrating on the sheet music, sawed on. More jaws dropped with every push and pull of Gary's bow. Gary told us he was going to play a medieval ballad. A similar rendition at a royal court four centuries earlier would surely have seen him hung, drawn and quartered. And that's before the King got really mad. By now I was thinking that the Mongolian throat singer I had seen years earlier in a Şile circus wasn't so bad after all.

Finally, I enjoyed the feeling you get when you are desperately trying to sleep and the sound of a neighbour's booming, quadrophonic stereo finally falls silent. Gary stopped. There was the merest ripple of polite applause quickly drowned out by the clinking of knives, forks and glasses as the diners resumed their expensive meals. Our entourage had already been served with, and despatched, pre-prandial drinks and now we were all hungry. But in the circumstances, we decided that accepting a follow-up gourmet meal would stretch even the sacred rules of Turkish hospitality beyond breaking point.

"We'd better get out of here," cautioned Danny. We jumped into Danny's car while Gary and his precious cargo followed in a taxi and sped off home. Soon after Gary left to travel to Israel. Apparently, Israel is home to the world's only theatre company comprised entirely of deaf and blind actors. Do they have an orchestra, I wonder? I'm probably being very cruel. Maybe Gary simply had an off-day.

Just as Danny's early adult days turned sour through his own ill-judged actions, so too did the final chapter of his life. Around 2008 when Danny was 63, he claimed he had fallen madly in love with a Turkish woman called Nesrin, a pharmacist, around 35 years younger.

"She makes me so happy, George," he told me in a telephone conversation. The next we knew he had made Nesrin and her daughter co-directors of the Karafatma Hotel. Unknown to Danny, Nesrin was a woman with a murky past and several very unsavoury friends rumoured to have Mafia links. She had had several run-ins with police. In one newspaper cutting she was accused of stealing from a pharmacy and making a false insurance claim. Danny was the perfect patsy. She went to a bank and, giving the Karafatma hotel as security, took out a huge loan - thought to be around £80,000 - and allegedly used the money to renovate a villa. Because the loan only needed to be authorised by "a majority" of the directors it was entirely legal. One version of the story also alleges she tried to put the deeds to the Karafatma Hotel in her mother's name.

When he learned what had happened Danny was distraught. He bought a wooden advertising A-frame and wore it while walking around the large tourist town of Bodrum displaying the full sorry tale under the heading: NESRIN CHEATED ME. Underneath was a placard saying: "Give me back my home and my money." According to one newspaper account at the time Danny claimed he was 300,000 US dollars out of pocket, although that appears to be grossly exaggerated. He was interviewed on national television but to no avail. The police said it was a civil matter and technically the criminal courts couldn't become involved. The indomitable, never-say-die spirit that had helped Danny survive all those years in some of Turkey's toughest prisons now kicked in. He pulled every string and bent every powerful ear he knew. He wrote to the local council, lawyers, newspapers and TV stations. But in vain.

"Why didn't I realise what she was up to, George," he wailed in another angst-ridden phone call.

Meanwhile Nesrin had launched a counter offensive. She told a senior police officer friend that he was likely to find cannabis at the Karafatma, where Danny still lived. The cops raided the place and sure enough Danny was nicked. Because of his previous record he faced the unenviable possibility of going back to jail. He was also threatened with deportation. Danny made a heart-rending outburst to one reporter.

"I love the area and want to die in Gümüşlük." Luckily the police's case file was passed to a local judge who Danny knew. He went to see the man in his chambers.

"What's going to happen to me?" asked Danny, a bleak looks on his face. The judge stretched across his desk and retrieved Danny's file. Then he put it on the bottom of a pile of other papers and folders in an in-tray.

"I'll get round to it in due course," said the judge ominously.

"Come on," said Danny. "Stop torturing me. How long will it take you to work your way through that stack?"

"Hmm," said the judge, eyeing up the paperwork for a second or two. "Given the normal regulations and the current speed of court procedures I would say your case is likely to come before the court in…," he hesitated.

"Yes, yes," urged Danny.

"In about ten to fifteen years," concluded the judge, smiling conspiratorially.

Danny went home, made himself a king-sized joint and contentedly strummed his guitar. He even wrote a song about the whole sorry affair called "The Nesrin Blues".

In 2012 on his Facebook page Danny, writing from England, claimed to have "won the case" against Nesrin. The hotel, he went on, "has been saved". Replying to the good wishes of a friend he added: "I'm not amazed. It was such a blatant scam I can't understand why it has taken five years and the bitch has still got away with 70,000 euros." Danny was still a fighter. In his twilight years he remained a rebel. He once posted on his Facebook page a New York Times story that Paraguay was contemplating legalising marijuana.

"Hooray," said Danny.

Several months passed and we lost touch with Danny. We had three telephone numbers for him but they all just rang out. A few more months passed. Finally, I decided to search back through scores of e-mails we had sent to each other over the years. On one I found that one of Danny's old London friends,

David Berkovitch, had been copied in. I e-mailed David. His reply wasn't the news I wanted to hear. Danny had died in London on November 22, 2012. A funeral announcement described Danny as writer, linguist, translator, tailor, traveller, teacher, musician, free spirit, table tennis and chess player, dog lover and charmer. That just about covered it.

In an e-mailed tribute, Pauline Crowe, chief executive of the organisation Prisoners Abroad, wrote: "He has long been a permanent part of Prisoners Abroad's folklore and his book still sits proudly on our bookshelf. I never met Danny but have read his book and was engaged and horrified in equal measure which I imagine was his intention for the reader. Gary, the viola da gamba man, wrote from Israel: "I lived closely with Danny for thirteen months from 2008 to 2009 and I can tell you that in his own very unique way he was the centre of a large group of colourful and vibrant Turkish people who will sorely miss him and always remember him. R.I.P. Mr Koplowitz; you lived your life in your own way, enjoyed yourself more than most people ever do, and you will not be forgotten." In an e-mail to a mutual friend, Gary added: "Danny was a big fan of the late Hunter Thompson, by the way, and with sunglasses on even looked a lot like him. May Nesrin, the fiendish Turkish gal, who messed things up so badly for everybody, find a special place in Turkish Hell, if there is such a place. And I'm sure there is."

Apparently, Danny had contracted lung cancer. He had come back briefly to the UK for treatment but sadly did not survive. He never had any children but he had two sisters. I tried to find them without success. But friends said they were very wealthy and independent and didn't have the same affinity for Turkey that Danny had. Whatever happened to his belongings in Turkey and the Karafatma Hotel I never learned until I started researching this book and one of his friends, Umut Uğur, provided the typically extraordinary answer. The last guest of the hotel became its owner or at least its keeper. Apparently, Danny had given the woman, in her forties, a hand-written and signed authorisation to "look after" the place and his dog while he went to England. He tried to return to Gümüşlük from a spell in London but at Bodrum Airport his entry was refused, probably because of the final drugs bust, orchestrated by Nesrin. He was sent back to the UK and died shortly afterwards. The lucky guest then claimed ownership until a legal heir appeared. Possible claimants included the two very old and rich sisters, who were not interested and his Turkish ex-wife, Sevgi, who said she had no intention of usurping the family members. So since 2013 the last guest, "always lonely and ill looking" according to Umut still occupies the place, renamed Altı Parmak Pansiyon, in homage to Danny's dog.

A Japanese pianist, Sachika Taniyama, who had stayed at the Karafatma, wrote a moving blog in Danny's memory. She called him: "A warm hearted, lovely man." Many other friends and hotel guests added their own special memories. For me Danny was a unique series of contradictions. Gregarious yet comfortable in solitude. Totally disorganised yet able to lead a team to build a hotel. Often smiling but never happier than when playing blues on his acoustic guitar. Passionate about football but a hopeless player. He could be sardonic but you knew it was just an act. Above all he was a giver not a taker. People who met him were always enormously richer for the experience. Although we saw each other sporadically, I am proud to count him as one of my truest friends. If he went to Heaven, I'm certain he is up there still breaking rules.

CHAPTER SIX

THE MONGOLIAN CIRCUS

If there's one thing that stirs a Turk's blood as much as the national anthem or a sense of pride in the Turkish nation ... it's football. I have attended thousands of matches in my life but nothing quite like one we saw in 1998 at Beşiktas's iconic Inonu Stadium on the banks of the Bosphorus, surely one of the best locations in the world for the Beautiful Game. Every football fan remembers when Galatasaray gave visiting Manchester United's players the "welcome to hell" treatment at Istanbul's Atatürk airport with flares, torches and hostile chants. But the fans of Beşiktaş, who play in black and white, with a black eagle as their emblem, can be every bit as intimidating. Their ultras are called Carsi and their motto is *Herşeye karsi* (Against everything). During the Gezi Park riots some of them stole a bulldozer and rammed it into police lines. On the terraces they sing: "Eagle you are my life. I would die for you my only love."

I had been invited to the Beşiktaş game by my friend Levent and with us were daughter Charlotte, then eleven, and a friend's son Matthew, ten. We arrived at the ground to find it was all-ticket match and police were using batons to thrash ticketless fans trying to get in. We watched the aggression for about ten minutes when suddenly Levent moved one of the temporary metal barriers and urged the four of us to follow him quickly up the stadium steps to a turnstile. I thought it foolhardy but we complied. The police were too busy with their pummelling to notice us and soon we were at the gate.

"Sorry, you cannot come in," said the turnstile operator. "We're full. There's no room and you don't have tickets." Levent pleaded with him.

"Brother, my friends have come all the way from England to watch the Black Eagles. Please don't ruin their day and send them away unhappy. Don't disappoint them."

Before the employee could speak again, an overweight police officer with a bristling black moustache and service revolver on his hip stepped in front of him. He eyed up our group through the bars and then waved an arm flamboyantly.

"Come in. They can be my guests." No money changed hands.

The ground was indeed full and we struggled to find a place to sit. Fans shuffled up on the hard-wooden seats and we eventually squeezed ourselves into a spot high up behind one goal next to a policeman standing guard. We thought it wise to regularly feed the officer sweets, which, as things turned out, proved a wise decision. Beşiktaş were expected to win easily against lowly league opposition, Gaziantepspor. The Black Eagles came into the game on the back of a 4-1 home win, followed by a 3-0 away victory. But as the following day's newspaper headline read: "Beşiktaş went from a feast to a nightmare".

The game was only seven minutes old when the away team broke clear. A Beşiktaş defender up-ended the forward and was sent off by referee Ali Uluyol. Fury erupted all around us. Our amiable, sweet-munching copper quickly drew his baton and gave a few fans a whack but fortunately not us. Then the referee refused to award a penalty when a Beşiktaş player appeared to be fouled inside the area. On 49 minutes the away team went 1-0 up. Again, there was hysteria all around us and again the cop gave a few fans another good leathering. A long way away to our left we could see a clutch of away fans, in a tiny segregated area, going mad.

Despite the one-man disadvantage Beşiktaş pushed forward and dominated the game. On sixty-four minutes they equalised. 1-1. Delirium now, as black and white flags were unfurled and waved enthusiastically in the air. But the referee soon returned to centre stage. On 85 minutes he booked a Beşiktaş player, to the ire of the fans. Then a minute later he gave a straight red card to another home player. Pandemonium. The Black Eagles were down to nine. Supporters were going mental all around the ground and the noise was deafening. Anything that could be thrown rained down on to the pitch, cigarette lighters, coins and pieces of wood. People were tearing up newspapers and showering the place with home-made confetti. At that moment a huge Beşiktaş fan, probably around 20-stone, somehow waddled past the heavily populated pitch-side police cordon, jogged on to the field and chinned the referee. The official collapsed to the ground in slow motion like a discarded parachute. The overweight fan was dragged off, doubtless to be used for more baton practice. Medics rushed on to treat the ref. All around us the fans were still going crazy, shouting, screaming, waving their fists.

Our friendly cop was now in overdrive, putting his baton to good use again, with everyone in a five-metre radius suffering, except us. Eventually the ref was deemed fit to carry on. And with order finally restored Beşiktaş tried to fashion a miracle. With almost the last attack the home side hit the bar. The final whistle went and at 1-1 so ended the craziest game I have ever seen. For the crowd trouble, Beşiktaş were fined and ordered to play one game behind closed doors.

Aside from this, holidays were usually an oasis of calm. But every holidaymaker knows the anxiety you feel about not being ripped off while abroad. It helps if you have protective Turkish mates who will do their best to seek redress, even if the monetary value is tiny. In the old days Levent and his extended family would constantly warn us to be careful when out shopping and they would check the price of everything we had bought when we returned. In Şile we had our own private trading standards officer, our friend Hüseyin.

Hüseyin came to England in his early twenties, initially working in catering and later married a one-time exotic dancer, by chance also named Carolyn. Like us, they had a property in Şile and regularly travelled between the two countries. Hüseyin loved a bargain and was adept at finding cheap flights or big discounts in Portobello market, near the couple's home in West London. Once in Şile market we bumped into Hüseyin who asked what we had bought.

"Some ingredients to make *börek*," we said.

He looked in our bag. His brow furrowed when he checked the cheese we had bought:

"They sold you *kırık peynir* but you need *lor*," he thundered.

To us it just seemed like crumbly cheese in a plastic bag. But Hüseyin marched us back to the stall and shouted at the vendor for giving us the wrong kind.

"You cheated them. Now give them *lor*," he demanded, as we shuffled awkwardly in the background.

Şile might have been small but we were never bored. I was 39 when we first bought the flat but still quite fit. Back home I was still playing amateur football and in Şile I used to go running most days. A lot of the time I ran on the main roads. I would carry a stick because at one house an angry dog used to come flying out of the front garden to guard its territory. It would growl menacingly and bark furiously but fortunately never actually attack. I often ran past the town's military camp, sometimes getting a wave from the guards. On Tuesdays the air force would hold shooting practice with jets firing at a target trailed behind another aircraft. Another jogging route took me to the village of Ahmetli. The locals would look at me curiously. Back then jogging wasn't a popular pastime in Turkey. Most people worked so hard in the fields or in shops they didn't have any spare energy for sporting activities. And Turkish holidaymakers anyway preferred to play volleyball. There was at least one court on the beach and in the summer, there was always a highly competitive volleyball tournament. The council would erect a small stadium which was always packed during the event.

Sometimes I would run along the beach to the community at Kumbaba about a mile away and back. One morning I was pounding along the sand when I came across a dead body washed up on the beach: a Turkish man in his early Sixties. In those days the safety arrangements were quite primitive and Şile was well known for its rip tide that could quickly take you far out to sea, especially if you were swimming a couple of hundred metres from the main harbour area. Around thirty-five people a year used to perish at the resort. When I got home, I called the Jandarma and they collected the body.

Most years there was a greasy wrestling tournament and a festival often featuring famous Turkish rock bands and classical music artists. One year there was even a high-end open-air fashion show. Another local to befriend us was a seafarer we called Fisherman Hüseyin to distinguish him from our other friend. He also went by the name *Kalaycı* (tinsmith) his father's occupation. When we first met, he was a very handsome man, not tall but athletically built with long flowing hippy-style hair. He didn't speak much English but he was a good ally and would often turn up for dinner at our flat with a huge fish, a lobster or crabs from his fishermen mates. He was like an unpaid Butlin's Redcoat always coming up with excursions, usually involving a fishing boat. But his Achilles' heel was beer or rakı.

After a few sherbets all common sense was forgotten.

His favourite outing was sailing along the coast to an enormous cave under some rocks. You could only reach it by sea but you could sail inside the cave, disembark and then swim or wade to a sandy ridge. Returning from one trip we were flanked by three dolphins happily leaping and plunging back into the water not twenty metres away. A beautiful sight. But the weather conditions in the Black Sea are notoriously contrary. One year when he took our family, and Carolyn's friend Kathryn Jackson and her son Matthew to the cave, the wind suddenly whipped up and the boat, which was like a cross between a long punt and a gondola, began pitching ominously, with spray coming into the craft. Hüseyin was at the back, working the rudder. The rest of us were lying flat on the floor, petrified. Kathryn's face was a whiter shade of pale and mine wasn't much better. Despite the pitching and the real possibility that we could capsize, Hüseyin ploughed on, probably buoyed by Turkish machismo, rakı or both. The thought of returning to the safety of the harbour was a clear sign of weakness. The twenty-minute journey felt like a lifetime. Finally, we made it to the cave. But whereas we were normally excited to arrive, this time we were just thankful to be on solid ground again, albeit only for a short while. We looked at each other like characters in a horror B movie trapped in a haunted house No one smiled or made a joke. We realised we still had to make the return trip. When we finally reached the safety of the jetty Carolyn whispered: "Never again."

Another time, Fisherman Hüseyin decided to take Carolyn, me, Charlotte and Sophie plus the other Hüseyin and his wife, the other Carolyn, down the coast. This time we were in a small fishing boat. We had been sailing for about fifteen minutes when Fisherman Hüseyin spotted a friend on the beach. He stopped the boat's engine, dropped anchor and swam ashore.

"I'll only be ten minutes," he said.

A few moments later we spotted him playing in a volleyball match. The minutes ticked by. We had no shade on the boat and no food or water. We were due to stop and pick up some provisions. The sun was burning hot, around thirty-five degrees. And in the resort the humidity is often very high, something like seventy-five per cent. We were about two hundred metres offshore and the sea was deep. There was no way we could swim ashore. A good two and a half hours passed before Hüseyin finally clambered aboard. We were absolutely frazzled. The other Hüseyin, about ten years older than him, gave him a volley of abuse in Turkish. But Fisherman Hüseyin just smiled, switched on the boat's ignition and off we went again.

Yet another time he asked me if I fancied a day's fishing. The fishing season usually starts in September and we used to sit on our balcony in the early morning and watch the flotilla of fishing boats going out to sea. They would come back with sea bass, sea bream, bluefish, red mullet, anchovies and many others. You could buy fresh fish daily on the side of the harbour from one of the many stalls. One day we were chatting in a beach cafe and I admired a piece of equipment propped up on a mantelpiece. It was a wooden frame in the shape of a large H with yards and yards of fishing line wrapped carefully between two central struts. Attached at every few feet on the line was a tiny hook. The idea was you would set off on the boat and pay out the line by simply turning the frame over and over. When the H frame was empty you could meander around for a bit and then, when ready, head home, winding back the line to hopefully land a decent amount of fish for supper and maybe extras to sell on the harbour side.

Off we went, the two of us, Fisherman Hüseyin steering the boat and me dutifully paying out the line. The sea was calm and this boat had a wheelhouse so we had a bit of shade. After two or three hours we headed back. I began spinning the frame to draw in the line. By the time we reached the harbour the line was back in place on the frame with not a single fish, not even a sardine on any of its hooks. I was bitterly disappointed but the more phlegmatic Hüseyin just put it down to unusual currents and trotted away to drown his sorrows in a bottle of rakı.

It was true the currents could have a spectacular effect on the sea and local marine life. One August we had arranged for an English couple Philip and Sarah Braund, good friends, to join us on holiday. But three days before they were due to arrive, the previously tepid sea near the beach bars suddenly turned Siberia cold. You couldn't even put your foot in the water for fear of hypothermia. It was incredible. The deckchairs and loungers were lined up in serried ranks as usual but no one was in the sea. Luckily on the very day our friends arrived the currents changed and the lukewarm bathwater sea returned.

On another occasion the wayward currents brought in a plague of annoying insects. The sea was like some Biblical movie. You couldn't go in without touching or being touched by one or more of these creatures. And they really carried a nip. The normally azure blue water turned a dark shade of green. But again, a couple of days later and everything was back to normal. Later our friends Carolyn and Hüseyin bought themselves a boat called the Dudu. It had one tiny bedroom and a large wheelhouse which afforded decent protection from the sun. Hüseyin would bring it near the beach and we would swim out. The beach bar waiters would wade out holding trays above their heads to brings us snacks and drinks. When our holidays coincided with Ramazan, these waiters, devout Muslims, would work sixteen-hour days without food or water and without complaint. The Dudu was very civilised but it too featured in a drama. One day we were meandering along the coast not far from the harbour when we saw two canoeists, a man and a woman, in trouble. They were in that dangerous rip tide area and their canoe was taking in water. They were shouting for help and Hüseyin reacted quickly, appreciating the danger and steering the Dudu alongside the couple so they could scramble aboard. It's maybe a little overblown to say that we saved their lives but on that stretch of coastline you just could not take chances. The swirling waters near the sea-bed were incredibly strong and my wife Carolyn, who was a very strong swimmer, often said she would never go in there.

I'll never forget the time a Mongolian circus troupe arrived in Şile. Their promotional advert featured a girl in exotic national costume lying with her chest on the ground and her face looking up cherubically to the camera with her feet impossibly stationed at the side of each ear. "Elastic Girls," screamed the poster. What a way to make ends meet. "And forty-five performers in all," the advert added. This we had to see.

The Mongolians had erected a Big Top near the beach and when we entered, the tent was already more than half-full with scores of people queuing outside. Eventually the show began and a Master of Ceremonies, wearing tight white trousers and sequinned royal blue coat, welcomed everyone. The first act was a Mongolian throat singer. If you haven't had the pleasure it can be summed up as a man gargling glass while playing a small cello. Next came six acrobats, dressed in white tee-shirts and skin hugging white trousers. They performed the usual stunts, cartwheels, flips, somersaults, high jumps and building a three-man high pyramid, with colleagues standing on each other's shoulders. Then came a trick which involved the strongest of the group lying on his back with his legs in the air. A colleague made a pick-a-back and a third man, a small and slim gymnast, leapt over him and flew through the air only to be caught by the feet of the strongman lying on the floor. He straightened his legs and with his feet cradling his colleague's buttocks, he lifted the lighter man up, as both extended their arms in a gesture of triumph.

One of the acrobats then asked for a volunteer from the audience to repeat the manoeuvre just performed by the lightest man in the troupe. A rather overweight man in his late thirties rose from his seat and, to fulsome applause, began walking down steps to the ring. As before the Turk had to jump over the man making the back and then be caught in mid-air by the chap on the floor. After a few seconds of explanation, the audience novice took his place like a man running a dad's race at school sports day. Given his size and apparent lack of athleticism, the plan looked risky to me. There was a drum roll followed by the clash of a cymbal, the signal for the volunteer to set off. Over five yards he gathered pace, put his hands successfully on to the back of the acrobat bending over and launched himself into the air. Unfortunately, he could not control his legs properly. Although the acrobat on the floor managed to catch the volunteer's right buttock the man's left leg foot landed heavily between the Mongolian's legs, catching him fully in the crown jewels. He yelled in pain as the audience member stumbled forward and fell flat on his face. The crowd howled with laughter. The volunteer limped away as did the catcher, clutching his groin, his face contorted in pain. The remaining men in white regained their composure and did a few more tricks.

They were replaced by two jugglers. The men flung their plastic clubs higher and higher, never once making a mistake. Then they juggled flaming hoops before a big finale which involved juggling eight clubs each. For this they swapped clubs, the new set being made of plastic but somehow luminous lime green. One by one, the first juggler would throw each of his clubs to his associate, who still had to juggle his own. The idea was that the second man would catch each one of his pal's clubs while simultaneously putting one club at a time into a nearby container. When all sixteen clubs were put away the men could take a well-earned bow. Sadly, after grabbing three or four of his friend's flying clubs the second man made an error and dropped one. His pal stopped sending his quota through the air and the act came to an abrupt end. Cue generous applause as the entertainers took a bow and left the ring.

There followed clowns, singers and dancers in traditional Mongolian costume. And finally came the Elastic Girls, who tied themselves in ever-more contorted knots to the crowd's delight. The Master of Ceremonies then re-appeared to invite all the performers into the ring for a final bow and a well-deserved round of applause. But having assembled his crew he grabbed a microphone and turned to the audience. In Turkish he said that the jugglers felt so bad that they had not completed the grand finale of their routine successfully that they wanted to give it another go.

"Will you give them have another chance?" he asked. There was a general murmur of approval. The ring was cleared and the two jugglers re-emerged with their sixteen luminous clubs. With each man back into his rhythm, juggler A began to launch his first club over to his colleague. At that very moment there was a power-cut and the Big Top was plunged into darkness. In the gloom all we could make out was the two men flailing about with their green luminous projectiles crashing down around them like a bombing raid. One juggler winced as a club dropped on his head. The paying Turks again roared with laughter and began trying to get a better look by lighting cigarette lighters, matches and the odd candle. The two distraught jugglers slunk away as Turks began leaving the tent, many with tears of laughter rolling down their cheeks. If the Ringmaster had any commercial sense, he would have kept that bit in the show and deliberately cut the lights at the crucial moment. It was priceless. On the way home, we passed a poster for the circus and, as it was the troupe's last day in town, I carefully peeled off the sticky tape at the corners and rolled it up as a souvenir. Later I had it framed and it now sits proudly in my office, a homage if not to The Greatest Show on Earth, certainly the weirdest.

CHAPTER SEVEN

EARTHQUAKE

Apart from the occasional dose of the runs and the odd allergy we rarely fell ill in Şile. We had a scare once when daughter Charlotte, then ten, fell and hurt her leg and we took her for an x-ray to the local hospital. After confirming that she had not broken any bones, a man tied up the x-ray with a pink bow and gave it to us as a souvenir. Actually, that's not quite the full story. When we arrived, we were confronted by a man in his forties in jeans and a tee-shirt. After explaining about Charlotte's slip on the beach he organised the x-ray. But afterwards he made her sit on a bench in reception. He then took out a metal tape measure and checked the lengths of both her legs. I had not seen that done on Holby City or Grey's Anatomy.

"Everything is ok," he said confidently. When I asked if we could also have a photograph of him as a keepsake, he beamed a wide smile, disappeared for a few seconds and returned wearing a white doctor's coat, with a stethoscope in the top pocket. As we left the clinic, I began to wonder if he was actually a doctor or a cleaner or security guard who just happened to know how to work the x-ray machine. Maybe he had simply given us an old x-ray image from the archives. Who knows?

Our favourite beach bar was run by a man called Sami Baba. He was a gaunt figure with an infectious smile, permanent stubble on his chin and a white sailor's hat on his head, who liked nothing better than generating laughter. One day we arrived to find he had taken delivery of two huge plastic jerry cans full of bootleg Martini. Normally, I can't stand the drink but after a few glasses I found myself in a beachside conga. Another time Sami sidled up to me.

"Have you ever seen a Turkish circumcision party?" he whispered. The *sünnet* is rather like the Jewish idea of the bar mitzvah, a boy's coming of age. The word *sünnet* comes from Arabic and means "busy path", referring to the path to God and the good or bad attitudes which may or may not take you there. In Turkey the boy is dressed in a white uniform with a special sequinned hat, fur-lined satin cape and baton and usually paraded around the town before his family host a lavish party. I once passed a shop window display with mannequins in *sünnet* outfits. Nearby was a tableau featuring a log with an axe embedded in it alongside a fake foreskin in a pool of blood (well, red paint). Gold or banknotes are pinned on the boy, in a similar fashion to the wedding ritual. In Ottoman times the sultan would organise mass circumcisions, with thousands of boys snipped in a single day. It was his way of bringing society together in a shared rite of masculinity.

"Well not first-hand," I said, answering Sami's question.

"Follow me," he said.

Sami led me into a back room of the beach bar. There, lying on a wooden bed, was a young boy who seconds earlier had been circumcised. A man (a doctor, a licensed practitioner or an enthusiastic amateur, it was hard to tell) was sewing up the remains of his foreskin. There was blood everywhere. The boy grimaced but wasn't crying. Maybe the screaming had come earlier. The operation is usually done without anaesthetic. His father, apparently proud to have a foreign visitor as on onlooker, urged me forward and vacated a chair next to the bed. I took his seat. It would have been impolite to move until the needlework was over. When the job was done the beaming, dad presented me with a huge piece of fruit cake, heralding the start of a party.

According to one report one sixth of the world's menfolk are circumcised and the practice is thought to be 15,000 years old. When explorers first discovered Australia they found aborigines were circumcised. Exactly how, I have no idea. I'll leave that to your imagination. I can't quite envisage Captain Cook handling over mirrors, beads and trinkets and then saying: "By the way, can I look under your loincloth?" Circumcision by unlicensed people is still a big problem in some Turkish areas. Children have sometimes been rushed to hospital with complications including, heavy bleeding, glandular injury, gangrene and even partial amputation of the penis. A survey in 2003 found that up to thirty per cent of circumcisions were not carried out by qualified people.

"Where have you been?" Carolyn asked as I returned to our sunbeds.

"You'll never guess." I responded.

We never had a television in the flat from the day we bought it until 2010 and then it was only for the World Cup. We would, however, often watch pirate videos on a laptop. I know law enforcement agencies around the world condemn the practice of buying knock-off CDs and DVDs because criminal gangs and sometimes terrorists are often allegedly behind the distribution. Then there is the not insignificant matter of copyright infringement. But it was very tempting when the little shop down the road was selling for 50p a Hollywood blockbuster that only premiered the week before. I recall our excitement in 2004 as we settled down to watch the newly-released cheapo DVD of Troy, starring Brad Pitt. We were approaching a key moment in the action when suddenly the battlefield was blotted out by the silhouette of a man standing up and walking left to right. We realised that the author of the dodgy disc had simply paid to enter a cinema, probably in the United States, and used a sophisticated camcorder to copy the action on screen, only to be undone by a fellow patron needing a pee.

Another source of annoyance was that, although the friendly shopkeeper always assured us the film was in English, it was often actually dubbed in Turkish with no subtitles. Sometimes it would come with English subtitles but apparently written by a dyslexic Turkish fourth former. In fairness, if this happened, he would always swap the DVDs for different fakes. Once or twice we would reach the film's denouement only for it to suddenly end just as the villain was about to get his comeuppance. Presumably at that very moment the camcorder man had his collar felt by the cinema management or police.

A far more Turkish form of entertainment was playing backgammon (*tavla*). The game, believed to be older than chess, can be traced back nearly 5,000 years to Mesopotamia (modern-day Iraq). The world's oldest set of dice, made from human bone, was discovered there. A version of the game surfaced in France during the 11th century, becoming a favourite pastime of gamblers. It was banned in 16th century England but by the 18th century, backgammon had become popular among the English clergy. The Russian-American socialite Prince Alexis Obolensky Jr, who died in 1986, is credited with being the "father of modern backgammon" after promoting the game in the United States and co-founding the International Backgammon Association which drew up an official set of rules.

Nowadays, Turkey has built a reputation for having more players per capita of population than anywhere else in the world. Most Turks are masters of the game from an early age and play at a ferocious speed. The quickness of your decision-making and movement of the pieces is a sign both of expertise and masculinity. Mulling over a move, as if playing chess, may well bring tuts or even catcalls from your opponent or spectators. When you take an opponent's piece you have to slam it down as hard as possible on the table. Turks also hate to lose, especially to a foreigner. So, some of their moves replicate the sleight of hand which made Paul Daniels famous. There really should be a video assistant referee.

There's also the rather ungentlemanly practice when your opponent secretes in his hand one of the pieces that you have taken rather than placing it on the side of the board. You then forget it is "resting" and foolishly leave yourself open to be taken yourself when it's your opponent's turn. And if you do lose, the tradition is for your opponent to put the closed-up board game under your arm as he tells you "*öğren de gel,*" which literally means, "go learn how to play and come back."

Daughter Sophie proved to be a dab hand at the game and once, aged about eleven, won an informal beach competition involving Turks and holidaymakers, young and old, in which she was the youngest competitor. We loved it when a certain Turkish man was a spectator. In his seventies the grey-haired man regularly frequented the beach bars, wearing white shorts and a white sun hat but no shirt. Local legend had it that he had been a decorated soldier and later a government spy. Whether this is true I have no idea. Turks love a rumour. But he watched any backgammon game closely. When Sophie had the choice to take one of her opponent's pieces or play a safer move he would roar in English "KILL HIM, KILL HIM" meaning she should take the piece. So that was the nickname we gave him. KILL HIM.

Because, as foreigners, we were a rarity in those days there was no shortage of people keen to talk to us. Among the many intriguing strangers, we met was a former military jet pilot who went on to start a business and made a fortune erecting all kinds of aerials all over the world. He claimed to speak nine languages. Then there was the fertility doctor who told us an amusing tale of a couple who seemed unable to make a baby. He examined the man and the wife and both seemed physically healthy. Further laboratory tests confirmed there appeared to be nothing to prevent procreation. It was only after several weeks of head scratching that he discovered the man was actually infertile and had been bringing in his brother's sperm to be tested because he was so ashamed. Turkish virility is, of course, very important.

A regular highlight of the summer holiday was the greasy wrestling, always very popular in Şile. One year we were invited to go to support a friend, Ahmet, who was running a burger bar at the event. Unfortunately, just as the mayor introduced the event's main sponsor and shepherded him to a ceremonial chair the size of an Ottoman Emperor's throne, an enormous cloud of smoke from Ahmet's grill wafted over and caused a coughing fit in the VIP stand. There were two prizes for the overall winner: a sum of money and a ram with fearsome horns. Try lifting that above your head FA Cup style.

Greasy wrestling in Turkey originated as a diversion for Ottoman soldiers in the 14th century. But the sport itself is believed to date back to Persia in 1065 BC. Turkey's premier event at Kirkpinar is the oldest continuously sanctioned sporting event in the world. According to one theory, the wrestlers covering themselves in olive oil stemmed from using the stuff as a mosquito repellent in bygone times. Another explanation is that it was used by gladiators in ancient Rome to make it harder for opponents to grab hold. Modern competitors, called *pehlivan*, which means hero or champion, come in thirteen categories from chief wrestler to best beginner. Each wears a pair of leather breeches called a *kispet*, often with a name written on the waistband at the back in metal studs. This can be the wrestler's own name, his club or his town. The *kispet* is carried to events in a special reed bag called a *zembil*.

The winner has to pin his opponent to the floor using any one of 350 special moves. They include shoving a hand deep inside your opponent's *kispet* in an apparently homo-erotic gesture. Excessive force, however, is not allowed and can lead to disqualification. Bouts had no time limit until 1975 when a forty-minute duration was imposed. Events last all day. They begin with a traditional ceremonial dance in which the wrestlers line up and walk across the arena in special slow steps before each puts a left knee to the ground. Then they all jump up with a shout in Turkish of "come on wrestler" and the show begins. Dozens of bouts start all over the cordoned off arena, each one with its own umpire. The carnival atmosphere is complemented by drummers and pipe players.

One hero of the sport was a man called Yusuf Ismail who in 1897 travelled to America to pursue a career in what would now be called unregulated Cage Fighting. Standing 6ft 2in and weighing more than 300 lbs, he was known as the Terrible Turk and billed as one of the world's three strongest men. He made a lot of money but on his return to Europe his steamer sank and, along with six-hundred other passengers, he perished. While some fellow travellers were rescued some reports, possibly apocryphal, claimed that Ismail sank because he was weighed down by his money belt containing up to 10,000 US dollars in gold coins. His story is now used as a Turkish parable against avarice.

I'm not a sun worshipper and I'm always careful to keep my head covered by wearing a battered Tilley hat. There's a rule among wearers of the famous headgear, launched in Canada in 1980 by Alex Tilley, that if you see someone else wearing a Tilley hat you must go and speak with him or her. That's how we met Jakob. He hailed from a small town not far from Şile called Polonezköy, founded in 1842 by a group of around a dozen Polish emigres. They had fled their homeland after a failed uprising. The community grew and ventures in forestry and farming flourished. But Polish culture and language were scrupulously maintained. After Polish Independence in 1918 many of the Poles returned home. Those who stayed took Turkish citizenship. Nowadays the village consists of around 1,000 people and around forty still speak fluent Polish.

Jakob spoke Polish, Turkish and English and ran a successful hotel in the village. But his obsession was vintage cars. He had three, including a cream-coloured Plymouth, each worth in today's market around £70,000. And every year he hosted a classic car rally attended by thousands of enthusiasts. His ambition was to produce a car magazine in Turkey, rather like Auto Express. He asked if I could help him launch a Turkish edition of a mainstream UK car magazine and when I returned to England, I made enquiries. The various publishing houses, however, requested huge sums of money for a licence to use their titles and the idea came to nothing. Two years later, back in Turkey on holiday, we decided to visit Polonezköy, for the first time. We hired a car and eventually found Jakob's hotel. But a gardener informed us he had died suddenly some months earlier. We were introduced to his widow who proudly showed us around the hotel and its extensive grounds, including the garage housing the classic cars. There was also a vintage motorcycle and sidecar. Apparently, Jakob had been driving when he felt unwell. He stopped by the side of the road and called an ambulance. Paramedics checked him over and advised him to go immediately to hospital for a full examination. He said he didn't want to go in the ambulance and felt well enough to drive himself. But minutes after they had driven away he had a massive cardiac arrest.

Sometimes I experienced Turkey's unique quirkiness remotely. For many years in the 1990s I would while away boring newspaper "graveyard shifts" trying to improve my Turkish by watching internet episodes of a wonderful TV show called *Maceracı* (Adventurer). It was about a reporter called Murat Yeni riding all over Turkey using a motorbike and sidecar looking for weird and outlandish subjects. Clearly the sidecar was for his TV cameraman pal but he was never in shot. One day *Maceracı* (pronounced mar-jer-a-jer) pulled up to see an old man dragging a stone on a sack truck.

"What are you doing?" he asked.

"I'm building a house," said the wizened old man, who claimed to be well into his nineties. Sure enough, a short way down the road, we were introduced to his creation, a stone edifice, not yet finished and not exactly fit for TV's Grand Designs but nevertheless quite pleasing on the eye. Another time Murat came across a fully functional barber's shop built into the base of a huge, centuries old tree, four or five metres in diameter, that had either been hit by lightning or had grown in a peculiar way. In yet another episode he drove into a dust-blown village of mainly adobe buildings, somewhere in

Anatolia where you assumed the only skills were goat herding, to find workers meticulously assembling a massive chandelier for some foreign country's embassy. Another show featured an incredible memory man. Many of the programmes involved tasting the local food of the places he visited. Dozens of scarfed-up ladies in baggy pantaloons (*şalvar*) would sit on carpets or blankets, with their cook pots in front of them, explaining arcane recipes and ladling spoonfuls into Murat's mouth.

Whether it was the many food tastings or the vida loca, which came from the fame that the show's success brought him, Murat's weight began to balloon. He wasn't quite at Elvis Presley proportions but you could tell something was amiss. But much worse was to follow. On July 19, 2016 the licence of the TV station where he worked, Samanyolu, was revoked and the channel was closed by the Radio and Television Supreme Council because it was owned by the exiled cleric Fethullah Gülen. Gülen and President Recep Tayyip Erdogan had been firm friends and political partners at one time but were now sworn enemies. The cleric, living in America, was blamed for the failed coup in 2015. Everything that Gülen owned was confiscated and anybody who worked for him was deemed a terrorist, unless they proved otherwise. Two years later Murat was arrested as part of the so-called FETO investigation and purge against Gülenists and later sentenced to at least fifteen years in jail. The prosecution claimed that Samanyolu was a propaganda tool for Gülen. Murat denied all the allegations against him, claiming he was simply a professional TV presenter. But it cut no ice. Was Murat guilty? Who knows? But I do know that a friend's wife had her teacher's licence cancelled and all her pension to date seized because, unknown to her, the college where she worked was owned by Gülen.

These two stories are good examples of why UK friends often ask me: "Why Turkey?" But if you stay out of politics it doesn't affect you. Saying that, the lack of free speech is often breathtaking. In June 2020, journalist Ender Imrek went on trial accused of "insulting" President Erdogan's wife by criticising her for wearing a 50,000 US dollar Hermes bag when many parts of the country lay in abject poverty. The indictment said he had insulted her "by not attributing nice qualities to her." Fortunately for him he was later acquitted but the decision was appealed and the case is still before the courts.

One year, Carolyn's sister Melanie, husband Tim and their three children, Eleanor and identical twin boys James and Edward, joined us on holiday in Şile. We went to an open-air restaurant for an evening meal. Diners were being entertained by a Turkish keyboard player. But when he went for a break Tim, a music teacher, asked the restaurant owner whether he could use the equipment to play a tune or two. We never saw the Turk again as Tim (or "Meester Tim" as the owner called him) belted out hits by Elton John, the Rolling Stones, the Beatles and other rock legends. With most of the diners now on their feet dancing frenetically, the owner produced a bottle of brandy, poured it on the floor and set light to it, so our gyrations continued around an ankle-high, meandering stream of flame. At the end of the evening the owner thanked Meester Tim for one of the "best nights of my life," pulled a large painting from the wall and presented it to him as a gift.

"We would love to see you play here again one day," he said, shaking Tim's hand like a long lost relative.

In 2003 we were sitting on our balcony in Şile when, for the first time, we saw a sea plane coming into land. It was quite a spectacle. A number of people got out and went ashore. A few hours later they returned to the plane and it prepared to take off.

Now I'm no aviator but I would have thought it was easier to get airborne by running parallel to the beach rather than heading out to sea, especially given the waves in the resort can be very strong. But that's exactly what the pilot attempted. We could hear the revving of the plane's engines and the aircraft bobbing up and down on the surface of the water. Each time it tried to take off it just couldn't seem to leave the water. It looked as if the pilot was struggling but he kept trying. The engine noise became ever more strident. Then, the plane's nose suddenly dipped. Carolyn was in the kitchen preparing our evening meal.

"Come here, quickly," I shouted. "I think this bloody plane's going to sink."

Within seconds there was a full-blown emergency. The plane, indeed, was shipping water. At the time the town did not have a proper lifeboat. But several fishing boats and a motorised rubber dinghy instantly headed towards the beleaguered aircraft. We saw men scrambling to board the makeshift rescue vessels. I decided to stroll into town and find out more.I quickly bumped into our friend Fisherman Hüseyin.

"Did you hear about the plane sinking," I inquired.

"Yes, I helped in the rescue." he said

"And do you know who was on board?" he added.

"No, who?" I asked.

He looked left and right, conspiratorially.

"Sedat Peker," he responded. Peker was, and still is, one of Turkey's most famous criminals. Born in 1971 in Adapazari, not far from Istanbul, he was tried for murder but acquitted and fled to Romania Police also wanted to talk to him about alleged protection rackets and many other offences. In 1998 he returned voluntarily to Turkey, pleaded guilty to a number of crimes but was also found guilty of building a criminal organisation. The prosecutor wanted a sentence of seven-and-a-half-years but the judge gave Peker less than nine months. Popular legend has it that Peker often gave money to the poor and to charity and therefore had a kind of Robin Hood status. If you asked people in the street few people had a bad word for him. Anyhow, the sea plane crash was hot news and I immediately called a Turkish journalist friend in Istanbul who got a front-page scoop.

The ill-fated plane had by now been dragged into the harbour and was lying half in and half out of the water. Peker had a villa in Şile but was rarely, if ever, seen walking around the town.

However, his henchmen, invariably carrying guns, often spent time in the beach bars we frequented. Two years after the plane crash Peker was in trouble with the authorities again and after a two-year investigation he was sentenced to fourteen years in jail for, among other things, running a crime syndicate, forgery and false imprisonment. By now our friend Fisherman Hüseyin had secured the job of maintaining Peker's speedboat. Following Peker's incarceration he gave us a few spins around the Black Sea in it. Peker's bodyguards continued to mope around, seemingly at a loose end. But after a while they simply disappeared.

It wasn't just the Turkish mafia who carried guns. Our next-door neighbour, a white-haired, retired policeman in his seventies, who we called Grandad, still carried his service revolver. He would take it to the beach and hide it under a towel. God knows why. Maybe he missed the thrill of always being on duty. Grandad didn't like sunbathing much. But he did enjoy playing backgammon and drinking copious amounts of *rakı*. One afternoon Carolyn and I, plus kids, were just packing up to walk back up to the flat when Grandad saw us leaving.

"Hey, I'm going back now, too. I'll give you a lift."

"OK, Grandad. That's very kind," I replied. We followed him out of the beach bar and all piled into his car. The smell of *rakı* filled the air. Grandad set off but we had not driven very far when we reached a stand-off in the town centre. A car was coming the other way and, because of some inconsiderate parking, the two vehicles couldn't pass. Grandad wound down his window and ordered the other driver to back up.

"I have right of way," he shouted with the authority of a man used to ordering subordinates around. But the other driver wasn't conceding. He didn't move.

"Do you know who I am," shouted Grandad, reeling off his former high rank in the police force. Still the stalemate continued. The other man gestured with his hand for Grandad to go back as if brushing something from the dashboard. Finally, Grandad pulled out his pistol and waved it in the air. Carolyn and I looked at each other in shock, wondering just how far the old man would go. But the appearance of the firearm did the trick and the other driver reversed. Grandad put the weapon in the glove compartment, muttered something under his breath and thrust the car into a forward gear with a contented smile on his face.

Fisherman Hüseyin was responsible for introducing us to one of the most colourful characters we ever met in Şile.

"George, Carolyn, meet Rambo," he said. The man sitting on the harbour wall looked nothing like the Sylvester Stallone character. Quite the reverse. He rather resembled comic and ornithologist Bill Oddie with a decent tan. Maybe they meant the French poet Rimbaud. About 5ft 6in tall, around fifty-five years old, with silvery hair, glasses and a lined and weather-beaten face he could have been mistaken for a poet or maybe a vicar or an accountant. Our other friend Hüseyin turned up and was able to translate Rambo's story. By all accounts he earned the nickname as a soldier.

"I was in the military when Turkey invaded Cyprus in 1974," said Rambo. "I was involved in some hand-to-hand fighting. I saw men die. It was hard to take. They were terrible days. Something happened to me.

"I can't explain it exactly. Maybe you might call it Post Traumatic Stress Disorder. I was having mood swings, psychiatric episodes, panic attacks. My life was a total mess."

Rambo was sent home and was in hospital for a while. Later he was allowed to leave the army on medical grounds and doctors told him to live as quiet a life as possible. He didn't mention family but we took it that he was either divorced or never married. He came to Şile and opened a gift shop selling knick-knacks. A year or so later a rich German businessman sailed into Şile on a large yacht intent on an early retirement and the dolce vita. Having bumped into Rambo, he asked the ex-soldier whether he could help him with odd jobs on the yacht. To earn extra money Rambo readily agreed. The arrangement continued for a few years. Then one day the businessman told Rambo he had been offered the chance of a highly-paid job back in Germany. He really wanted to accept the position but didn't want to take his yacht. He also didn't want to leave it accruing harbour fees in Turkey. Why he didn't try to sell it I have no idea.

"He cooked up a plot," Rambo went on. "He asked me if I could help him to sail the yacht a little way out to sea and then deliberately sink it so he could claim the value of the craft from his insurer. He said he would make it worth my while, so in the end I agreed."

The conspiracy worked perfectly. The German collected his insurance pay off and returned to the Fatherland never to be seen again. Rambo took a deep breath and continued.

"After a while, I got to thinking. I wonder if I could salvage that yacht. So, I got some helpers together, hired some lifting equipment and one day we pulled the yacht off the sea bed and dragged it back into the harbour.

"I spent months pumping out water and cleaning it up, ensuring that the engine worked properly and that it was seaworthy. The work was very therapeutic. I enjoyed it. It was like a new hobby for me. And here it is, look, just behind me. How about I take you and your family out for a sail in it?"

I glanced at the gleaming craft tied up along the quayside, mainsail neatly folded. Then I looked at Carolyn and our children and they looked back at me. For a few seconds nobody spoke.

"So, let me get this right," I said to myself. "We are being invited by an ex-psychiatric patient who suffered panic attacks after being shell-shocked to go for a sail in a yacht that once sank."

I turned to Rambo: "Yes, of course. Great idea. What day would be convenient?"

The summer in 1999 will be etched on my memory forever because of three natural events. They were all documented in Sophie's school diary, designated homework, on how she spent the holiday. First came a huge tornado which thankfully stayed far out at sea. Then on August 11 we experienced a total solar eclipse. For people in the UK, it was the first full eclipse seen since June 1927. We pasted a pair of special cardboard sunglasses into Sophie's dossier. And finally, six days later, came a terrifying earthquake which killed around 17,000 people and left more than 250,000 people homeless.

The epicentre was Izmit about eighty miles away. Staying with Carolyn and me, Charlotte and Sophie were our friend Kathryn and her son Matthew. Because of the heat I was asleep on the lounge sofa with the balcony windows wide open when at one minute after 3am I sensed a deep rumbling noise. I thought at first it was thunder. But then our apartment building began to shake like a washing machine on full spin. I could hear Carolyn running to the kids' bedroom as Kathryn and Matthew quickly dressed. Nobody can predict how they will react in a major crisis but I was remarkably calm, standing in the corridor with a hand, rather pathetically in hindsight, placed on each wall. The shaking lasted for forty-five seconds. Everyone else headed for the stairs but, foolishly, I was more concerned that I could not find my keys. I was still looking for them when I heard Carolyn shouting from below.

"Get out of there. Come down," she bellowed. I had just located my keys, at last, when a neighbour Ibrahim appeared at the front door.

"Come on. You shouldn't be here." He had bravely climbed the sixty-four stairs to persuade me to leave. We stood around in the small car park at the front of the building as Ibrahim tried to gather information. Telephone lines were out of action. After an hour or more, our friend Hüseyin arrived in a car and ferried us to his house on the other side of town. We sat in his garden listening to events unfold on a radio. In the aftermath there were reports of a large amount of dead crabs and jellyfish turning up two days before the earthquake in Degirmendere, a small town near Gölcük, not far from Izmit. The phenomenon was explained as the release of methane gas in the prelude to the quake. During the quake itself part of the town of Gölcük, including a hotel and several shops and restaurants, collapsed into the sea. In Izmit, medical workers smashed pharmacy windows to obtain supplies for hospitals swamped by the injured. All through the region, even in Istanbul, buildings collapsed. Many were later found to have design or construction faults. Some had been made of concrete fashioned with sand from beaches.

"We have done the most that we can," said Mustafa Erdik, head of earthquake engineering at the Bosphorus University in Istanbul. "But existing building codes are simply not being applied".

The Turkish Ministry of Public Works and Settlement had tried to improve compliance two years before but suggested legislation was resisted by the construction industry and was not passed by parliament. The earthquake also caused a near eight-foot high tsunami in the Sea of Marmara, believed to have killed 155 people. At the time I was freelancing and doing a lot of work for The Sun newspaper. I took a taxi to the post office and rang the paper's news desk. They asked me to file a first-person account of our ordeal which appeared the following day with a picture byline. That night we slept in a makeshift tent in Hüseyin's garden. At exactly 3am the following morning there was a powerful aftershock which saw several of us sit bolt upright. More than fifty search and rescue teams from all over the world headed to Istanbul. It took a while for them to be effectively assigned because local people would stop vehicles and beg those aboard to follow them to a collapsed building to hunt for loved ones. The tragedy led to a new blueprint for use in similar disasters, focusing on better communications so teams could be redeployed quicker to where they were most needed. The idea of a "gold command" was developed to deal with communities, journalists and other volunteer help and rescue agencies.

Over the following days we bought many national Turkish papers and clipped out graphic photographs detailing the damage for inclusion in Sophie's diary. Before the holiday I had, strangely prophetically, made the front cover to resemble a haunted house, with the vampire from the 1922 silent German horror movie Nosferatu peeking out from the windows. Never for one moment did I think some of the entries would be every bit as macabre. Sophie stuck her airplane boarding pass on the final page under the words "we're glad to be home." Indeed, we were.

I used to enjoy telling people I was a millionaire. A Turkish millionaire. Then on January 1, 2005, Turkey introduced a new currency. It lobbed six noughts off everything and proudly announced the New Turkish Lira. At one time the lowest denomination of paper money was the 100,000 TL note. For a while shopkeepers and market traders still talked in millions.

My eyebrows were raised again in 2018 when the government decided to make it easier for people to change their family name. Turkish names had fascinated me for years. Our neighbour Birgül's name, for instance, which means "one rose". There's also an actor called Mahsun Kırmızıgül, the surname meaning "red rose". It wasn't until 1934 that Turks were obliged by law to adopt a surname. For centuries before that people used a first name and were addressed with titles like *hacı* (pilgrim), *hoca* (teacher), *ağa* (master), *paşa* (general), *hafız* (someone who has completely memorised the Koran). In her book Surname Stories in the History of the Republic, Emine Gürsoy Naskalı explains how people chose their new names. Some arose from the father's physical appearance like *pehlivan* (wrestler) or *sakallı* (bearded), while others preferred linking to personality, like *çalışkan* (hardworking) or *güleryuz* (smiling). Many people took surnames related to their ancestors and historic events, for example *kılıç* (sword), *Osman* (founder of Ottoman Empire), *Sakarya* (a battle during Turkish War of Independence), and *yılmaz* (fearless fighter).

Levent's surname is Uçak, which means aeroplane. Yes, Mr Aeroplane. But he believes this may have derived from a mistake by a clerk sometime in the past. He thinks his adopted family name may actually have been Üçok, meaning "three arrows". But clearly some people were unhappy with their names. According to a story in the Guardian many people wanted to change the names their ancestors took or those that were obviously misspelled. Among more than 75,000 applicants, unsurprisingly, was Mr Testicle. Also, in the queue were Mr Naked, Mr Jackal and Mr Sold.

Carolyn's sister Melanie, husband Tim and family have contributed to many of our Turkish memories Once we sent the identical twin boys, James and Edward, then aged around fourteen, to the shops in Şile to buy some *lahmacun*, the traditional ultra-thin Turkish pizza, topped with savoury mince. They had been gone for about twenty-five minutes when they rang our flat on a mobile phone.

"Uncle George, what's the Turkish word for *lahmacun*?" they asked. They are still having to live that down fifteen years later. Once returning from a shopping trip, again in Şile, Tim found himself with a decidedly suspect tummy. To make matters worse he had "gone commando" that morning, wearing only khaki shorts. Still two hundred metres from home his bowels involuntarily opened and soon a brown pool was forming at his feet. Didn't the same thing happen to Gary Lineker in a World Cup match? Tim reached for his mobile phone and immediately rang our flat for help. But while explaining his plight, a car full of Turkish tourists pulled up and asked him for directions. Having got rid of them, he stammered into the phone.

"Come quickly, and bring a towel." James or Edward (I can't tell them apart) raced to the rescue and a few minutes later appeared at our door, tears rolling down his face.

"Dad's shat himself." Having cleaned himself up, Tim threw the soiled shorts into a bin immediately opposite our flat. A few minutes later we looked out from the balcony to see them being retrieved by a gang of gypsies who regularly raided the refuse for anything they could use.

We were on holiday in Turkey in 2010 when the World Cup in South Africa opened but we didn't have a television in our flat. If we wanted to watch a game we would always go to a local bar or restaurant where the atmosphere created by football-mad Turks added to the enjoyment. But knowing how important football is to me and for greater convenience, my friend Hüseyin offered to give me a spare black and white TV.

"Now you can watch the World Cup in the comfort of your own home," he said. He delivered it with a basic aerial to plug into the back but the picture we got resembled a fuzzy grey forest viewed from outer space.

"Ah, you need a satellite dish," said Hüseyin. We called a TV engineer and the following day, after a lot of drilling and hammering, the dish was erected on the back balcony. But when we plugged the dish's lead into Hüseyin's set it was clear the two devices couldn't talk to each other.

"You will probably need a special de-coder box," said Hüseyin. We found one in a shop in the town but when we brought it home, we realised it required a SCART connection which Hüseyin's set didn't have.

"Well the television is quite old. But you can get a more modern one cheaply from a second-hand shop," said Hüseyin, helpfully. "There's one about three hundred metres down the road." Off we went to the *eskici* (seller of old stuff). He had a television with a SCART connection but it was the size of a trunk you could hide a body in.

"Does it work?" I inquired.

"Of course," said the *eskici*.

"Unfortunately, I don't have an aerial. But I can turn it on, look." He twisted a knob and sure enough another fuzzy forest filmed from a satellite appeared, only this time in colour.

"OK, we'll take it," we said. Later that day two helpers, grunting and groaning, manhandled the thing up the four flights of stairs to our flat. We plugged in the SCART lead from the decoder and twisted the knob, hoping to see Gary Lineker, Alan Hansen or Alan Shearer and hear the sound of vuvuzelas. Nothing. Just the fuzzy colourful forest. The helpers looked crestfallen and were soon grunting their way back down the stairs. We walked back to the shop but there was a sign on the door. "We are closed".

"Damn. Just our luck," I thought to myself. Fortunately, there was a telephone number on the sign and when I rang the owner answered.

"I'm so sorry," he said. "But I just learned that my brother has a much better television, smaller and in good condition. It definitely works and I'll bring it tomorrow." For once the famous "mañana" meant what it said and not sometime next month. This time the owner came in person. The set was still an old model, not a flat screen, but when we plugged it in we got a decent picture.

"Fantastic. At last. Does it have a zapper?" I asked.

"Ah, I forgot. No." said the *eskici*. "But I can get one." He made a phone call and fifteen minutes later a boy arrived with a plastic shopping bag containing no fewer than fifty remotes. None of them had batteries. We took two AAA batteries out of an old flashlight and began working through the selection.

Eventually we found one that worked. The *eskici* smiled broadly and bade us farewell. Given England's performance, scraping through the group and then being thrashed by Germany in the first knock out round, we really shouldn't have bothered.

CHAPTER EIGHT

MAD ABOUT THE KÖY

It had long been our intention to move to Turkey full time. But something always seemed to get in the way. One day Levent sent me an e-mail. He had also been planning for his retirement. As you have read, we first met in Istanbul in 1972 when he was just fourteen. He claimed our chance encounter inspired him to pursue an interest in English and that had led to a number of job opportunities. He had mostly worked in Turkey in a variety of jobs including selling petrol pump equipment but also spent seven years in Saudi Arabia building infrastructure, mainly water reservoirs. Speaking English had been invaluable. He was now in his late fifties, tall, slim with greying curly hair. Levent, who was now divorced and living with his mother, had spent three years scouting the Izmir area, where years before he had done his military service. Eventually he cultivated a jovial estate agent, Ismail, in a town called Tire, about forty-five minutes inland by car from the Aegean Sea. Thus, he was alerted to a run-down property in a nearby village called *Kaplan* (Tiger) part way up a mountain overlooking the town. Then he realised the plot opposite was also for sale. This was the crux of his e-mail. He forwarded several photographs.

We came, we saw, we conkered. The area was awash with chestnut trees. In "our" garden there were also fig, walnut, olive, quince, apple, sour plum, pomegranate and loquat trees. A cornucopia of culinary comestibles ... as the Aristotle of alliteration Leonard Sachs might have said on The Good Old Days music hall television show, on which the curtain dropped in 1983. Looking back, it was probably a foolhardy decision at our time of life to buy almost 2,000 square metres of land with three virtually derelict buildings in a traditional Turkish village (*köy*). I was sixty-four and Carolyn fifty-three and, although we had renovated properties in both England and Turkey, this was on a different scale. Apart from having a friend living nearby there was one highly motivating factor. We had tried and failed to do something similar in England more than thirty years earlier. Over a twelve-month period, we pursued (but ultimately were unable to buy) five run-down farmhouses or barns on the Derbyshire/Cheshire border. Here was a chance to exorcise that dormant frustration and fulfil a latent dream.

The area is known as *Yeşil* (green) Tire for its fertility. People say if you put a finger in the soil and leave it for a few minutes when you pull it out, you'll have six on that hand. Visions of Richard Briers and Felicity Kendal living frugally off the land in the Seventies' British sit-com The Good Life flooded in. But if we went ahead this was going to be more like Changing Rooms meets Last of the Summer Wine. Carolyn and I had talked many times about the idea of living permanently in Turkey. We agreed we did not want to pursue the traditional expat life, watching Match of the Day in smoky bars with other Brits and doing karaoke She had a special dislike for leathery-skinned, gravelly-voiced British women whose vocal cords had been smoked in Marlborough and marinated in vodka. But was Levent's suggestion taking "going native" a bit too far?

The plot was part of a clutch of seven dwellings, mostly owned by traditional, inter-related villagers, but one, only forty metres away, was renovated to a very high standard as a summer house by one of the richest men in the area, petrol station owner Fikret Namlı. The views were magnificent. Mountains behind us and to our left, a valley, which a couple of million years ago had been sea, and then in the distance another mountain range, the highest point of which has been made into a ski resort called Bozdağ, about two hours' drive away. In the valley and around the paths leading down to it were thousands of trees. But in clearings, some of which looked like unworkable slopes, ambitious locals had created gardens and allotments. Every so often we would see a huge JCB ripping up small trees on the steep hillside abutting the road the next time we passed the spot the road would be half covered with huge rocks, smaller stones and mud. On the third pass we realised that someone was making an access road to arable land and all became clear. Most days a stream of villagers trundled off with various implements, by lorry, motorbike or on foot to work the fields.

Accessed on two sides by two narrow roads, the plot was on three levels bordered to the west by a tiny stream. Unfortunately, on the other side of the stream was an area which historically had been a refuse tip. The council had prohibited the dumping of waste but old habits die hard and many villagers simply ignored the official bins and continued to roll their rubbish down the bank into the stream. We'll return to the subject of Turks and litter later. There were three buildings: a large two-storey house which we called Number One; a smaller two-storey house, we dubbed Number Two and an old single-storey, roofless stone barn which somehow reminded me of a trip I once made to Hadrian's Wall. Ruin didn't cover it. The site was actually an amalgam of two different title deeds (*tapular*), which had been owned by one large family. The previous occupiers had used only the top floors of both houses. The downstairs was for animals, their body heat in winter helping to warm the rooms above.

Both main properties, built in a combination of stone and rendered brick, were in complete disarray. Groping one day in the murky downstairs of Number One, I thought I'd stumbled across dozens of human skulls only to find the Pol Pot-style graveyard was actually a pile of gourds, awaiting decoration. The Turks love to use them as light shades or hanging ornaments. Lütfi Çakir, a Kaplan restaurant owner, who was one of the first to befriend us, delights in drawing ornate patterns on them and then, following the pencil lines, drills hundreds of tiny holes to make unique artefacts. Coincidentally, while writing this, forty real skulls were found in a cave in the south eastern province of Mardin. Human Rights Association Mardin chairman Fevzi Adsız said he believed the skulls belonged to victims of unsolved murders in the 1990s. There had clearly been some kind of fire downstairs in Number One and many of the thick support beams showed signs of damage. The other basement rooms were littered with rusty farm implements, including two horse-drawn ploughs and a plethora of trash: dozens of odd shoes, discarded medicine containers and empty bottles. Around the walls were the concrete food troughs once used by the family's animals. The remainder of the ground floor was just earth. All muds cons, you might say.

Upstairs, among more detritus, we found an old wooden crutch and an ancient fuse box. A few of the windows were intact. But not many. The metal shutters outside were rusty and in poor condition. Renovating them was out of the question. All in all, it was what estate agents describe as a property "with great potential, in need of some TLC." Dilapidated, to you and me. On the first floor in Number Two we discovered a bird's nest with baby swallows. We spent a long time just watching the birds fly back and forth to build their home and feed their young. Nearby was an old fashioned "squatter" Turkish toilet. According to a blogger called Johnny Vagabond "the squat toilet was invented by an early side-branch of humans who had a third eye in their butt." We wanted local authenticity but that would be one of the first things to go, we both agreed. Later another incarnation of the poo hole in a shop in Tire got its revenge when Carolyn's best friend Kathryn dropped a £300 pair of sunglasses down the smelly orifice. Despite the valiant efforts of the shopkeeper, who was happy to lend not just a hand but a whole arm, it ended up as a dubious but genuine insurance claim.

The plot's garden, despite many promising fruit trees, was a complete mess. Rubbish was strewn all over the land nearest to Number One, including part of a reinforced concrete column about four feet long. There was a small bank of soil which was home to three unkempt rose plants and two lavender bushes that wouldn't produce flowers. The outside of Number Two looked like a still from a Pathé newsreel of the wartime Blitz on London. The roof on a one-time shed at the front of the house on the ground floor had collapsed and there were beams and hundreds of broken tiles and shards of glass to be cleared. In the corner of the courtyard at the side of the house was a huge pile of aggregate from some unfinished building work that now blocked the front gate. The floor was a mixture of broken paving, soil and weeds, flanked by a tangle of untrained vines and other fruit trees. Just above head height was a crazy lattice-work of wires carrying more vines.

The village comprised around seventy houses. There were many more horses and donkeys than cars. Our neighbours, should we sign up, seemed kind and helpful, although they were obviously curious. It was unusual enough for an Istanbulite to buy a house in the village but what about a foreigner (*yabanci*)? They must have wondered whether we had plans to build some of the same avant-garde concrete monstrosities that had gone up in many Aegean and Mediterranean coastal towns. Unlike in the UK, where many would only become acquainted with their neighbours if an unexploded Luftwaffe bomb was discovered in the street and everyone had been evacuated to the local church hall, a Turkish village is very different. Ayşe, in her mid-eighties, for example, scarf around her head and wearing baggy pantaloons (*şalvar*), regularly walked through "our" garden to a field below where she picked herbs or collected firewood. Other neighbours would pop in to collect vine leaves for stuffing. Also wandering in at all hours were any number of chickens, goats, cats and dogs. Then there was the tradition of neighbours giving each other food from time to time. If a Turk hands you a plate of something you can't give the crockery back empty. And so the ritual continues.

Originally called *Arpacılar* (meaning barley sellers), Kaplan was renamed after 17th century buccaneer Kaplan Ahmet Pasha, the so-called Conqueror of Crete. For reasons unclear the swashbuckling adventurer was exiled to the village and, pining for the high seas, whiled away his days building water channels from there to Tire. His grave, to the west of the village, carries an ornate tombstone. When we first arrived to survey the house and the area Kaplan had two restaurants, the *Dağ* (mountain) and *Çam* (pine). The first, owned by Lütfi, has been reviewed in the New York Times and diners arrive from all over Turkey to enjoy its fare, especially the starters (*meze*). Later Lütfi's son Serkan opened up a third restaurant, called *Gastro Tire*, with many experimental dishes. It instantly became a commercial success. Day-to-day, nothing much happens in Kaplan. People work their plots or move their sheep and goats from A to B and back again. And at the weekend excitement reaches fever pitch with the village women's own tiny market in the square, selling all manner of home-grown produce, from tomato paste and soap to cherries and almonds, depending on the season. Peace and tranquillity reign, except when a car backfires, a dog barks or the muezzin begins his call to prayer.

Saying that, shortly after we arrived there was a murder. To this day the details are unclear and several differing versions of the story still do the rounds. What I am about to reveal comes from a Turkish newspaper report I spotted on the floor of the lavatory in a cafe we sometimes use. It was probably a bit unhygienic but I wanted to see what passed for journalistic fact rather than rely on village gossip, so I salvaged the discarded newsprint. The report said a man called Hüseyin, thirty-seven, from Tire was stabbed to death by a twenty-seven-year-old villager called Coşkun in the tea garden, opposite where the ladies hold their market. But the motive was unclear. One rumoured explanation was that the sale of a not-so-roadworthy car might have been involved. There was an argument, then a struggle and finally a knife was drawn. Another indisputable fact is that the manager of the tea garden, Soner, bravely or foolishly, maybe both, tried to intercede, grabbed the murder weapon and ended up with a nasty cut across the palm and the fingers of one hand. We will hear more of Soner later.

The murder aside, crime is unheard of. Like the owners before us, we are able to leave out chairs, garden tools, sunbeds, anything really, knowing it will never be touched. Sometimes we even accidentally leave the key in the front door. While we were making up our minds whether to buy, we stayed at a hotel in Tire and Levent gave us an extensive guided tour of the area over two weeks. We were only thirty-five minutes' drive away from Ephesus, one of the world's greatest archaeological sites. There were other attractions, too, such as Şirince, the only place that was predicted to survive the end of the world on December 21, 2012. New Age spiritualists convinced themselves that this really was Doomsday, verified by studying Mayan hieroglyphs. According to the cult, Şirince, home to six hundred souls, and close to an area where Christians believe the Virgin Mary ascended to heaven, had some kind of special positive energy. That, and the Mayan prophecy, sparked a tourism gold-rush and tens of thousands flocked to see it, including some Americans who booked in, hoping to beat Armageddon. Today Şirince is a picture postcard place, surrounded by olive groves, tangerine and fig gardens and vineyards and famous for its fruit wine outlets. Founded following the decline of the city of Ephesus by Byzantine Greeks, it was originally named Çirkince (meaning rather ugly). They deliberately chose the novel negative PR to keep away annoying visitors and to increase security. Would it work nowadays for overrun Cotswold villages, I wonder? It was Kazim Dirik Pasha, a governor of Izmir during the first years of the Turkish Republic, who suggested changing the name again from Çirkince to Şirince (meaning charming).

Other nearby attractions included the towns of Selçuk and Birgi. Wandering around Birgi one day we saw a piece of a Greek or Roman column used to support a door jamb. This casual attitude to antiquities reminded me of a wonderful story, told in a website called turkishtravelblog.com, about a young photographer in the 1950s driving to Aydin to photograph a new dam. He lost his way and ended up in a village called Geyre. As he sat there, drinking tea with the locals, he noticed houses built with odd-looking stones. Villagers shrugged their shoulders, said the stones had always been there and were amused at his excitement. He took photographs and eventually contacted the famous Turkish photographer Ara Guler, who alerted a Turkish archaeologist Prof Kenan T. Erim from New York University. Erim came to Turkey and quickly realised that the photographer had accidentally discovered the lost city of Aphrodisias. From that day Erim dedicated the rest of his life to excavation work. He died in 1990, but the Turkish government rewarded his dedication by burying him within the ancient city, next to the Tetrastoon, the gates welcoming pilgrims on their way to pay sacrifices at the Temple.

From Tire the bustling holiday resort of Kuşadası is only about seventy-five minutes away by car. And roughly the same driving time brings you to Izmir, Turkey's third largest city. Tire itself is a hotbed of history dating back to the Hittites and full of architectural archaeological gems. It is believed to have been founded 5,000 years ago by three tribes of Pelasgians, settlers from Asia Minor. The name Tire supposedly comes from the word "three" in Indo-European languages. It was home for a while to the French poet Alphonse De Lamartine. It survived the Roman occupation, when it was called Teira, and began to really flourish in the Byzantine Period. From the fifteenth to eighteenth centuries it had its own mint and fire brigade, such was its importance. It was certainly a major provincial centre. Tire had been one of the final stops on the Silk Road before merchants took their goods to the port at Ephesus for transportation to Europe and elsewhere. It still boasts several decrepit but wonderful *hanlar*, the ancient "motels" where the journeying traders would sleep upstairs while their camels or horses rested in stables below. There was also a *bedesten*, a vaulted indoor market place, reputed to be more than 800 years old, which the local council has now lovingly restored. Just as work started, we peeked inside one day and, true to Turkish hospitality, a project manager in a white hard hat spent twenty minutes showing us around and explaining how the renovations would proceed. Tire also boasts a possibly unique structure: a mosque that sits immediately above a church, like a duplex apartment block. The stone-built church downstairs has bars on the windows and is ideal for taking funny "prison" style pictures when family or visitors from England come to stay. For many years the church was empty but in 2019 a Baptist minister based 25 miles away in Torbalı began holding services there.

Possibly even stranger, Tire was also once home to a thriving Jewish community. Someone who also became our friend, Murat Sanus, then working as the council's director of external relations and social projects, was curious one day to find some old photographs of well-dressed Jewish people in the 1920s and 1930s. Researching in the town's archives Murat, well-educated and very well-travelled, unearthed more than 150,000 documents and after months of painstaking work produced a wonderful book called The Jews of Tire. According to some sources, the first Jews were exiled to Tire during the reign of Alexander the Great. Centuries later they taught locals the rules of fair trade, tailoring, shoe-making, dressing well, the importance of education, and how to play the game of *karambol*. In the game, now virtually extinct in Turkey, balls are directed with a special kick technique to small targets made of wood and planted at regular intervals. It was played on a polished concrete floor of four by twelve metres, by two or four people. The word *karambol* is still used to describe a scramble or melee. The Tire Jews were also famous for *pandispanya*, a kind of cake and *sübiyye*, a drink made from roasted watermelon seeds. Murat also found nearly three hundred old tombstones, many buried undergrounds and collected them at a new Jewish cemetery, after painstakingly collating every one. He built a sophisticated database logging every Jew who lived in Tire from the 1800s to the 1960s, plus some from previous centuries. In all round 6,500 souls. Attempting to connect with the descendants of every one of those people, from all over the world, he also created a Facebook group to share information. People began supplying their photographs and memories. One poignant story that Murat unearthed was of three siblings who moved to Paris only to be captured by the Nazis and killed at Auschwitz. He is trying to make it into a television documentary. He also discovered the wife of the first Israeli astronaut Ilan Ramon, who died in the Columbia space shuttle disaster, was from Tire Many came as part of the Jewish diaspora, fleeing persecution and later drifting away again, some to Israeli settlements in the second half of the 20th century Such is the detail of Murat's intricate family trees that he still receives a steady stream of inquiries from people seeking knowledge of their ancestors in order to apply for citizenship in countries where their forebears once lived.

Tire is mainly known for diary produce and handicrafts. Wander through the town and you can see saddle-makers, clog-makers, weavers and many other tradesmen and women at work. One especially interesting shop is owned by Arif Cön. He is a *keçeci* or felt-maker and he exports his beautiful products all over the world. They include hats, scarves, hangings, doormats, waistcoats, slippers, vests and toys. They are mainly handmade and sometimes finished on a pressing machine that is more than a hundred years old. Nowadays, most visitors to Tire come on a Tuesday when the town hosts what council chiefs claim is Turkey's largest street market. Every road in the town centre is packed with stalls, where you can buy everything from a pitchfork to a kilo of kiwi fruit. One man even sells plastic bottles full of live leeches. This is totally unlike the markets in tourist towns like Bodrum where vendors sell "Bolex" watches, "Burbor" coats, "Guchy" and "Abibas" tracksuits and "Parada" handbags. There, you hear Turkish cries in Mockney of "cheap as chips" to lure the British holidaymakers into buying. Turkey prides itself on its ability to create "genuine fakes". In Istanbul's Grand Bazaar, for instance, a replica Mulberry bag can change hands for £300. I know because daughter Sophie once had a salesman running everywhere to bring her samples, only for her to reject each one due to (she argued) obvious specific counterfeiting errors. At one knock-off stall I once saw a Turkish man proudly displaying a tee-shirt, he had just bought with the word BASTARD across the chest in large letters. When my Turkish friend Hüseyin asked him if he knew what the word meant he shook his head. Having been enlightened he chased the stallholder down the road.

Tire's market is fundamentally different, run by locals for locals. Many herbs grow around town and nowhere else in Turkey. The market offers wild asparagus, mallow (from the hibiscus family), pincushion, nettle, cabbage sprouts, wild radish, acanth, blessed thistle, scapwort, phlomis lycia, chicory, rumex patientia, stellaria holostea, soleirolia soleiroli, plantago, witloof, leaf mustard, pigweed, poisonberry, chard, common hackberry, purslane, watercress and more. So restaurateur Serkan often runs cookery workshops on Tuesdays where foodies investigate the market and then learn to cook the produce they buy.

The hotel we used while discovering the area, Gülcüoğlu Konakları, created from two old Ottoman houses, was idiosyncratic and friendly, with creaky wooden floorboards and beautiful overhanging oriels (*cumbalar*), which I had previously seen, among other places, in Malta. One night just before bedtime I decided to unplug what I thought was a light in order to charge up my mobile phone. Unbeknown to me I had inadvertently disconnected the room's small refrigerator which defrosted and sent a small rivulet of icy water through the floorboards and on to the head of the manager of the local football team, Tirespor 1922, sleeping below. Sportingly he didn't complain at the next day's breakfast.

After a fortnight of exploring the village and the area beyond, the day finally came when we had to make a decision about living permanently in Turkey, or at least to commit to an elaborate ruse in which Levent would pretend to buy the plot to keep the price realistic. He argued that if the sellers learned foreigners were interested the cost would rocket. In truth it was a big decision. But it was not as if we were strangers to the Turkish culture and way of life. As you have read, we had experienced most things Turkish including eating sheep's brain soup. So, what could possibly go wrong? Although she never articulated it, I suspect Carolyn would have preferred a house that was more modern and completed. However, she also relished the chance to design new buildings from scratch and appreciated the quaintness of the village and the superb views. Her two reservations were that Kaplan did not have its own corner shop or a bus service, despite the council building a shiny bus shelter.

There were a lot of conversations that started: "What do you think?" My mantra when buying houses was always to buy something you can add value to. The Kaplan project took that idea to the limit. Back home daughters Charlotte and Sophie were both supportive and intrigued. We told Levent to go ahead and seal the deal. A run-down, sixty-square-metre garage in Stoke Newington, London, was sold around the same time for six times what we paid for our plot. Estate agent Ismail, who had acted as a go-between and negotiator and who was due a handsome commission (from seller and vendor, as is the custom in Turkey), was now even more jovial than ever.

Portly and sporting an impressively thick black moustache, Ismail invited us all for a dinner which we later named "the never-ending meal". It was a meal we'll never forget. Actually, several meals. He took us to a village about twenty minutes' drive away where we were joined by two of his relatives. The open-air restaurant was in modest surroundings but the food was superb and it kept coming. Meze after meze, followed by kebabs, chicken on skewers, lamb on skewers, fish, steak, salads of many varieties, rice, bread, pasta. Then a whole series of wonderful desserts, all washed down with beer, wine and *rakı*. We sat down at 7.30pm and it was well after midnight when we finally admitted defeat. We could eat no more. For a moment I wondered if I could even raise myself off the chair without a hydraulic lift. During one break in courses, I asked about the restaurant's impressive garden fountain, nearby.

"Is it spring water?" I asked the owner.

"Yes. We found it by using a water diviner," he replied.

"You are joking. Are those people really effective?"

"Oh yes," he said.

"He came with his funny stick, wandered around for several minutes and then told us just where to dig. We hired drilling equipment, went down twenty-five or thirty metres and there it was, exactly where he said," explained the restaurateur.

"And what did he charge?" I inquired.

"Oh, we just gave him a free meal," said the proprietor. I don't suppose water divining gets much of a plug from careers advisers in Turkish schools.

Apart from Levent's tour, we had done plenty of research of our own, spending hours on expat internet message boards and corresponding by e-mail with other Brits who had taken the plunge. I also received a lot of encouragement from the keyboard of an English chap called Chris Chesher, whose internet musings entitled Cukurbaglı's blog never fail to entertain. But we broke one of the golden rules of purchasing property abroad: view in all seasons. We bought in summer, seduced by the thirty-five degrees of heat, Turneresque skies at sunset, the buzzing of the cicadas, fulsome bunches of grapes and the aroma of chicken grilled on the barbecue. But we did not move in until December when, just our luck, the region experienced its worst winter in forty years and at night temperatures dropped to minus fourteen. Snow was such a rarity that Tire town dwellers drove up the hill to Kaplan to collect it and rode home triumphantly with mini snowmen on their bonnets to shock and upstage their neighbours. Our plastic water pipes, partially situated in the garden, froze. To heat the property, we relied on the traditional Turkish village soba, a rectangular metal box with a cylindrical tin inside and a configuration of thin metal pipes that theoretically disseminate the warmth before exiting through a wall. An economical and effective way of keeping warm it seemed, although the incidence of people dying from carbon monoxide poisoning were disconcertingly high. It burned wood and coal. But lighting it seemed to require skills only Bear Grylls possesses. We took to using barbecue accelerants and even soaking small pieces of rag in petrol to place between the kindling. Sometimes we would check outside to see smoke billowing out of the chimney section but nothing much apparently happening in the body of the soba. Then suddenly there would be a mini-explosion and the whole thing would rattle as puffs of smoke emerged from the box itself. Sobas come in a range of colours, all of them brown. And if you don't fit the pipes together securely, you'll have droplets of brown tar all over your floor and furniture. You also have to regularly check the joints in the chimney section outside. In spring the whole contraption has to be taken down and cleaned.

The first-year neighbour Hüseyin helped and the soot and tar inside the pipes was like what I imagine surgeons find in the lungs of a sixty-a-day smoker. The hole in the original fourteen-centimetre diameter pipe can shrink to five or six. The usual cleaning solution is to wrap a sack around a stick and repeatedly push the stick up and down inside each section of pipe. That seemed like hard work to me and our eighty-something neighbour Ayşe Hanem clearly agreed.

"Benzine!" she recommended. Eschewing all maternal warnings about playing with fire, Hüseyin was encouraged to fill an empty plastic spray-topped bottle of cleaning fluid with petrol and coat the inside of each tube. Then he lit a piece of paper and dropped it into one of the pipes. Whoosh. There was a dull, mini-explosion and a modest plume of smoke. But incredibly the method, doubtless forbidden in every health and safety manual, proved most effective. When the pipes cooled, I got to work with a wire brush and before you could say Chim chiminey, chim chiminey, chim chim cher-ee!... the pipes were ready for re-assembly next winter.

I never thought we had made a mistake but it's fair to say the project was proving harder than we anticipated. If Carolyn was having reservations, she didn't share them. With monsoon-like electrical storms of Biblical proportions, our first task was to make the main house, Number One, habitable. A crew of workmen arrived and hid the Heath Robinson array of tree branches that constituted the rafters and purlins behind thin, white-painted hardboard. The grass huts of the Hottentots or the thick blankets of nomadic desert tribesmen would have provided more effective insulation. The red terracotta roof tiles themselves looked serviceable. But, when it rained heavily, water cascaded down the interior walls rendering our back-up electric heaters a fire risk. With our furniture still waiting to be shipped from England, we bought a second-hand bed and a new mattress and slept fully clothed. Rough sleepers on London's embankment have fewer layers. Then one day Carolyn's resolve finally broke. I was working in the garden when I heard a woman's scream from the shower room that would have satisfied Alfred Hitchcock. I ran as fast as I could to find Carolyn dripping into a towelling robe, sobbing but no cross-dressing, knife-wielding maniac.

"What's wrong?" I asked.

"There," she pointed to her left.

"I knew coming here would be a disaster," she whimpered. I looked but saw nothing untoward.

"Where? What?" I asked.

"There," she insisted, flailing an arm, as if trying to stop a bus. On second glance, at head height, what looked like one of many cracks in the plaster of the decrepit farmhouse we had just bought, was actually a 25cm long green-grey lizard (*kertenkele*). It was motionless. Clinging to the wall like a jail-breaker caught in a searchlight. It was a toss-up who had had the bigger shock.

"I'm sure it's not poisonous," I reassured Carolyn, wafting the creature with my ancient Tilley hat. It immediately bolted downwards and disappeared up the blackened inside of the former fireplace and onwards up into the chimney. Maybe it was imitating the legendary Bill the Lizard from Disney's *Alice in Wonderland*.

"Why did we ever come here? That's it," said Carolyn. "I'm done. Enough." She's just being over-theatrical, I reassured myself. Ever the amateur dramatist. A modicum of extra heating at night was supplied by our two rescue dogs Darcy and Willow, more on them later. Our idea was to live in Number One while renovating one floor of Number Two. I made a sign to hang outside of the front gate saying *Kismet Konak*, which roughly translates as Destiny House. Before we started work on the houses properly there was one last piece of administration to sort out. As previously mentioned, the house was purchased in Levent's name to avoid a price hike. Now we had to swap the names over on the deeds. But under Turkish law, before you can do this (at a notary by the way) you have to get a certificate from a psychiatric doctor saying you are of sound mind. We went to the hospital, paid our £7 and sat in the shrink's waiting room. Eventually Levent's name came up on the screen.

"I'll wait here," I said.

"No, it's ok...come in with me." The doctor, let's call him Cemre, turned out to be crazier than most of his patients. As we walked through the door, we saw his face was turning purple with anger.

"Who's the sick person? You or you?" Levent explained why we were there but by now the doctor was now almost apoplectic with rage. He kept muttering under his breath. The veins on his neck were bulging. He told me to sit down and, grumbling to himself, took Levent into a nearby cubicle. He asked him his name, date of birth and where he lived. Then he walked to his desk, bent down to pull a form out of one of the lower drawers and signed it. Then he waved his arm dismissively.

"There you are. Take that to the office." Levent could have dementia or been nine shades of bat crazy for all he knew. He could have been the Anatolian Ripper or the Josef Fritzl of Istanbul. Where was the Rorschach Test with the ink blots? Chastened, we trooped out and walked to the appointed office where an official put another stamp on the document and signed it again. The Turks really love their stamps. Levent leaned over the stamp holder.

"He's a bit strange is that Doctor Cemre." The official looked up and laughed.

"Oh him, yes he's a complete nut job," he said. And out we came clutching our vital piece of paper.

Pinning down builders to provide workable quotes and starting times was like untying the Gordian Knot blindfold. Mañana may be a Spanish word but the Turks are Olympic gold medallists at promising to work and not turning up. As one Turk ruefully shamefacedly admitted: "We always arrive for work eventually but on the day after mañana." We decided to use our near neighbour Birgül's twenty-something son, another Hüseyin, to help with some basic preparatory work. As ever with DIY we knew there was always a risk of a Frank Spencer moment and it duly arrived. Above the balcony of house Number Two were two large, galvanised water tanks, part of a long defunct solar energy system that had already been partly dismantled. The tanks measured 120cm by 60cm, (about 47 inches by about 24 inches) and resembled the sort of thing Barnes Wallis might have strapped underneath a Lancaster bomber. Hüseyin and I attempted to disassemble the contraption but soon found the lower tank appeared to contain a wasps' nest. After pumping in a full can of insect spray, we stood to await a reaction. There was none. Hüseyin duly climbed the rickety metal structure that held the tanks, like a trapeze artist, oblivious to health and safety precautions. We later discovered he was a keen motorcyclist, never wore a helmet and had come off three times, once sailing like a human cannonball into a nearby tree. He had more stitches than the Bayeux Tapestry. If the local hospital had a loyalty scheme he'd certainly be a gold card member.

The higher tank proved fairly easy to dislodge and he duly pushed it off its moorings on to the muddy ground below. The one below, however, was a lot heavier, suggesting it was full of water, rust and sludge, dead wasps or all four. First Hüseyin bored into the underside with a power drill. Nothing. Then he used a grinding machine to make a cut along a seam. Again, nothing emerged. It was too heavy to push ... so there remained just the nuclear option. We would have to cut one of the support legs and hopefully guide it to fall more or less in the same spot as its predecessor. Like some manic pole dancer, and armed with the heavy grinder, Hüseyin contorted himself around the structure cutting here, cutting there. Then he broke off, went to his house next door, returning with a length of mountaineering rope, which he tied to the frame just beneath the tank. The other end he secured to a pomegranate tree. What happened next was like one of those never-to-be-forgotten Firework Night incidents when your rather tipsy uncle decides he is going to light the giant Catherine Wheel that he bought for £20. Hüseyin made one final cut and ......

KERRASHHHHHHHH. With noise like a motorway pile-up, the whole structure toppled over from the roof of Number Two....on to the roof of Number One. Luckily, a huge fig tree was in the way and broke its fall, otherwise the tank might well have ended up in our makeshift kitchen. Fortunately, the "Dambuster bomb" merely dislodged three tiles and squashed about twenty Turkish liras worth of figs. At last it began disgorging the rust-coloured sediment that we had suspected all along was inside, all down the side of the house. A few tugs of the mountaineering rope and the tank, frame and all were safely grounded. Red faces and rueful glances all round. But mission accomplished. It was a start.

CHAPTER NINE

TALKING TURKLISH

I began trying to learn Turkish in the Seventies. I bought cassette tapes produced by a government department in the USA called the Foreign Service Institute and used mainly by foreign affairs professionals, diplomats and the military. The dialogue was dull and the method of learning built on tedious repetition. Since then I have acquired eight or nine books to help me. Several are by the Oxford professor Geoffrey Lewis who died in 2008 and who is generally hailed as the doyen of linguists exploring Turkish. I can speak enough to complete everyday tasks but I'm still far from fluent. I quickly discovered that Turkish is an incredibly regular language. Pronunciation is quite easy, much easier than English. Can you imagine trying to teach a foreigner the pronunciation of a sentence like: "Although he went all through the cookbook, he found it tough to make dough on a plough"? But Turkish sentence construction is much different to English. It loves suffixes and uses verbal nouns and verbal adjectives in unfamiliar constructions. For example: "I lost the gift that I bought" in Turkish turns into "my having-bought gift, I lost" It is also partial to expressing in one word an idea that in English would be seven. There's actually a seventy-letter Turkish word often quoted which means "as though you are from those whom we may not be able to easily make into a maker of unsuccessful ones." All right, it's just for show. But you get the idea.

Then there are the words with twenty or more meanings One such is *çıkmak*, which means to go out. But it can also mean to stem, to emanate, to climb up, to be dislocated, to no longer merit its name and so on. You also use it to float shares, to date someone, to flirt with someone and in a variety of other situations. What can you make of a language where the word for to play (a musical instrument) *çalmak* also means to steal? Quite often, dictionary in hand, I would look at a sentence in a Turkish newspaper story and find myself able to identify every word and its meaning and yet not have a clue what the journalist was writing about.

I'm not a natural linguist. I passed O-level French and German and I have a good ear for mimicking foreign words. But I let myself down badly when acting as best man to an English friend who married a German girl in a small town near Hanover. Instead of, or sometimes as well as, a best man's speech and a groom's speech, it's traditional in some parts of Germany for the bride to write a speech. My pal's *liebling* (favourite) asked me to read out loud to the guests. Although I didn't understand most of it, my pronunciation was pretty good. All was going down like lager at the Oktoberfest until I missed off the umlaut on the word *schwül* (which means humid) and instead called everyone at the gathering homosexual. Luckily the guests took it in good part and after a few seconds of bewilderment there was thunderous laughter.

I have had similar, but not quite as embarrassing, situations in Turkey. I once asked a market stallholder selling clothes for *çorba* (soup) instead of *çorap* (socks). Then there was the time we thought we had been given a wedding invitation in April (*Nisan*) when we were actually being asked to an engagement party (*nişan*). We bought a wedding present but took it home because no one gave the couple engagement presents. Another time we went into a shop intending to buy *yufka* (filo pastry) but used the wrong word *hamur* (dough). We put the stuff in the fridge only to return a few hours later to find the dough had expanded like some alien monster. We had pizzas morning, noon and night for about four days. Another potential trap is to mispronounce the girl's name Halime as *Hamile*, which means pregnant.

Someone else who has slipped up wrote of the experience on Facebook. The expat wrote: "We lived in Bangkok and the Turkish community was very close. While my father in-law, a retired army colonel, was visiting we decided to have a barbecue in our poolside garden and invited the Turkish Ambassador and his wife. After we had eaten, we men retired to the balcony to smoke and drink our *rakı*. You know the nickname for *rakı* is aslan sütü or lion's milk. I thought I would be clever and used the phrase in conversation but for some reason it came out as *adem sütü*, literally the milk of Adam or semen. The Ambassador and my father in-law sprayed their drinks out in shock and laughter."

Of course, not a century ago, Turks themselves were stumped by their own language after Atatürk's sweeping, revolutionary reforms. He argued that the increasingly obsolete Ottoman language, written in the Arabic script and riddled with Arab and Persian borrowings, was holding Turkey back. Atatürk also used the changes to weaken the power of Islam on the country. If Turkey was to move to a more secular, Western-facing, culture it had to adopt the Latin alphabet and modernise its dictionary, he insisted. Just imagine, the impact of the UK government deciding that everything should, virtually overnight, be written in Arabic. Parliamentarians had to return to their constituencies and organise the re-education of their people. Special schools were established. Atatürk himself travelled the land with a piece of chalk and a blackboard. A lot of chaos ensued, especially over vital documents, for example the drafting of laws, business transactions and buying property.

On a more cultural and aesthetic level, linguist Geoffrey Lewis claims in his book The Turkish Language Reform: A Catastrophic Success, that some Turks were left groping to find a satisfactory way of delivering their own thoughts. Atatürk's slash-and-burn approach, he says, prevented what might have been a better natural development. Change was certainly needed. But using a linguistic guillotine created massive problems. For example, *Nutuk*, a 36-hour long speech Atatürk gave over six days in 1927, later became largely incomprehensible to younger generations and in the early 1960s had to be translated into modern Turkish. As we all know, language is ever evolving and as Lewis points out, the speech was updated yet again less than twenty years later. The difficulty in recruiting teachers to work in rural areas meant that the literacy and educational gap with the big cities widened. I suppose it's like Elizabethans, used to reading Shakespeare, suddenly being given a copy of The Daily Mail.

Today many educated Turks have serious reservations about the reforms. But with laws prohibiting any criticism of Atatürk they are reluctant to voice their opinions. Vahdet, a banker friend, told me: "I love my country, I love my history and I love Atatürk. But he is not God. There was no proper compliance when the language was altered. The Ottoman Empire was a great civilisation, certainly in the fifteenth and sixteenth centuries. A lot of important books were trashed.

Meanwhile many people became illiterate." He claimed that many important Ottoman archives were sold to Bulgaria.

Back in England, still struggling with Turkish, I enrolled in a class run by a Turkish teacher from Izmir called Korhan, whose main occupation was teaching English to foreigners. Once a week I would join two or three other students in the lounge of his cosy Cheshire home. Korhan was thorough and his lessons were always interesting. Upstairs he had a room which was a shrine to his favourite football club Galatasaray. But to really succeed, a student has to immerse himself in a language. I made better progress after moving to Turkey full time. In Kaplan virtually, nobody except Levent speaks English. And in Tire it's much the same. Being forced to use the language certainly concentrates the mind. Saying that, I know expats who have been in Turkey for ten years and still cannot speak a word.

What the grammar books don't properly explain, though, is that Turkish is also peppered with bizarre sayings. For example, the Turkish for "we're in trouble" or "we're screwed" translates as "we ate a quince". The etymology, I am told, is that quince is difficult to eat and can stick in your throat. I'm sure Turks learning English are similarly bewildered, for example, by Cockney rhyming slang but they really do love a metaphor and an idiom. Saying two people are suited to each other is expressed by the phrase "a cooking pot rolls on the floor and finds its lid". A lot of Turkish sayings are very rude. For example: *ayranı yok içmeye, tahtırevanla gider sıçmaya.* It translates: "He doesn't have any yoghurt drink but he travels to have a shit in a sedan chair." The English equivalent might be "all fur coat and no knickers", in other words someone who is poor but still loves to show off. If someone asks you a stupid question you might reply: *ben diyorum hadımım sen diyorsun çoluk çocuk nasıl.* It translates: "I say I'm a eunuch and you ask me how are my wife and kids?" Then there's *imam osuruyor, cemaat sıçıyor*, which roughly translates "the vicar farts, the congregation shits." In English: "give some people an inch and they'll take a yard." And singing from the same hymn sheet becomes *Ikiside ayni kaba siciyor*. They're both shitting in the same cup.

While grappling with Turkish, I decided I might as well try to cash in on my native speaker status and teach English. Before moving to Turkey, I had taken a teaching course and gained my CELTA (Certificate in English Language Teaching to Adults). I was the oldest in the class by almost forty years but being back at school was fun. The college in Manchester recruited guinea pig students for the wannabe teachers by advertising free English lessons and a mixed bag of learners arrived daily. One was a guy in a wheelchair, Aimen, a twenty-nine-year-old Libyan from an elementary class. Aimen was born with spina bifida in Cardiff where his parents were working. When he was five the family moved back to Libya where his father was working in Tripoli teaching medicine. Aimen returned to the UK in 2013 to study, hoping to settle. Despite his handicap he always smiled broadly and was keen to learn. We hit it off immediately and, when I was tasked with writing a mini-thesis on the differences between languages, I chose Aimen as my subject.

His mother tongue turned out to be Amazig, an obscure Berber language and one of the world's oldest, with its own unique script. He learned Arabic in school in Libya and spoke Amazig only with his immediate family. He was unable to properly explain the difference between Amazig and Arabic. It quickly became apparent that Aimen's problems with the English language were the same as most Turks' difficulties. In both written and spoken language Aimen tended to miss out the definite and indefinite article and prepositions or to choose an incorrect preposition. He would also say "brudder and fadder" instead of "brother" and "father". Turks have similar issues with "th" and the word "healthy" usually comes out as "heltly". I would later draw on Aimen's experiences.

A friend in Tire put me in touch with a local, fee-paying private college which was recruiting and, after a brief interview, I agreed to work two days a week, Tuesdays and Fridays. Unfortunately, the college's building in Tire was being renovated and local teachers and pupils were being bussed to a sister site thirty-five minutes' drive away in Ödemiş, which had its own students but room for the overspill. It led to some interesting bus journeys.

"Are you a Christian?" sixteen-year-old student Orçun asked me one day as we sat next to each other on the back seat. I had long ago learned that in Turkey you speak about two things religion and politics at your peril. I was trying desperately to be non-confrontational.

"Well, I am more of an atheist really." As soon as the word had left my mouth, I realised I had committed a cardinal error. Orçun, a pharmacist's son, slim, good looking and quite bright seized on the remark.

"Then you are going to hell. And when you are there you will be tormented for all eternity by Zebani."

"Who is Zebani?" I queried.

"She is a devil who will inflict great pain on you," he said cheerfully.

"She sounds awful," I said. "But probably not quite as bad as my wife," I joked.

The humour was lost on Orçun. In reality, Orcun probably paid as much attention in his religious studies class as he did in mine. None. Zebani is not actually one woman but a collection of women, also known as the Angels of Punishment or the Guardians of Hell. The Quran also mentions them as the Nineteen Angels of Hell.

I caught the bus at 7am sharp and for the first thirty minutes we meandered around the town picking up pupils and staff. The driver, we'll call him Burak, was unbelievably patient if the kids were late. And most of them were. A lot of Turkish children are incredibly spoiled as discipline in the home is often sadly lacking. Boys are usually more indulged than girls. I once saw a five-year-old boy repeatedly punch his own mother when she tried to take a robot away from him. He faced no sanction whatsoever. Even his father sat motionless as the attack continued, with his mother cooing in token disapproval. One American friend told how she once saw a twelve-year-old boy on a beach being feted like a Pharaoh by his mother and aunt. As he lay on a sun bed, they took off his loafers, put on beach shoes, rubbed cream on him and brought him drinks.

On my school bus run, you could easily spot the potential troublemakers. They would emerge from their homes, invariably after keeping us waiting, wearing the latest Fenerbahçe or Galatasary football shirt or designer training shoes. You could guarantee young boys with shoulder length hair would be difficult. There was the usual childish banter and tricks on the bus. But for the most part it was good humoured. Burak would often put on loud Turkish music and staff and pupils would sing and sometimes dance in the aisle, oblivious to health and safety regulations. One girl lived on a farm up a narrow lane with high foliage on both sides. Burak would drive along this single-track road at foolhardy speeds, bits of leaves falling in through the open windows on both sides. Having dropped off his charge, when he reached the main road again, he would drive on the wrong side of a dual carriageway for two hundred yards or so before making a turn in order to avoid a lengthy detour.

We would usually arrive at the Ödemiş campus about five minutes before the first lesson was due to start. In the corridors, pupils would call me *hocam* (my teacher). But that's where any respect usually started and finished. The lessons were invariably a nightmare. If I am generous, I would say it was probably exacerbated by the enlarged classes due to the building work. Sometimes I looked out on as many as thirty-five faces. But this was also St Trinian's on speed. The college was kitted out with high-tech teaching aids, including interactive touch screens instead of blackboards. The problem was the screens often froze. This was the signal for five or six pupils to run up to the front of the class and jab their fingers at it or at the keyboard of the integrated laptop computer on my desk. I soon learned the word *dokunma* (don't touch). But it fell on deaf ears. A few, maybe ten per cent, wanted to learn English. But the vast majority certainly did not. And some clearly wanted to use the class time for surreptitious activities of their own, usually catching up on homework, but occasionally reading novels, embroidery or knitting.

The concept of not talking in class seemed entirely alien to them. Indeed, the attitude seemed to be that it was actually quite all right to talk during lessons. The default position was: our parents have paid the fees, so we'll do what we like. This did not go down well to someone who had been to a boys' boarding school in the Sixties, where corporal punishment from staff and fellow pupils was routine. I fully realised I could not give anyone a whack. But I also wasn't going to be a pushover. Unfortunately, graduated sanctions proved totally useless.

"OK, I have had enough," I would say. "The next person to talk will be sent outside."

No sooner had I turned my back than not one but half a dozen conversations started up. Initially I would try to put disruptive pupils in the corner at the front of the class, facing the wall. But they would turn around and make silly faces so out they would go. Sometimes four or five pupils per forty-minute lesson would be ejected. It had little or no effect on maintaining order. Before the end of the lesson a member of the college's management would often come in, claim the kids had apologised and intercede on their behalf to have them reinstated. At first, I agreed. But as the term wore on, I regularly refused. In one lesson with eleven-year-olds I had walked to the back of the class explaining some grammatical point or other and spun around to return to the screen. One kid had deliberately sprinkled water on the floor and my foot slipped causing me to throw my hands in the air and lurch to and fro like some stoned rock fan at Glastonbury. I regained my balance, just, but inside I was fuming. The older kids were no better. I would often turn up for one class, comprising nine or ten students aged sixteen or seventeen to find five of them asleep on their desks.

"Look," I said. "If you don't want to listen, I have no problem with you sleeping. "But I don't want you talking or messing around because there are people in this class who really want to learn." Sure enough, moments later some of the "sleepers" would start throwing empty water bottles at each other when my back was turned. In one lesson I confiscated six such bottles before finally ejecting almost half the class. It was a shame because some pupils, usually the girls, wanted to make progress. Strangely, those ejected never seemed to bear a grudge. The next time in the corridor it was still all smiles and a friendly "good morning my teacher." Another time, with the same class, one idiot took off his quilted and hooded jacket and put it on again back to front, as if it was a straitjacket, his face buried in the hood. I said nothing, ignored him and he stayed like that for the whole forty-minute lesson. But I took his picture to show colleagues in the staffroom and management.

"Oh, Omer," they would say. "He's a real case."

Another time, after putting up with the empty water bottle throwing and loud chatting for a few minutes, I'm afraid I finally lost it.

"Will you shut the f*** up?" I shouted. At breaktime I was summoned to the director's office. My friend Göksen, who also taught English, was already there.

"Some pupils tell me you swore at them," the director said gravely.

"Yes," I confessed. "They are making my life misery. They won't stop talking and they disrupt every lesson."

The director and Göksen consulted for a minute or two. Then Göksen turned to me and said: "You did right. They deserved it." I heard no more about it. I consulted my wife's sister Melanie, a teacher for more than thirty years. She gave me a few tips but admitted that really there is little I could do. Her school has a regime where disruptive kids are sent to an empty classroom supervised by another teacher. But it's really only moving the problem around. The worst offenders are sent to another school. But, of course, you have to take your fair share of miscreants in return. I also sought advice from two other English teachers at the college, my pal Göksen and Mustapha.

"Is it me? Is it because I am a foreigner that they are being extra naughty?" I asked.

"No," they concurred. "They are exactly the same with us."

For another class, of nine-year-olds, I would regularly enter the room to find one girl missing.

"Where's Müge?" I would ask. I've changed her real name.

"We don't know," came the chorus from blank faces. I knew only too well that Müge was in fact hiding behind some furniture but I wasn't going to give her the satisfaction of launching a hunt. I knew she would emerge when she got bored and that was invariably within ten minutes. She really was a piece of work. Stroppy didn't cover it. One day, exasperated as she turned around to speak to a kid behind her for the umpteenth time, I tapped lightly her on the head with my finger knuckle to gain her attention. She immediately fell on to the desk as if I'd hit her with a baseball bat. Other kids crowded around her, concerned. A female teacher was summoned and with great difficulty Müge limped out of the room, like she was at death's door. It was an Oscar nomination performance. Her parents came to take her home but, unbelievably, there were no repercussions for me. Next day she was back hiding behind the furniture again.

The funniest kid, without doubt, was a lad we'll call Ahmet, aged about ten. He was one of those children who look about forty-five. He had large brown eyes, a shock of black hair and thick black glasses. You could visualise him in thirty years running a shop or being an accountant. He loved to play football in the playground but obviously was the last boy to be picked for any team. He would run around the pitch as the ball whizzed this way and that but he rarely touched the thing. On the odd occasion it accidentally came within his ambit he would thrash out a leg and send the ball hurtling into the fence, sometimes over it. But he never lost heart, was always smiling and seemed to be well liked by his peers. In English class, whenever it was his turn to read aloud, he would wave both hands in front of his chest and simply say "no, no."

"Come on Ahmet, you can do it."

"No, no, no." One day I was asked to invigilate during an English examination. All I had to do was sit there, eyes wide open, and stop any cheating. For once all the kids were quiet and kept their heads down, even Ahmet. I was impressed. When time was up, I collected the papers. As I glanced at the pile, I noticed that Ahmet's paper, apart from his name at the top of the page, was completely blank. At break I told Göksen and asked whether Ahmet would be punished.

"No," he confided. "We'll just give him a pass mark."

"Let me get this straight," I asked. "Most if not all of these kids will eventually want to go to university. Right? And to do that they will need good English. That's correct isn't it?"

"Yes," Göksen replied.

"So, what will happen when they apply?" Göksen smiled.

"Well, how can I put it? Often their dad will ask if the university needs help with a new library or equipment for a laboratory. That kind of thing."

At least these kids were in school. In Anatolia many children's school attendance is patchy to say the least and some drop out after only a couple of years. They are needed to work on the farms. On our road trip back in the Seventies we had seen plenty of kids as young as ten or eleven changing tyres in a garage. Even nowadays in and around Kaplan it is quite common to see young children tending flocks of sheep or goats. In Turkey's social etiquette many families will take more pride in a daughter getting married than passing her exams to go to university. Ironically, in society teachers are respected far more than they are in the UK. They are given special concessions on transport and at places such as museums and art galleries and there is even a Teacher's Day, when they are presented with an official gift by their school or college and sometimes by the pupils, too. Like my male colleagues, I was given a shirt and tie on Teacher's Day while the women received blouses and scarves.

Carolyn's sister Melanie was miffed.

"I've worked in teaching in the UK for thirty-plus years and have never had a bean." To be fair, there were some fun times. School plays or concerts, especially on the anniversary of a famous day in history when elements of Atatürk's story are told and retold, were very impressive. Not quite so riveting was a celebration of the day Pi was discovered. The school's theatre was packed as around thirty students, young and old, waited to take part in a contest to see how many correct decimal points they could regurgitate. A prize was at stake and their scores were highlighted on an electronic board. There was an element of excitement and tension at first and some of the students were quite clever to remember thirty or forty correct numbers after the decimal point. But after a while it became incredibly tedious, especially as students began to get stuck. No one had thought to make a rule that you were disqualified after so many seconds of brain freeze. So, we sat and watched as stymied contestants scratched their heads and looked up to the rafters for inspiration.

A number of commentators have raised alarms about Turkey's state educational system. An article in 2019 in the Hurriyet newspaper carried worrying statistics from that year's university entrance exam sat by 2.3 million students. Using official government figures it claimed students on average answered correctly only five of twenty-four questions on Turkish literature, four out of twenty-one on history, four out of twenty-one on geography and two and a half out of twelve on philosophy. Marks in science subjects were worse. The author blamed the rise in religious schools, insufficient qualified teachers and an outdated curriculum. Meanwhile, in 2017 a module was introduced to teach the concept of "jihad" while prohibiting any instruction on the theory of evolution. Darwin was a complete no-no. The article claimed parents were being pressured, if they could afford it, to send their children to private colleges.

Finally, the end of the school year arrived. We all shook hands and said: "See you next term." But I had already decided enough was enough. The director had invited me to sign on again for another year. But a few days later I sent him a message via Facebook, thanking him for his offer but adding that sadly I had to decline.

"I'm afraid there's insufficient discipline and respect from students for teachers at the college," I wrote by way of explanation. His reply was refreshingly honest.

"I agree. But we have a duty to educate these children." I admired his commitment and vocation. But I also noted from his Facebook page that he was the main organiser of the college's foreign trips. The scores of photographs on his timeline from destinations all over Europe and beyond were clearly worth the aggravation of dealing with a caucus of spoiled brats, especially given how difficult it is for most Turks to get travel visas. The smug Judith Chalmers-like smile told the real story.

A better option, for me, was to teach English to private students one-to-one. I quickly built up a group of eight or nine learners. One, Cem Kaan, the son of a dentist friend Cem, and his wife Zeynep, was to become involved in an extraordinary twist of fate. Dad Cem wanted the boy to spend at least a year being taught in an English school. He had explored some private boarding schools but the charges were prohibitive, around £30,000 for the year. Then he discovered a little-known agreement between the British and Turkish governments whereby Turkish students can attend a British state school if certain conditions are met. They had to travel with a parent who had to promise to set up a business in the UK. Because Cem already had a Turkish friend living in Chester, he decided son Cem Kaan would be schooled in that area and gave Carolyn and me a list of three state schools for us to assess.

"Could you look at all the relevant reviews of these schools and let me know which one you believe is the best?" he asked. When Carolyn saw the list, she burst out laughing. The head teacher at one of the schools was one of her oldest and best friends. What are the odds on that? Cem filled in all the relevant paperwork and Cem Kaan and his mother Zeynep set off for an adventure in England that lasted almost a year.

I also responded to an appeal on Facebook which launched a friendship with Zeki, the boss of a company organising weeklong English tuition camps. They were divided into two kinds, purely academic or a mixture of work and play. A good example of the latter was one held during the World Cup of 2018. Attendees certainly went home with a good knowledge of English expletives as we watched many of the matches together. That camp, based in a small hotel near Fethiye on Turkey's famous turquoise coast, included excursions in buses with no windows. As we waited at a garage and superstore complex for other buses to join us, I was bemused by some adults and children buying toy guns and rifles. We hadn't driven more than ten minutes when a similar windowless bus passed us from the opposite direction and I had my answer. A giant water pistol fight began and almost everyone was soaked. Some tutors, clearly more experienced than me, had smuggled aboard plastic containers filled with water as ammunition.

Our first stop was a cafe bar where the counter was a channel containing live fish. At the back was a pool of freezing cold mountain water. The bar owner proclaimed that anyone who could stay in the pool for five minutes would be given free drinks and a young Australian tutor from our group immediately stripped to his underpants and dived in. He claimed his prize despite appearing to have hypothermia. His chattering teeth prevented an acceptance speech. One of the learners at the camp was a wealthy Kurdish businessman planning to set up an English tuition television channel in Erbil in Iraq. He claimed to have a budget of twenty million US dollars. He asked me if I would help in the project.

"It sounds very interesting. But is the place safe?" I asked.

"Of course. It's the new Dubai," he replied. "How do you say in English? Safe as houses."

A month later I was still mulling over the idea when an ISIS cell, armed with automatic weapons, attacked a government building in Erbil, killing an employee and wounding five security personnel. The Arabian adventure hit the buffers.

CHAPTER TEN

THE RED CRABS

Carolyn and I fed our addiction to football by following the local club Tirespor 1922, playing in the fourth tier of Turkish football. Even there, emotions still ran very high. During one home match the mayor jumped from his seat in the small main stand and ordered police officers to manhandle away a home fan shouting abuse at the club's management. The beauty of watching Tirespor 1922, nicknamed The Red Crabs, was that you could rock up ten minutes before kick-off and still get a seat with an excellent view. Until the club moved to a shiny new stadium, the seats were plastic fixed on to concrete so we soon learned to bring cushions. After one match we forgot to take them with us at full-time. We went back the next day. The ground was unlocked so we walked in and there were our cushions, exactly where we had left them.

For our first four years the team played in a huge, roofless bowl near the town centre. Home fans sat along one side and the away fans, if any, occupied a tiny, covered stand opposite. The ends behind the goals were empty. The average attendance was around a thousand but the atmosphere could still be frenetic. When the team was losing expletives ranged from "louse" and "pimp" to "prostitute's child". And a match rarely ended without the popular chant *ibne hakem*, (the referee is homosexual). At one game we attended the heavens opened. With no protection, except in the VIP area, the fans were drenched. At half-time about fifty fans decided to simply walk across the pitch to take shelter in the empty "away" stand opposite. The mayor was livid. He immediately ordered several policemen to eject the soggy spectators. Only this time they had to walk around the perimeter of the ground, or face the consequences. The miserable fans plodded back to their seats, damp and despondent.

A few minutes into our first ever game I remarked to Carolyn: "Watch the Tire number eight, he's mustard." Mert Hakan Yandaş, was a midfielder with a musketeer's facial hair and a keen eye for goal. He was a bit of a prima donna and would roll around as if pole-axed at the slightest challenge. At the end of one game, when Tirespor 1922 had lost, he sat crying in the back of one goal and stayed there for several minutes after all the other players and officials had left the pitch. But he had rare skills, energy and bravery, in abundance. He was also a great showman. After a victory, Mert would grab a microphone and act as a conductor while the team and the fans exchanged chants before the whole Tire squad, including substitutes, coaching staff and team doctor engaged in a maniacal dance. Although he got through a lot of work in midfield, he was rarely seen in the opposition's penalty area. Mert had that uncanny knack of popping up at the vital moment when the ball was in what a one-time English tactician famously called POMO, the position of maximum opportunity. Mert was a natural goalscorer. Right foot, left foot, head, volley, tap-in, penalties. He missed sometimes, but very rarely.

We turned up at a match a few weeks later not realising that the clocks had changed. We were more than an hour early and the ground was empty. Pacing up and down outside, wondering whether we should kill time at a coffee shop, we were suddenly approached by one of the club's management.

"Hello," he said. "Come, please, come inside." He led us through a door marked "officials" and took us to the stand where the mayor usually sat, finding us two seats in the back row.

"You'll be fine, here." he said. The players were already on the pitch warming up.

"I really like your number eight, Mert Hakan," I said.

"Really?" he replied. "Wait there." He disappeared and a few minutes later returned with the player himself in full kit.

"Nice to meet you," said Mert, who had a few words of English.

"It's my pleasure," I responded and chatted for a couple of minutes.

"I hope you take three points today." Mert smiled.

"Don't worry. We will. And I will score a goal, just for you," he said. And with that he returned to his hamstring stretches and five-a-side drills. I cannot recall the details of the game and I don't even remember if Tirespor won. But I can still visualise Mert lashing the ball home from almost 30 yards in the second half. It was one of more than thirty goals he scored that season.

Mert turned up in the *Dağ* restaurant in Kaplan one evening and was persuaded by the owner, our friend Lütfi, to be filmed on a mobile camera wishing me all the best. "See you at the next match, George," he said. The clip was uploaded to Facebook. It was no surprise when Mert was transferred to a club called Menemen in a higher league. Later he moved to Superlig outfit Sivasspor, mixing it with the big boys including Fenerbahçe.

Galatasaray and Beşiktaş. And in August 2020, still only twenty-five, he made a big money move to Fenerbahçe.

On one occasion we went on an away trip to Altay in Izmir. Just outside the city our supporters' coach was stopped and everyone was searched by two dozen police officers. We continued with a police escort to the ground. Having left the bus, we were surrounded by police all the way to the stadium and back again after the game.

In 2016 mayor Tayfur Çiçek launched a project to build a new football stadium for Tirespor on the edge of town, a wonderful construction holding fifteen thousand spectators. There were grandiose plans that the venue could be shared with Izmir-based Superlig outfit Göztepe, whose ground was much smaller, but sadly they did not materialise. It opened for the last few games of the 2017-18 season and mayor Tayfur decreed entry would be free. At the old ground you never had to queue for more than five minutes to get in. For the first match at the new stadium, we suspected there would be a lot of interest and arrived more than an hour before kick-off. We made it through the turnstile just as the first whistle blew. Despite the huge number of empty seats, it was obvious the players enjoyed playing in such a wonderful structure with its carefully manicured pitch. Tirespor reached the play-offs that year but couldn't quite gain promotion. There were high hopes for the following campaign. The team had a change of kit from all red shirts to red and yellow stripes, apparently the club's original colours. Turks have a phrase *O sene, bu sene* which literally translates "that year, this year" but means something like "that was then but this is our year." Fans' expectations were high. Again, Tirespor qualified for the play-offs. But in the second leg of the semi-final, having drawn 0-0 away, they lost 0-1 at home and missed out on promotion once more.

Meanwhile, there had been a lot of local gossip about off-field issues. The final weeks of the league saw local elections and conspiracy theories flourished. Tayfur, the mayor who helped build the stadium, was not re-elected and the new mayor seemed reluctant to financially support the club. Rumours had it that the players had not been paid for months but this was denied by council chiefs. A players' open-air protest meeting on the evening before a match was filmed and put on Facebook. The players were seen standing around chatting near a famous statue in the town as one of the club's officials made an announcement to camera. It was clear that behind the scenes all was not well. And in one of the final leagues matches of the season the players staged a bizarre demonstration. At kick-off the club's captain Gökhan Erdöl kicked the ball to the opposition, who were clearly party to the act of defiance. Tirespor players stood stock-still in their line-up positions while the opponents passed the ball around for about a minute in their own half. Then they hoofed the ball back to the home side and the match proper began. At the final whistle many of the Tirespor players took off their shirts and ceremonially dumped them in the centre circle. A harassed kit man was seen collecting them and pushing them into a sack as the crowd disappeared.

After the play-off defeat more speculation emerged. A rich businessman from Izmir had bought the team, it was said. He was going the take the whole club to the big city and merge it with another club. There were other fanciful scenarios. Sadly, the gossip was correct. The new mayor declined to bankroll the club and the players sought new employers. According to the Hurriyet newspaper, businessman Cihan Aktaş, the president of a former Superlig club called Bucaspor which had fallen on hard times, had taken over Tirespor and would form a new club called Buca FK He would be its president. Among its players were former Tirespor skipper Gökhan Erdöl and team-mate Berke Bıyık. Buca FK would play in the professional leagues in the same yellow and dark blue colours worn by Bucaspor, which would play in an amateur division. But for the 2019-20 season there appeared to be another twist in the plot with 1928 Bucaspor reappearing in the Turkish Football Federation's Third League, where Tirespor once competed. That season the impressive stadium in Tire was used only by the town's amateur team. The new mayor had already changed its name from that of the former mayor Tayfur Çiçek, to the Gazi Mustafa Kemal Atatürk Stadium.

"What will happen to it?" I asked a friend Selo.

"Maybe it will be used for camel wrestling," he quipped

In Kaplan there's always plenty to do, especially working in the garden and walking the dogs. Every now and again there is a special event such as a wedding. Turkish weddings are especially crazy. They usually involve a procession of cars honking their horns, each decorated with ribbons or flowers. Sometimes at the head of the cavalcade is a truck carrying musicians, including a drummer and a flute player. If the family is wealthy the celebration may include a lavish firework display. At the reception the bride and groom traditionally greet the guests. Sometimes money or gold is pinned on the bride before the meal. But there's a newish practice nowadays where gifts are placed in a large box at the end of the festivities. There's always loud music and dancing, sometimes prefaced by prayers. The whole thing is captured by a battery of movie cameras. Some photographers use sophisticated robotic cranes to film revellers. Recently drones have been used. Often you can buy a framed picture of yourself or the happy couple on the way out.

Surprisingly, there is never any alcohol. Well, not in my experience.

The staple wedding food is *keşkek*, like porridge with meat in. If the wedding reception is held at home, members of the family often get up very early to make this dish in a giant drum.They use chickpeas, wheat and pieces of lamb, pounded for hours and then slowly cooked until the wheat breaks down. Traditional village weddings involve elaborate ceremonies and last several days. Large transfers of wealth are often involved. In some areas a man may still give a dowry to the father of his son's bride and also pay for the wedding. The total cost can often amount to as much as, or even more than, one year's total income for an average household. As Carolyn and I arrived I saw a group of lads with a rifle. They began firing into the air.I was invited to join in and handed the weapon.

"Be careful you don't hit the electricity cables," said a relative of the groom. I didn't. But soon after, on a trip back to England, I failed a residue test for explosives at Stansted Airport and had to undergo a detailed body search before being sent on my way. I wondered whether the test was faulty or whether the gun activity at the wedding could have been to blame. It is a certainly a dangerous tradition. One of the male tellers at the bank we used in Şile was fatally wounded when a wedding guest pulled a hand-gun out of his pocket and accidentally fired it a split second before raising the weapon to the sky.

In Kaplan, we have the internet and television, of course, and we signed a contract for a Turkish version of satellite TV called D-Smart. For around £100 a year we could watch around five-hundred channels including thirteen film channels. Others channels include BBC World, CNN, Al Jazeera and the Discovery Channel. But most importantly we could watch live Premier League football. The broadcaster covers five or six games live every weekend and whatever midweek matches are on. We needed to arrange a satellite dish and in choosing the supplier I had to avoid one particular business. The Turkish word for sound is *ses* and the business owner's initials must be AR. So, he called his company ARSES. And that is the name printed in huge letters on all his satellite dishes.

CHAPTER ELEVEN

ARMS LENGTH FROM DEATH

The first winter in our new home eventually gave way to spring and summer, with temperatures sometimes rising to forty degrees, occasionally higher. Instead of being a walk-in deep freeze, the bedroom in Number One had turned into a hot house, akin to the gun deck on one of Nelson's battleships. The summer sun is so hot it can perish the seals in your car windows. A friend who bought an expensive second-hand car was caught in a freak summer rainstorm as he drove home from the purchase and the floor of the car suddenly filled with water. We bought a portable air conditioning device and several fans. We slept with no covering and the minimum of clothes. But we usually needed four or five cold showers during the night, risking meeting up with more lizards, possibly scorpions and snakes too. We had seen all three species in the garden and neighbours warned us to keep the doors and windows firmly closed at night but many of the windows in Number One were either missing or jammed open. When we told neighbour Ayşe about the snakes she just looked dismissively and said *"geçer o"* which toughly translates as they will run away.

There are around forty-five species of snakes in Turkey, around ten of them poisonous. The most common venomous snake is the black viper. We once found a dead one in the garden. It comforted me to learn from Google that between 1995 and 2004 (the latest period for which data is available), while five hundred and fifty people visited clinics or hospitals in Turkey with snake bites, there were no deaths. Most snake bites were in the Marmara region, Central Anatolia and along Turkey's Black Sea coastline. There were also ominous scratching and scurrying sounds in the roof space above, which we desperately hoped were birds and their young and nothing more sinister. I recalled a time in Greece in a friend's rented house when a fruit bat fell from the rafters on to my face. Not a pleasant experience. One night I woke to find one of the dogs had caught a mouse and proudly left its disembowelled body at the foot of the bed.

The good weather meant it was finally time to consider the garden. Fixing that was always going to be a case of trowel and error. Neither of us was exactly green-fingered. Some things clearly grew well without any attention, olive trees and roses, for example, and especially all manner of weeds. Our first task would be to ensure our stone-walled borders were solid and secure. Next, we wanted to create a lawn on a piece of ground at the side of the old, derelict barn. On two sides it formed a border to our property and on a third side was a sloping bank of soil that we earmarked for some colourful shrubs. With both tasks we were going to need help. Decades ago, when I was a university student, I would earn holiday money working as a van boy for a furniture delivery and removal company in Hackney, East London. The boss, "known to police" as newspapers sometimes put it, only employed ex-convicts, apart from me. His catchphrase, instead of asking "how are you?" was "how's your belly off for spots?" As Eric Morecambe used to say ... there's no answer to that. Every morning a dozen workers and I lined up in front of his lorry yard and waited to be chosen. Sometimes we were lucky, other days not. They were exciting, often wild and invariably humorous times. The worldly-wise drivers got up to all kinds of tricks and villainy and opened my eyes to what life was really about. One driver claimed he had axed his wife to death. Either he was vastly exaggerating or there must have been extenuating circumstances because, according to him, the judge told him he would not go to jail if, instead, he agreed to join the British Army. So, he did.

The system of hiring casual labour in Tire was a little different. If nobody in the village was available, you turned up at a certain cafe in town around 8am and asked who wanted a fair day's work for a fair day's pay. That's how we recruited Ibrahim and Efe. Ibrahim was the muscle, bald and built like a bull. Efe was the brains, although he could also lift weights at which contestants on television's World's Strongest Man might well have baulked. Their first job was to repair the wall surrounding the plot. Eager to impress, the two men readily jumped into the ankle-deep stream, which we had only just learned doubled as the village's sewage outlet. The council had a blueprint for a brand new, purpose-built concrete sewer pipe but were trying to find a budget for it, we were told. The two men ignored (or were "undeturd" by) the awful whiff and began to clear brambles and salvage stones that had collapsed over passing years. We bought some tractor loads of extra stone from local suppliers. Then one day workers starting on a nearby house construction invited us to take whatever stone we wanted from a steepish slope at the back of the property, overlooking our clutch of dwellings. We dislodged about two tractor loads.

But when rolling them down the escarpment we had to be careful not to hit any parked cars or passing vehicles.

I don't think hired hands are particularly well looked after by Turks during their shifts. They are lucky if they are given a cup of water in eight hours. But we brought ours regular cups of tea and chocolate biscuits. And at 5pm there was a small glass of *rakı* for our heroes. Their happy grins revealed a very casual attitude to the benefits of dentistry. Their daily rate was very reasonable, about £15 each, given the exchange rate at the time. But they had no transport and as we had not yet bought a car, our friendly local taxi driver Ibo had to bring them to the village and drop them back home. His fares added about 30 per cent to their cost. Within a fortnight the work was completed.

Next came the lawn. We chose an area below Number One house with a panoramic view, which contained five olive trees. Our idea was to hang a hammock between two of them. Turf, *hazir çim,* which literally means ready grass, is relatively cheap, less than £2 a square metre at the time. We visited a few suppliers and eventually struck a deal. Before delivery we had to prepare the ground carefully. It was on a slight slope but I was comfortable with that. We didn't want to create a Hampton Court croquet arena. I had already single-handedly removed a huge amount of rubbish that had been dumped there. In all I cleared twenty-five sackfuls containing, among other things, dud batteries, medicine bottles, empty tubes of cream, cigarette lighters, old shoes, broken blades, lengths of chain, a child's plastic toy gun and multiple tins cans.

Ibrahim and Efe turned over the soil, removing as many small stones as possible. Sod's law (excuse the pun) the turf lorry arrived unexpectedly on a day the labourers were unavailable. It snaked its way down the narrow street to our door, with a few centimetres to spare on either side. There seemed to be enough rolls on the back to re-turf Wembley and only the driver to help unload them. Because of the layout of the property you either had to carry the turf twenty metres across a concreted courtyard and then down some steps or use a slightly shorter route around the outside of the plot which included a tricky ten-metre descent down a steep and rock-strewn path less than half a metre wide. Although our octogenarian neighbour Ayşe often navigated this route without incident, Carolyn and I always found ourselves gingerly inching our way down with arms outstretched like novice tightrope walkers. So, we usually chose the courtyard way. To attempt it while carrying rolls of turf seemed foolhardy to say the least. Eventually the lorry was empty. The following day the labourers were back to lay the turf with the help of carefully positioned lines of string.

Once down the lawn looked spectacular. As green and straight as a (slightly sloping) snooker table. But sadly, it didn't stay that way for long. Although I watered it carefully, the summer heat, ammonia-filled urine from local female street dogs, and possibly a mystery virus soon contrived to turn the lush green sward into a brown, crunchy stubble. It was like walking on a street sweeper's broom head. I bought a sprinkler but although it sent water into the air like a fountain its head didn't rotate as it should. I thought it was something to do with the water pressure. A villager walking down a nearby path saw my dilemma. He came over, muttered something in Turkish and began meddling with the three heads on the device. A jet of water shot out straight into my face. But his intervention did the trick and the sprinkler was now rotating and throwing out water as it should. But regular watering couldn't revive the grass. A friend's mother, a professor of botany, visiting from New Zealand said that, given the climate, maintaining a traditional lawn in Kaplan was nigh on impossible. But the following summer the original turf grass made a surprise comeback and the area, though not exactly the outfield at Lord's, looked passable.

We had other jobs for the labourers but Efe began not turning up for various, doubtless spurious, reasons so we had to stand them both down. We soon learned that when some Turkish manual workers have a bit of money, they like to let their hair down. In addition to the obvious haunts men enjoy, we discovered there was a thriving underground and illegal cock fighting scene. We were told tens of thousands of Turkish lira were gambled on each fight. One day a villager even showed us his own fighting cock. But the following day it ran off never to be seen again. Now it was time to add a few shrubs and flowers. We were soon on first name terms with the man at the garden centre and his boisterous dog Gingo, who wore a small cow bell. The owner had a vast array of plants, shrubs and fruit trees and we would often fill the back of the car, yet never spend more than the equivalent of £15. We were also intrigued by the myriad of plants that grew wild.

Digging them up, even from a forest, is a criminal offence in Turkey. But we decided to risk it while driving past a huge lake at a place called Belevi about twenty-five minutes away from Tire. Gingerly we rescued some water lilies and also two species of what looked like reeds. The water lilies survived in large plastic bowls only for a week or two. But the reeds loved their new home. One was small, about eighteen inches high, with tiny yellow flowers. The other, a type of bulrush (*saz*) was probably the inspiration for the children's story Jack and the Beanstalk. Although we only planted one, it propagated like mad. Within two weeks we had sixteen or seventeen stalks, two or three metres high, dominating the bank bordering the brown lawn. As fast as you cut them down more grew. Maybe the author of

Day of the Triffids had holidayed in the area. If we were not careful, we would soon have a whole battalion of bulrushes blotting out the landscape.

If we had committed an offence by removing them from the lake, then Izmir Big City Council should have been indicted for crimes against ecology. While widening the road from Belevi to Tire, they dumped thousands of tons of rock, gravel and aggregate around its circumference. That along with the constant passage of noisy lorries and heavy machinery and the fumes from the asphalting, contrived to kill off every single bit of flora and fauna in the area. Strafing with napalm could hardly have been more destructive. The forest of bulrushes disappeared. So too did all the birds, frogs and insects. Not even the annoying black flies survived. It had been a popular picnic area and a spot where fishermen would regularly come to cast their lines. But in a year, it was reduced to desolation. Two years later, when the road was nearly complete, it was only just beginning to show signs of recovery.

We had long admired the wonderful jacaranda trees and bougainvillea that beautified the up-market seaside towns of Alaçatı and Çesme. But we quickly learned that Kaplan was too high for them to thrive. After losing several plants, we finally coaxed a jacaranda to grow to about two metres with three lonely looking leaves at the top and no flowers. An Irish friend of Carolyn's gave us some anonymous looking bulbs that grew into two-metre high plants, canna lilies, with spectacular purple-brown leaves and a gorgeous orange flower. They needed little attention and grew everywhere. So-called "Bodrum plants" also worked well, growing about a metre tall with a pretty blue flower but they needed plenty of water. Further down the garden, in front of the old barn, we wanted to create a lavender bed, despite the lack of blooms on the two bushes we owned already. We bought thirty small plants and set them out in six rows. On a trip back to the UK we bought a soil tester, like a stopwatch with two parallel knitting needles sticking out, and discovered, to our horror, that the ground was acidic when lavender liked it alkali. Google told us to mix in lime, embers from the soba heating device or barbecues and leaf mould in a bid to alter the soil's chemistry. Despite our best efforts all but six of the plants quickly died. We were crestfallen. Maybe the lime or the embers took time to infiltrate, maybe Mother Nature is capricious, malevolent, or both, or maybe a few sacks of neighbour Birgül's goat-poo fertiliser did the trick. But the following year the surviving six really spread, just as we had hoped, and also yielded an abundance of eye-catching blue-mauve flowers.

A wisteria plant we placed near Number Two, and invited to climb up some metal mesh left by the builders, suddenly sprang into life too. At the far end of the lawn, we created a small bed and planted three hydrangeas. They don't like direct sunlight but a nearby olive tree provided just enough shade. Soon they, too, yielded gorgeous flowers for the house. You cannot teach Turkish villagers much about flora. But Carolyn's trick of plunging the hydrangea stems into boiling water for ten seconds, before putting them into the vase to make them live longer, amazed Birgül, who was convinced they would quickly wilt indoors.

Soon afterwards Birgül's son suggested growing fruit and vegetables. He earmarked a patch at the bottom of the garden and dug it over. He found some discarded branches, built a fence with chicken wire and planted tomatoes, red and green peppers and courgettes. I brought back from England some mange tout and pak choi seeds. Nearby in an unfenced area we positioned melon and watermelon plants. To our astonishment, and true to the local soil's famed virility, virtually everything grew. So, well, in fact, that the produce attracted a large number of tortoises. The official collective noun is "a creep" by the way. Recalling that at my old Oxford college Oriel we had a tortoise reputed to be ninety years old (they can actually live to 150), with the college crest painted on its back, I decided to number the interlopers. Using white paint, I quickly reached number ten but never found a left winger to complete my team. Despite the fact that tortoises have no teeth they made short work of the melons and watermelons. But the protected produce in the veg patch grew well and soon we had our own supply of marrow, courgettes, tomatoes, pak choi, mange tout and two kinds of peppers, one like swallowing a red-hot poker.

We had found a reliable builder with a crew who said he could transform house Number Two. We agreed a budget, materials arrived and he set about taking the roof off, storing the tiles, and creating a new floor throughout the building. He was assisted by a welder, Volkan, a small, thick set man built like a prop forward, who looked like he cut his own black hair. He made several frames, which were then welded on to long pins drilled into the existing walls. The frames were covered with hardboard and then thin strips of metal and finally concrete was poured on top. Metal props were put into the cellar to bear the weight. Outside other workers began building a balcony. First, they had to make an extra column to support the weight. They made a vertical metal structure using rods and wire, then surrounded it with shuttering and poured in hand-mixed concrete. When it had set, they did the same again but this time horizontally outside the front of the building.

But soon Volkan had a problem. One of two lanes to our plot is on a slope. The gradient is not severe but when it's wet, or if the vehicle is large, it can prove difficult. If parked in the garden of Number Two the trick is to get your revs high before starting off and then keep your foot down as your drive out of the front garden and turn hard left on to the road. Full throttle (*tam gaz*) and nerves of steel are required as there is a small wall on the other side of the narrow road facing our garden. On this particular day Volkan made the turn well enough but with too few revs. His flat back truck was stuck. Cursing, he put on the handbrake. I heard a metallic crunch as he put the thing back into gear and revved the engine so hard smoke poured off the tyres like a boy racer on a British sink estate. The smell of scorched rubber assaulted the nostrils. But the lorry moved not one centimetre. What Volkan should have done next is carefully reverse into our garden and begin the manoeuvre all over again. Instead, with typical Turkish bravura, he opted to simply roll backwards hoping to find enough purchase lower down the road. He failed to realise that the block paving runs out about ten metres after our front entry and the road then becomes a dirt track. Or on this day more like a mud track. Volkan's predicament was now worse than before.

Such situations, however, bring out the best in Turkish villagers. Immediately a near neighbour, Aytekin, appeared out of nowhere and so did Levent. Another neighbour was summoned and I joined in. The four of us climbed on to the back of the truck. Aytekin gave Volkan the necessary instructions and he revved up as the four of us, me hanging on to the back of the vehicle for dear life, jumped up and down to hopefully give the rear tyres some bite. The lorry lurched forward a few metres but then slipped further backwards. We had passed the spot where villagers dumped their rubbish and, to my left, I was now looking at a sheer escarpment and some rocks about thirty metres below. The distance to the edge was less than the length of my arm. Just how compact was this track's subsoil, I mused?

One false move now by Volkan and we'd be front page news in the Tire Bugle. I desperately wanted to get off but that would have been cowardice and I didn't know when Volkan was going to make his next escape attempt. A few seconds later the engine roared again, the four of us jumped up and down like maniacal disco dancers as the truck shuddered forward once more. Mud squirted left and right as the vehicle gained a metre or two before coming to a complete stop again. Then, even with the handbrake on, it slid further backwards. I felt a clammy sensation as the wheels thankfully kept parallel with the track.

Clearly, it was time for Plan B. Aytekin drew his mobile phone from his pocket and rang a number. The four of us dismounted and waited for a few minutes until we heard the rumble of a tractor. Salvation. The driver said something to Aytekin which I could not fully understand but was probably: "What sort of mess have you got yourself into now?" Then, smiling ruefully, he tied a length of thick rope to a tow point on Volkan's lorry and the other end on to his tractor. Slowly the two inched their way up the slope, back on to the brickwork and up past Aytekin's house on to level ground. From then on Volkan would always park in the small square nearby.

The interior of Number Two was plastered stone. We decided to leave this in place in the bedroom but to chip away and expose the original stonework in the living room and kitchen. It was a dirty, choking job but the results were spectacular. Incredibly, in the corner of the living room we discovered what had once been a primitive shower area, at least one hundred years ago, maybe more. There was even a ledge on which people placed their soap. Our neighbour Birgül's son Hüseyin helped. With the roof gone we quickly realised that extra stonework would be needed to build on top of the existing partition walls to fill in the empty spaces up to the roof. We were advised the two best men in Tire for this job were Mehmet Ali and Bayram Usta. *Usta* means expert in Turkish and is a sign of respect. The men's stone masonry rivalry was the stuff of legend. Depending on who you spoke to one was a little better than the other. Everyone knew them, however, and seemed to have an opinion.

We found Mehmet Ali up a ladder helping to restore the town's famous 800-year-old market (*bedesten*). A slightly-built man with a rather pinched face, by all accounts he had just fallen out with someone in charge of the project and was free to work elsewhere. Our good fortune. Having negotiated his services, we did not bother to contact his rival. But he would work for us soon enough. Mehmet Ali (or M'dali as locals called him) was punctual, a good worker and finished the job in no time. We were so impressed we asked if he would work on the derelict out-building in front of Number Two that I had ear-marked as a study. I had cleared the rubble, fractured tiles and broken glass. But the whole front wall needed rebuilding with space for two small windows and a front door. M'dali happily agreed to carry on.

During July and August, the building work continued but with substantial siestas. Carolyn wanted white painted tongue and groove wood for the interior ceiling of Number Two. But she insisted it should be built around and above the original beams, most of them old bits of tree trunk so they would be left exposed. The carpenter we engaged was called Onur, an obese Alfred Molina with a broad smile and a can-do attitude. He was dubious but climbed my aluminium ladder to take a closer look and turned each step into a large horseshoe. He agreed it was feasible and set one of his men to work. Carolyn also had a brainwave about the doors to the bedroom and newly-created bathroom. With space at a premium why not have sliding doors? In a scrapyard we had spotted some wheels about thirteen centimetres in diameter attached to rods forty centimetres long that were ordinarily used on old horse-drawn ploughs.

"Why can't we use those?" she asked Onur, who clearly thought Carolyn was insane, despite always calling her *patron* (boss). You could see the incredulity written on his face.

"Bits of plough on a door?" He sucked his teeth. Then he called over welder Volkan, whose shop was nearby. Together they sharpened their chins with thumb and forefinger. Volkan went away and returned a few minutes later with a runner wide enough to take the old plough wheel and together they scratched their heads and stroked their cheeks while carrying out a quick feasibility study.

"We'll give it a go," Onur confirmed.

About six months after the practical and impressive sliding doors were installed, we saw something almost identical in a glossy magazine featured in a multi-million-dollar farmhouse owned by Hollywood film star Meg Ryan. A small galley kitchen was created where the squatter loo had been, the poo hole now thankfully buried under several centimetres of concrete. A toilet, sink and shower were fitted in the bathroom, at the opposite end of the building. Fortunately, we found an excellent plumber/electrician called Saygın. In Turkey it's quite normal for one person to be proficient in both trades. Saygın was actually far more than proficient. He was meticulous. Normally in their haste to finish the job as quickly as possible the Turkish plumber/electrician will leave no end of snags. A regular annoyance, even sometimes in top hotels, is finding that the hot water comes out of the tap with the blue marker and the cold tap is coloured red. That's because the plumber cannot be bothered to learn which is the hot feed and just guesses.

Saygın didn't fret at installing a number of hanging light fittings we had brought from England. He skilfully fixed them to the old tree trunk supports that criss-crossed the kitchen and dining room, hiding the wiring on top. Because the walls in the living room of Number Two were all rough stone he cleverly installed a large light fitment we bought in Istanbul and ensured it switched on and off via a small zapper. Again, the control box was hidden in the rustic roof supports. The first-floor area was then tiled throughout. By now the builders had completed the new balcony for the front of the house which joined up with the existing one at the side. In summer we would now be able to sit in the sun, if we so wished, from about noon until it set. During the work one of the builders volunteered that his son was serving a life term of imprisonment for the knife murder of his wife in a "crime of passion". He was clearly distraught by what had happened and was too upset to fully explain the circumstances. It reminded me of the day our restaurant-owning friend Lütfi took me for a hike in the hills above Kaplan, where he foraged for wild sorrel, oregano, sage and, when the climate was right, wild mushrooms. A car came towards us and the driver stopped to chat. When the nattering stopped, and the vehicle moved off down the hill and Lütfi turned to me.

"Nice chap. Known him for a long time. He served fifteen years for murdering his wife."

I was beginning to get a sense of the hot-bloodedness of the Turks. With the wooden ceiling at last completed, it was time for the roof to go back on. Only a few extra tiles were needed to replace broken ones. There were several other final external jobs. Volkan fitted railings up the stairs from the courtyard and around the edge of the now two-sided balcony, which was tiled by the same man, Serhat, who worked on the interior. We also asked him to tile the floor of my study. But when we returned from a day out we found he had used the balcony tiles instead of the interior house tiles as instructed. I didn't have the heart to tell him to pull them all up. We would have to live with it. Volkan also installed an ornate black front gate and a more functional fence and gate at the rear to create an area where the dogs could safely run. A huge glass window about 120cm by 210cm and an adjoining glass front door were then installed and a traditional sun-heated hot water system was erected on the roof. We could now move the wood burning stove (*soba*) from Number One to Number Two. The chimney section poked out above the new balcony. To catch the external leaks, we hung a plastic bucket over on the horizontal section before it turned through ninety degrees. When it rained, however, the bucket filled to the brim and emptying the thing required the strength and dexterity of a hod-carrier, otherwise negotiating the newly laid tiles became like sliding through molasses.

Around this time our furniture arrived from England. It had been transported by sea in a container to Izmir, then by lorry to Kaplan. But the lorry was too big to negotiate either of the two narrow lanes to our house. The last fifty metres would need a tractor and trailer so another Hüseyin, who had already delivered sand and cement to the property, was summoned. Whether it happened on the container trip, the loading on to the lorry or the move from lorry to tractor I have no idea. But when the delivery men finally grunted and groaned their way through our gate for the last time there was one box missing and the doors of our dismantled double wardrobe were badly damaged. The freight-forwarding company's insurance firm later compensated us but the loss was a blow, especially as the missing box contained a number of valuable and sentimental items. The damage to the wardrobe was also disappointing. But when we measured it we realised it was three inches too high for the bedroom anyway. A huge central beam was in the way. We called Onur. The wardrobe doors were half mirror and half wood. A fragment of glass was missing from a corner of one mirror. And there was an ascending identical crack in the wood of each door, as if they had been bent against something while packaged together in transit.

"What do you think, Onur?" I asked.

He said he could put a supporting piece of wood on the inside of each door but there was little he could do about the cracks.

"What about the height?" I asked. "I don't suppose it's possible simply to cut three inches off the back and the sides, is it? Give it a haircut, so to speak."

He sucked his teeth once more and promised to give it a try. I'd discovered long ago that the Turks are great fixers and bodgers. Whereas in the UK we will simply often just throw away a problematic washing machine or a vacuum cleaner and buy a new one when faced with a costly repair, Turks are thriftier. I'm with them, which is why Carolyn's Turkish nickname for me is *cimri* (miser or cheapskate). I remember on that first trip to Turkey in the Bedford van our dynamo burned out. In the UK you would hunt down a replacement in a scrapyard. But such things did not really exist in the 1970s and finding one with Bedford parts would have been like winning the national lottery. Instead a back-street mechanic spent hours to re-build the old one with copper wire.

Onur was certainly up for the challenge. From the back of his truck, he brought a portable band-saw and soon chippings and sawdust were flying in all directions. I returned an hour later from a shopping trip to find our old wardrobe tucked neatly just under the awkward beam, the shelves in place and not listing like the Tower of Pisa either. All right, the doors looked like two giant exchange rate graphs showing the value of the Pound sterling climbing inexorably against the Turkish Lira. But a bit of wood filler and maybe a coat of varnish or two might be able to minimize the impact. Home, sweet, home.

CHAPTER TWELVE

PAWS FOR THOUGHT

Dogs have always been important in our lives. In England we took in a red setter called Sally, rescued after being thrown out of a car on a motorway. She was a beautiful dog but a little schizophrenic and prone to incontinence, probably because of how she had been treated. Later we bought a pedigree flatcoat retriever named Ollie. The dog was so clever he could identify the sound of your car engine from 500 yards away and bring your slippers to the door. I cried for the first time since childhood when Ollie died in my arms of old age. That was after our regular vet (with whom we had spent a lot of money) came out on an emergency call and wanted £150 to administer a lethal injection. I refused. Not through parsimony but because of his uncaring attitude. Ollie was in no pain and faded away an hour later. My friend Gavin helped me to bury Ollie in our garden with his toys and favourite blanket.

When we first moved to Turkey full-time, we initially lived in our holiday flat in Şile, four floors up with no lift. Keeping dogs there was really not an option. However, one day we found a really beautiful abandoned brown and white English setter on the beach and named him Bradley. We cared for him because waiters at the beach bars were throwing stones at him, perceiving the hungry dog would dissuade customers from renting sun beds. We took Bradley home, gave him a good bath, groomed him and with the help of Levent's sister Dilek and several telephone calls to dog charities, we found him a home in a nearby village. His new owner wanted to use Bradley for hunting and over the next year, at the man's invitation, we visited the dog several times. Then one day we learned thieves had stolen Bradley. Luckily, a neighbour had noted down the number plate of the villains' car and within hours the police had caught the culprits in Istanbul and returned Bradley. Sadly, a year later, Bradley disappeared again. This time there was no trace and we heard no more of him.

Soon afterwards, we became the proud owners of English setter puppies Darcy and Willow. They had been rescued by an animal welfare group in Istanbul, after being dumped in a forest. We never understood the logic of them being abandoned because hunting dogs are regularly sold in Turkey for £400 or more. Carolyn spotted a heart-breaking internet appeal for a "forever home" and we drove from our flat into Istanbul to collect them, aged just two or three months.

"Which one do you want?" asked the group's kind and hard-working coordinator Şule (pronounced Shoo-lay) and immediately re-named "Shoelace" by daughter Charlotte.

"We'll take both of them. You can't split sisters," said Carolyn. That night they snuggled together in our flat in a furry oval dog bed. Darcy soon grew to normal size but Willow, who had flecks of brown among the traditional black and white fur, was a little smaller than expected.

"Don't worry," said the local vet. "She is a *manken* (model)." Although they were no trouble, there were clearly practical difficulties, especially when negotiating 64 steps down to take a leak before bedtime. By this time, we had already decided to move to Kaplan. Having the dogs merely hastened our schedule. True, they loved the beach and early one morning were even invited to take part in a magazine photo-shoot when we bumped into a photographer and a lissome model in a red swimsuit. Another bonus for "the girls" was chasing, and once or twice catching, seagulls. But we surmised they would also like the mountain terrain above Kaplan. Once we had moved to the village, however, we had to take care. If they liked gulls these hunting dogs were also going to be partial to the neighbours' free roaming chickens. Whereas Turks have an almost maniacal adoration for babies they have a distinct ambivalence towards dogs. Muslims are taught from a young age that they are dirty. And possibly because of the large number of ownerless street dogs that are allowed to roam freely in towns and cities, a disproportionate number of Turks are irrationally very afraid of canines.

As well as Darcy and Willow, we looked after a number of these street dogs. For starters, there was a white mongrel bitch called Daisy, abandoned at our front gate as a puppy and a light brown female dog Tilley. Later a gingery male, Mutley, joined the gang. They would hang around the garden hoping to be fed. They barked a lot but never bit. But one day, one of three workmen coming to install an air conditioning unit scrambled three metres up a tree when Mutley and Daisy approached. Of course, not all our villagers were saints. There's one we called The Mad Man. Over six-foot tall, sinewy, and usually four days unshaven, he earned the soubriquet because he looked like he was auditioning for a Turkish version of Rambo. His head was adorned with a special scarf associated with camel wrestling fans and he rarely travelled without a rifle and a huge hunting knife. Later we learned he had previously grabbed neighbour

Aytekin around the throat during a dispute. One day we were walking our dogs on a track when the Mad Man came into view leading some sheep and goats. We had Darcy and Willow on leads and they would never "worry" such animals. But the Mad Man began to shout.

"*Yol ver!*" (get out of the way). He gave us a withering look. We didn't argue.

It was the street dogs that caused the bust up with another villager Hayrettin. He was a relative newcomer to the village, buying a run-down structure on a hill above our plot and building an expensive summer house with a swimming pool. He brought with him two dogs, a small white, fluffy mongrel and a rather handsome brown retriever. Whereas we always kept our dogs fenced inside our property, Hayrettin allowed his to roam the village. Although he had erected a metal frame around his property it had no panelling so the dogs could simply climb through. One day Levent alerted us to the fact that Hayrettin was not happy. He claimed that Mutley had bitten his retriever. It seemed unlikely. Mutley, who would never win any beauty contests and whose ears had been cut off as a puppy to prevent predators from grabbing them in a fight, was an amiable mutt. Now he was facing a charge of grievous bodily harm. When challenged, Hayrettin agreed he had not seen the incident himself but had allegedly been told about it by a neighbour. The more likely culprit was another village dog we christened Scarface because of the huge, healed up wound across one cheek, who often prowled around the village square not far from Hayrettin's house. Scarface and Mutley were very similar in colour, build and size and Scarface was always spoiling for a fight. Hayrettin, thick set and overweight, was fuming. At his permanent home about 45 minutes' drive away he claimed he kept five pit bulls.

"Do you want me to bring them to the village?" he threatened. "I will you know."

He insisted we paid the vet's bill for his injured dog. So, to keep the peace, we drove to the surgery. Hearing the full story, the vet was reluctant to take our money.

"*Boş ver,*" he said, which means "forget it, don't worry." But to keep the peace we insisted and handed over about £40. Two days later we heard a commotion in our garden. I went on to the balcony and there was Hayrettin again, shouting and bawling and this time waving a huge lump of wood above his head.

"Come down here," he thundered. He now claimed Mutley had attacked his other dog, the white mongrel. Again, he had no evidence.

"Come down," he shouted again. Looking at the David v Goliath odds and deciding discretion was the better part of valour, I decided to decline his offer.

"I'm going to call the Jandarma," he proclaimed and turned on his heels.

"Why don't you build a fence," I shouted in Turkish as he shuffled away. The cavalry was already on its way to help us in the shape of our neighbour Birgül's feisty son Hüseyin. Such kerfuffles are rare in a village and the commotion had alerted all the nearby properties. Hüseyin, thin and wiry, was already in fighting mode and threatened to punch Hayrettin's lights out. His mother had to grab him and pull him away. It might have been super heavyweight against featherweight but my money would certainly have been on Hüseyin. Somewhat chastened, Hayrettin, cursing, stomped off to his luxury new-build and phoned the Jandarma. Now it was Birgül's turn to intercede. When the police officers arrived, she told them in no uncertain terms that the dog attack was "nothing to do with George and Carolyn". The Jandarma, instantly bored, decided no further action was necessary and departed without even getting out their notebooks. Even if it had been Mutley, which we later discovered it wasn't when another villager admitted her dog was to blame, he was a street dog.

In fact, technically that wasn't true either. He had an owner. A man called Mustafa. Mutley definitely didn't belong to us, we merely fed him every now and again. This was indisputably true. When Mutley first arrived on our doorstep, we rang Mustafa and he promised to come and retrieve him but never did. Probably due to the "day after mañana" syndrome. A few days later we walked Mutley home and handed him over to an elderly woman at the property. The following morning, he was back in our garden, looking for breakfast. We went to town, bought a three-metre chain and took Mutley home yet again. This time nobody answered the door. So we chained Mutley to a tree near the house. Sure enough, the following morning he was back at our gate with that "feed me" look. Either this was a canine Houdini or Mustafa really didn't want the bother of him. So, we gave up trying to take him back to his real home. Tilley was the offspring of a neighbour's gentle giant of a dog called Marco, a kangal, a famous breed often used by shepherds for protection. The Kangal can weigh up to sixty-six kilos and reach speeds of up to 30mph. Marco looked fearsome but would then roll over and invite you to rub his belly. We found Daisy abandoned, as already mentioned, six months after we arrived. At first, I thought she had a broken leg. But I quickly realised her pronounced limp was the result a deformity in her rear right leg. As she grew to adulthood either the deformity partially corrected itself or she learned to cope with it. Unless you knew her history, you would not tell from her gait that she had had a problem.

Realising street dogs' puppies are an awful nuisance in a village we paid for both Daisy and Tilley to be neutered. Tilley's operation was relatively straightforward. But Daisy's was rather messier. Getting her into our Renault Dacia Duster was tricky enough. Unused to having a collar, being on a lead or travelling in a vehicle she kicked and twisted in a frantic bid to escape. Finally, Carolyn and I managed to bundle her on to the car's back seat and I set off alone to the vet. I had only travelled 300 yards when an awful smell alerted me to the fact that Daisy had already exacted a measure of revenge. A dirty protest, you might say. Looking back, I saw a pool of black faeces. Tying a handkerchief over my nose and mouth, I tried not to retch and drove to town as fast as I could. The vet's clinic was in the town centre and parking was difficult. I found a space about 75 yards away from his surgery, jerked Daisy out of the car and guided her on to the pavement. She was reluctant to move. I yanked at her collar and in response she lurched forward and emptied her bowels again all down the left leg of my best khaki chinos. She adamantly refused to move. There was only one thing for it. I lifted her up and carried her in my arms the rest of the way to the clinic.

Warning of my imminent arrival had already wafted through the open door. Seconds later I stumbled in and with great relief dropped Daisy to the floor. She immediately decided to spray the linoleum with the remaining contents of her innards. A woman, waiting with a cat in a small cage, grimaced. But the vet, Erhan, seemed unfazed. He ordered a helper to clear up the mess and ushered me into his surgery room. He instructed me to lift Daisy on to a metal table and within minutes had knocked her out with an anaesthetic jab. I assumed I would be dismissed from the room but Erhan was quite happy for me to stay and admire his surgical handiwork. Eventually the sleeping Daisy was sewn up and I carried her back to the car and drove home. She made a quick and full recovery and joined our extended animal family.

Whenever we went out in the car Daisy and Mutley would run ahead like US Presidential bodyguards. If we visited a restaurant in the village they would wait by the car while we enjoyed our meal and would resume their close protection duties again on the journey home. If driving to Tire they would come with us for the first few hundred yards before deciding they could not keep pace and return to our garden. About six months after turning up, however, Mutley disappeared, suspiciously while we were away. Neighbours claimed a villager had taken him in. But Carolyn suspected he had been shot or poisoned. Winston, another dog who regularly visited but who had an owner, died by poisoning. A local claimed he was trying to "kill rats" but we had our doubts.

Turkish villagers treat dogs as working animals. They are never allowed inside the home. Some have better lives than others but we have seen some dogs shackled on one or two metre chains in gardens for 24 hours a day. A very sad sight. In another part of Turkey, a man was jailed for dragging a dog along the road from the back of his vehicle. A video of the despicable event was posted on Facebook and drew widespread condemnation. To be fair, Turkey actually has laws protecting dogs, even street dogs, against cruelty. A far cry from 1910 when all Istanbul's strays were rounded up and sent to an island where, it's said, many of them ate each other. But nowadays you still regularly see men and women bend down and pick up rocks to throw at ownerless dogs. We had a massive row, one day, with a villager who chucked a stone at Mutley as we drove through Kaplan. By contrast, at the Migros supermarket in Tire, staff routinely looked after street dogs and their litters, building cardboard shelters for them in the store's underground car park. And the internet is crowded with animal welfare groups, appealing for funds, volunteers and homes for their charges.

Our day usually started early (6am in summer) with a dog walk. At first, we would walk from our house, using one of two paths that led down from the village. Street dogs and even some with owners would join in. Following along, hoping for a biscuit at the half-way turnaround spot would be Winston (later poisoned), Corbett, Marco (sent away to a relative), Mummy (who later died), Scamp (taken in by a neighbour), Daisy and Tilley as well as our two, Darcy and Willow. Knowing our dogs' hunting pedigree, we only let them off the lead when we were well clear of the village and its livestock. On the way back up the hill we would have a routine whereby either Carolyn or I would go ahead and catch Darcy and Willow before they entered chicken territory. There was a bush on one walk where we would always hear an ominous hissing sound and would quickly walk on. But come the spring we worried that one or more of the dogs would dig up the fruit and vegetable plants in the many gardens dotted about. One day Darcy doubled back soon after being unleashed and ran to a spot near our house to snatch a neighbour's chicken. There was no witness but I confessed, apologised and handed over twenty lira by way of compensation. The owner of the dead chicken seemed happy enough with that.

So, we decided to abandon the village walks and either drive fifteen minutes to the top of the mountain above Kaplan where there are no gardens or else drive to Pamucak beach where we could also feed the strays there. When going up the mountain we began by passing Fadime's house. At 6am she, too, was up and had already lit a fire in her garden where she often cooked. We would drive through the village square and turn left before the Dağ restaurant to begin our ascent. We had to pass a small dog who always came flying out to bark at the car and gave chase for a few hundred metres. The higher we went the fewer houses we saw. If anyone passed coming the other way, we always exchanged nods, waves or a toot on the horn. We parked at a fountain near the top and walked twenty minutes almost to the summit and then walked back. Alternatively, we would go on a loop which passed the actual summit (and several wind turbines) before dropping down and back to the car. That took about an hour and twenty minutes. We never saw anyone else on foot except on the occasional Sunday when hunters assembled to seek out and shoot wild boar.

The strays at Pamucak beach were a rum lot. At one time there was Mummy and Daddy and their three pups, unkempt Scruffy with cream-coloured fur like the late Ken Dodd's hair, Bella, Poppy and Curly Watts (so named after its tail). They were all in one pack except Scruffy, who would sleep on her own at one end of the beach and Curly Watts, who was a newcomer to the shoreline. They would recognise our car engine and come running as we pulled up. Sometimes we would have to drive 400 yards down the beach to wake up Scruffy and then encourage her to follow us back to the others for the doggy buffet. We usually stopped at a supermarket in Selçuk about ten minutes' drive away to buy three packets of cocktail sausages and a multipack of biscuits. The dogs would wait patiently to be fed and then join us on a walk along the sand. Over the years we have found a variety of objects on the beach from a virtually brand-new life belt and a fishing rod to an armchair. Tragically, during the height of the migration crisis, we also found the shredded remains of a large rubber boat and many flimsies, and probably unseaworthy, life-jackets.

One day we saw that two new dogs had arrived, a large black dog and his sidekick, the aforementioned Curly Watts. They were at the far end of the beach near where Scruffy used to hang out but they quickly sussed the routine and trotted to where we parked the vehicle for feeding time at our pop-up kennels. The usual suspects lined up and waited patiently for their treats. But the black dog and Curly, either through excitement or starvation, were more anxious to dine. As I handed out the fare, I accidentally dropped a cocktail sausage. Bella went to pick it up but the black dog leapt in to try to snatch it away. A very rare fight ensued. Stupidly, instead of reaching for a hiking stick in the car, I tried to separate the combatants with my bare hands and the black dog bit me on the little finger of my right hand. Order was quickly restored. The wound was superficial but it was bleeding.

"You'd better get a rabies jab," said Carolyn. "Maybe a tetanus injection too."

"Don't be silly," I argued. "It's only a nip." At home I checked on Google to find that only two people in Turkey had died from rabies in the previous year, pretty favourable odds. But Carolyn carped on until I gave in and we headed off to the hospital. No sooner had I walked through the door of the Accident and Emergency unit that my eye was drawn to a huge poster. DANGER OF RABIES. I didn't bother translating all of it but it was clear that the Turks took the disease very seriously. I checked in as usual, paid my £7, and waited in casualty. Never mind the four-hour wait in the UK, I was called within four minutes. A doctor heard my story.

"Where is the dog?" he asked.

"Still on the beach, I presume," I replied. I later learned the Jandarma also take it seriously and biting dogs are routinely tracked down and tested for diseases. I was given a rabies and a tetanus injection and the broken skin at the base of my finger was bandaged.

"That's it then?" I asked the nurse.

"No. You need to come back for four more rabies' injections at regular intervals," she said, handing me an appointment card with the relevant dates already inked in. The following week we were back at Pamucak and the black dog was still there but now apparently contrite. This time it waited in line like the others and only ate when it was its turn. After that, we never saw it again. Whether someone took it for a pet or it was simply made unwelcome by the long-term inhabitants of the dunes, I have no idea. There's a Korean restaurant in nearby Selçuk but I don't want to think the unthinkable. Poppy, a lovely, small dog probably only six months old, also vanished. We learned from a Turkish woman dog lover, who we met one day as she dropped off a dozen loaves of bread, that people do give the strays homes from time to time. How the animals deal with the searing heat of summer and temperatures up to forty degrees with little or no shade I have no idea. Then one day we drove on to the strand to find that Scruffy had died. It was a heartbreaking moment. We didn't know whether or not to bury her. But a local told us the council would deal with it.

Springtime brings special problems for all dogs: ticks (*kene*). The nasty vampire-like creatures latch on to the skin and fill their bodies with the dog's blood. Sometimes they grow to the size of a small grape. To combat them you have to squeeze a plastic phial of medicine on the dog's neck and trail it down to its tail, rubbing it into the fur. We always carried an extra-large packet of biscuits in the car in case we saw a hungry dog. We couldn't save every stray but we liked to think we could bring a little joy into the lives of those who found themselves left on the street. There's a wonderful film called Hachi: A Dog's Tale, starring Richard Gere about a college lecturer who finds a stray and takes the dog in. The dog follows his master to the train station every day as he goes to work.But one day the man has a heart attack and dies. Hachi patiently waits at the station. Then he returns the next day, and the next. He carries on with the same routine for ten years until he dies. The screenplay is based on a real Japanese Akita dog Hachiko, who was born in Ōdate, Japan, in 1923. After the death of his owner, Ueno Hidesaburō in 1925, Hachiko returned to the Shibuya train station the next day and every day after that until he died in March 1935.

The story also mirrors that of Greyfriars Bobby, a Skye terrier who became known in nineteenth century Edinburgh for spending fourteen years guarding the grave of his owner until he died himself on 14 January 1872. In both cases local people erected statues in memory of the dogs. You would have to be stone hearted not to respond to the innate willingness of a dog to give love and affection.

CHAPTER THIRTEEN

FOOD GLORIOUS FOOD

Turkey's cuisine regularly tops international lists as the finest in the world. The variety is astounding. We have one Turkish recipe book which is almost four hundred pages. One of the first words you learn in Turkey is *ye!* (eat!) We like almost all of it. But when one day we saw our neighbour Birgül blowing up a two-metre length of sheep's intestine like a balloon, planning to fill with a mixture of rice and herbs, Carolyn and I swapped knowing glances. We were both thinking: "If we are offered some, we cannot offend our lovely friend. But we are definitely not eating THAT!" When it duly arrived, the dogs lapped it up.

Levent's mother is an especially good cook. It seems like an essential skill that mothers pass on to their daughters. What constantly surprised me was that she would often prepare something that we have never seen before. The taste was always wonderful. So, what's on the Turkish menu? Well, so much more than *döner kebab* and *şiş kebab*, tasty as they both are. One of our favourite dishes *Iskender kebab,* is long strips of lamb döner meat cooked in tomato sauce and served over rice and pita bread with yogurt. Not far behind is *mantı,* a kind a miniature ravioli and supposedly Turkey's national dish. In the villages you can sometimes see women painstakingly making the tiny beef or lamb dumplings. It is often served with yoghurt and a drizzle of garlic and tomato sauce. Then there is *köfte* – meatballs – but not always a ball. In Tire there is a tradition of long thin sticks of meat.

Another staple is flat and crispy *lahmacun,* an ultra-thin pizza served with a topping of minced meat, salad, spices and lemon juice. *Menemen* is an ideal way to use leftovers to make a wonderful breakfast dish. Essentially, it's scrambled eggs cooked with sautéed vegetables, including onions, peppers, paprika and oregano. It is similar to shakshouka, the only difference being that the eggs in this dish are beaten. Then there are all the stuffed vegetables, aubergines, peppers, tomatoes or zucchinis filled with a mixture of rice and onion before being cooked in water and butter. And we haven't started yet on the myriad of soups, pastries and tantalising desserts like baklava. Also, we haven't mentioned street food, including the wonderful grilled fish butties you can buy in many places, especially seaside resorts and in Istanbul at the side of the Bosphorus.

One Sunday at about 9pm Levent and I were sipping tea at his house when his mobile phone rang. It was carpenter Onur. Levent lowered the phone for a moment.

"Do you want a pig?" he asked.

"What? A pig?" I queried. "A live one?"

"No a dead one, for the meat," said Levent. "I mean a wild boar. Onur says he has shot one," he added.

Wild boar (*domuz*) are everywhere in Turkey. In some seaside places they can be quite friendly and come to people's front gates for food. During the Covid-19 crisis of 2020 whole families of pigs roamed through deserted streets. But they can also be incredibly vicious. Many have sharp curly tusks that can virtually amputate a man's leg. We have seen their heads hung on walls as trophies, snarling in perpetuity. Around Tire, hunters regularly track them because they damage gardens and crops. Of course, in Islam they are considered dirty, so no Muslim will eat wild boar meat. However, I was prepared to give it a try. If we don't like it, I thought, we can always give it to the dogs.

Getting the beast from its resting place about fifteen miles from our house at such a relatively late hour, then dismembering it and storing the meat, however, was going to take planning akin to the Normandy Landings. First, Levent summoned a lorry from a workman with whom we had previously done business. Then he rang a man who had sold us a fridge. He agreed to loan us a second, larger fridge for a couple of days and to deliver it to Kaplan right away. On a Sunday night. How's that for customer service? We were actually waiting delivery of a deep freeze but the fridge would suffice meantime.

"Who is going to chop it up?" I asked. Levent shook his head.

"No authentic butcher will want to get involved. If customers learn he has been slicing pig they'll disown him and bankrupt him."

I made a suggestion, a man we'll call Ali who I knew. He had previously worked on a supermarket meat counter.

"OK," said Levent. "We'll give him a try." Amazingly he was free and agreed to help. Our plan was coming together. As we waited for everyone to arrive, I stretched out a brand new, white tarpaulin in the garden. Soon Onur showed up and together we laid the animal out on the plastic sheeting. It was around fifty kilos. No curly tusks but large teeth and stubby hair on its body. Our ex-butcher pal Ali turned up on a motorbike, bringing a meat cleaver and several knives sharper than a Gurkha's kukri. Illuminated by a large outdoor nightlamp Levent had given us, nicknamed the "Gestapo light", Ali set to work. First, he made an incision in the chest. As he opened up the carcass the fresh night air was suddenly sullied with a disgusting smell that made me retch. Rivulets of blood meandered across the tarpaulin. The boar's innards were removed and thrown into a black bin liner. Next, off came the head as beads of sweat rolled down Ali's temples. After skilfully skinning the pig he began crunching the cleaver into bone, fragments of which leapt this way and that. Ali said the rib cage and back of the animal were difficult to cut and would not yield much meat.

"The real treasure is the legs," he insisted.

By now the fridge man had delivered and four sizeable legs were quickly wrapped in black bin liners and tucked away on the shelves.

"Here," said Ali, handing me his assorted implements. "I borrowed these from a butcher friend but I cannot take them back. It's not right. He won't use them now they've been near a pig. Give me forty lira for them. I'm sure they'll come in handy. Plus, sixty lira for my time, of course."

So for around £25 we had a lot of meat and a set of knives.

"How much do I owe you, Onur?" I asked.

"Just enough for a box of shotgun cartridges," he said.

"What about the head and the rest of the offal?" I asked Ali.

"I know a place. It's like an official rubbish dump. Just follow me." We bagged up the remainder of the wild boar and set off down the hill towards Tire. After a few minutes Ali stopped beside a normal council wheelie bin.

"Just dump it in there," he said.

"But, but," I protested. "Surely it will smell?"

"Don't worry. The bins are emptied every day. It will all be gone by tomorrow afternoon."

"Are you sure?" I queried.

"Yes. Hurry up. We don't want to get caught." The next day, around midday as we headed to the shops, we drove down the same road and approached the dreaded bin. We had visions of a scene from a horror movie with blood seeping out of the bottom or worse, a crowd of neighbours trying to learn the identity of the late night entrails dumpers. Happily, neither was the case. As Ali predicted, the bin was empty. I just hoped the refuse collectors didn't get the shock of their lives.

The same day I bought a huge pan and lid, more than fifty centimetres in diameter, and cooked one of the legs in boiling water on one of our two-ringed electric hobs. By now I had read on the internet that in Spain, where people regularly shoot and eat wild boar, the vast majority have the meat checked first for parasites. I couldn't imagine Tire had a civic microbiology laboratory and even if it did, would it really agree to undertake such an investigation? Reviewing the dilemma in hindsight, maybe our favourite vet might have done some blood tests for us "as a foreigner" so to speak. Then again, maybe not. Working with pig, even a tiny phial of pig's blood, might be a one-way ticket to ostracization. I was reminded of the time Carolyn and I had been checking in for a flight to Turkey and needed to lose some weight from one of our hold suitcases. She unzipped the thing and began moving no fewer than twenty packs of ASDA bacon into some carry-on luggage. Distracted by the need to be quick, she failed to see that immediately behind us were six Muslim pilgrims in full robes en-route to Mecca, looking horrified. I left the cauldron boiling for almost three hours.

Finally, I cut a piece of the brown meat. It was tender and tasted like game.

"You'll get worms," warned Carolyn, who decided she wasn't partaking. And after a couple of sandwiches worth, my own courage deserted me. Darcy and Willow and the street dogs, however, happily scoffed the lot. And there was enough left over for about a fortnight's worth of canine meals. Even after buying the cleaver and knives our outlay was equal to around twenty-five tins of shop bought dog food. So certainly, a result.

There are of course, strict rules about butchering meat anywhere other than in approved abattoirs. But, inevitably, the restrictions are circumvented. This is especially noticeable at *Kurban Bayram* (literally Sacrifice Festival), a major feast of thanksgiving, a bit like our own Harvest Festival. People are expected to sacrifice an animal, a sheep or a goat, sometimes a cow. The resulting meat is distributed to family, friends, neighbours and to the poor. It's really not the best time to be a vegetarian. Actually, it's quite sad to see sheep and goats being carted around in trailers, their fate sealed. Traditionally, it's the head of the household that slits the animal's throat. I remember once reading a letter sent to an English tabloid newspaper which read something like: "We went on holiday to Turkey and some savages murdered a sheep in the street right in front of our hotel." Villagers, of course, ignore the rules and cut up their own carcasses, which is why one year seventy-one of them ended up in the Accident and Emergency unit of our local hospital. When we visited neighbour Birgül during *Kurban Bayram* her husband Yalçın had a fresh bandage on his hand, the result of a self-inflicted wound. In a pan on an open fire a sheep's head was merrily boiling away to make soup (*kelle paça*). Villagers swear by the soup's medicinal properties. A little later I went into our garden to find what I thought were the remnants of a devil worshippers' ritual. On the grass were a goat's horn, a cloven hoof, and what looked like a fibula and a jawbone. In more time that it usually takes Columbo to solve the case, I finally worked out that the street dogs had been raiding the local dustbins.

The garden of Number One was an eyesore so instead of growing flowers we dug a pond and bought some ducks. Efe and Ibrahim started the project and Birgül's son Hüseyin finished it off. We bought two ducks from the local Tuesday market and took them home by car, Carolyn carefully confining them in a shopping bag. Later a neighbour offered us two more. And soon after that another villager wanted rid of four ducks, so we also gave them shelter. Sometimes the ducks would produce four or five eggs a day. Then they would stop, sometimes for two or three weeks on end. We tried different feeds. Ducks can eat a wide variety of things. They include small fish and fish eggs, snails, worms, slugs, and molluscs, small crustaceans such as crayfish, grass, leaves, and weeds. They also wolf down algae, aquatic plants and roots, tadpoles, aquatic and land insects, small berries, fruits, nuts, seeds and grain. Some ducks will even eat sand, gravel, pebbles and small shells, which apparently provide grit that aids their digestion. Ours loved lettuce most of all, running and squawking as I approached the gate and also certain types of grain, including corn, wheat, barley and oats. However, we had to beware of weasels (*sansar*) that relish duck eggs. Often, we would find empty egg shells in other parts of the garden. Eventually, when a particularly crafty weasel began stealing chicken eggs from neighbour Birgül's garden, her son Hüseyin decided positive action was required. Armed with a rifle, he staked out both gardens overnight and his diligence paid off. The following morning Birgül called me over and proudly held up one dead weasel with an egg still in its mouth. We had no further trouble for many months.

As far as we could tell we had five female and three male ducks. We tried to breed from them but it's a tricky business. Eggs require around twenty-eight days to hatch. We inspected daily as one female duck took it upon herself to sit on about seven eggs. Eventually the chicks were born and began frolicking in the pond. They were a joy to watch. But sadly, the many cats that inhabit the village attacked and all but one chick died. Birgül agreed to take the mother and the one surviving baby into her garden where she had a hutch and after about two months the chick had grown big enough to fend off any predators. But soon after it returned to the others, we found a fully-grown male duck floating one morning in the pond. Whether it died through natural causes or after a confrontation with a weasel or some other animal was impossible to tell. So, our flock was back to eight and stayed that way.

When it comes to eating out, we are truly spoiled in the village. As already mentioned, there are three restaurants. But we really only patronise two of them the Dağ and Gastro Tire. That's because Carolyn and her friend Kathryn, dining without me one evening, found the previous owner of the village's third restaurant the Çam a bit creepy. A new owner has since come in and spent the equivalent of hundreds of thousands of pounds on a total revamp including a three-storey lift. The Dağ is situated at the end of the village down a narrow, wooded lane. With its wooden windows, beams and interior ceiling it exudes rustic charm, augmented by an eclectic array of decorations, including gourds, dried flowers and plants. It began as a cafe and owner Lütfi built a lot of the structure himself. In May 2015 one of Spain's most famous chefs, Joan Roca i Fontané, visited to make a television programme. Lütfi told a journalist: "When we decided to open this place in 1993 everyone, including the people we know and strangers, said the same thing. Who comes to a restaurant on top of a mountain to eat herbs?" But he persisted and clearly produced a winning formula. The restaurant's reputation spread by word of mouth and also through regular mentions in magazines and newspapers. One paper hailed it as among the top ten restaurants in the whole of Turkey. The great and the good eat there. While visiting we have been introduced to leading lights in Turkish theatre, the regional governor, the chief of police and the town's mayor, among many others.

The Dağ has a four out of five rating on Trip Advisor. One reviewer said: "Whether you are a vegetarian or an omnivore you will be pleased. The vegetarian meze dishes are numerous and unique, using hand foraged items from the surrounding forest, such as nettles and mushrooms. "You could easily make a complete veggie meal or you could sample the varied Turkish meat dishes, including famous Tire *köfte.* After lunch or dinner, you can explore Kaplan, a classical working farming village that is becoming rarer as Turkey progresses with its rapid modernisation." A reviewer on Foursquare wrote: "Perhaps one the best regional restaurants in the world, simply among the best ten in the Middle East. Meet the owner/chef, he is a charming humble man." Lütfi doesn't serve chicken or fish. But there's still plenty of choice with more than two dozen starters alone. We have eaten there many times and never once had a bad experience or sub-standard dish. All the dishes have a special taste. As a starter you might choose fresh garlic with lamb meat, *haydari* a dip made by adding garlic, and fresh herbs such as mint, basil, and dill to thickened yogurt, fava bean puree, stuffed courgette flowers, stuffed vine leaves or Cnicus benedictus, a thistle-like plant in the family Asteraceae. Elsewhere, artichokes, broad beans, baby onions, aubergines, lentils, spinach, dried tomatoes, mushrooms, carrots, dried okra, parsley, arugula, nettles and many more ingredients are subtly woven into mouth-watering cuisine. For the main course you can have steak, mixed grill, a range of *köfte*, lamb kebabs or lamb chops. And for dessert more variety, including caramelised walnuts and a type of cheesecake with a coating of mulberry sauce. Apart from the odd tweak to the mezes, Lütfi's menu doesn't change.

But in contrast at Gastro Tire his son Serkan's menu alters almost weekly. When we go, we simply say to him: "You choose." It's more nouvelle cuisine, smaller dishes but more of them and all creatively presented. The first thing you notice as you enter the outer door is the wonderfully ingenious restaurant logo and the dazzling display of hydrangeas. Where his father has more than enough customers, you can tell that Serkan is an expert marketeer. His Facebook page is regularly updated with very funny or informative videos, often using time-lapse techniques and intriguing, professionally shot photographs. And the same invention and attention to detail is carried over into the restaurant's ambience and food. Gastro Tire's rating on Trip Advisor is five out of five. The venture began as a workshop/restaurant and Serkan trained a number of university students who were hoping to break into the catering industry. At one time he also toyed with the idea of staging culinary tours and cookery classes for foreign visitors. Originally the venue was one building and an outside terrace. But as its popularity grew Serkan expanded the seating area and enclosed the terrace with glass panels. The subtle, romantic lighting plus the beautiful mountain view make a hypnotic combination.

But the food still has to be right. And it is. My favourite are the salads, invariably different, sometimes using arugula, accompanied by peas, white cheese, green apple and apricot slices, sometimes strawberries or pieces of squash, and marinated with black mulberry molasses. Another winner, often known as samphire salad uses salicornia, europaea, common glasswort, a plant found in the sea or salt marshes, served with radish, fishnet almond, basil and sweet-sour sauce.

One of the clearest paradoxes in Turkish life is the country's attitude to alcohol. In a survey in 2019 around eighty per cent of Turkish people claimed they did not use alcohol. Per capita consumption of alcohol in Turkey is on average two litres per year, well below the average of the World Health Organisation European region (9.8 litres). That's because a lot of people simply don't drink wine, beer or spirits. Alcohol users, however, in Turkey consume almost twenty-nine litres per capita. From my own empirical studies, I would say many Turks love a drink. Drive up the hill to Kaplan on most summer evenings, especially at weekends, and you will lose count of the number of parked cars with picnickers enjoying beer, wine or *rakı*. Unfortunately, the country's President Mr Erdogan does not. Since the AK Party's rise to power an enormous amount of tax has been added to booze. In 2020 a 70cl bottle of rakı was around 152TL, a rise of around five hundred per cent from 2004. Nearly eighty lira of that, more than half, is tax. Consider that a labourer's daily wage in 2020 was around 125TL.

In response, huge numbers of Turks now make their own booze, including *rakı*. Of course, drinking home-made or bootleg booze is a dangerous activity. In 2005, twenty-two people died in Istanbul from a contaminated version of *rakı*, sparking a panic in bars throughout the country. And in recent years there have been many similar stories of people falling ill or sometimes dying after drinking illicit alcohol, often laced with methanol. Nevertheless, home-made production is a massive growth industry. There are secret groups which share recipes and methods. And it's likely to grow further as the government's anti-drink crusade continues.

The tipping point (of should that be tipple point?) as Alev Scott details in her book Turkish Awakening may have come in 2011. During that year Erdogan was allegedly enraged when a diner at a pavement table outside a restaurant in Galata, Istanbul lifted his glass in a mock toast as the then Turkish prime minister's motorcade swept past. Al fresco drinking in the area was banned, despite eatery owners having legal contracts to serve alcohol on the pavement. A year later Erdogan pressured brewer Efes to withdraw its sponsorship of the annual One Love music festival held on a university campus in Eyüp, Istanbul and the sale of alcohol was banned. Erdogan was quoted as saying: "They want all our youth to be alcoholics." As a follow, up the sale of alcohol was banned in popular campus restaurants. Erdogan later went on record to declare the national beverage of Turkey, always considered to be *rakı*, was actually *ayran*, a yoghurt-based drink. Legislation followed, ordering that all films or TV programmes showing alcohol being drunk should have the offending bottles and glasses pixelated out. The same applies to cigarette smoking.

During elections all sale of alcohol is banned. Once in a restaurant in Şile during a day of voting, I unthinkingly asked for a beer. The waiter, keen to help a valued customer, looked around nervously as if in a 1920s speakeasy before finally bringing me a coffee mug filled with Efes. Then for extra security he ordered me to hide it behind a large menu and to sip it "only when no one is passing by". The rule of the AK Party has seen a ban on drinks licences for establishments within a hundred metres of a mosque or a school. In most built-up areas virtually everywhere falls into this catchment area. High taxes and the political frowning on alcohol consumption have caused many bars and restaurants to close and put others on the brink. Of course, there were protests. But they fell on deaf ears. Bars are commonplace in the big cities. But in smaller towns they seem to be rather furtive places, a bit like betting shops. Despite this perceived stigma there is one bar in Tire called "Las Vegas".

One day a villager invited me to join him for a beer. We drove from Kaplan to Tire, parked the car and made our way on foot to the pub. It was a place I had been to once before but as I was about to step through what I thought was the front door, my friend grabbed my arm.

"No, no, no," he remonstrated. "The entrance is here," he said, pointing to a sliding glass partition to the left. "Don't go through that door. There are women upstairs." he added, with a frown.

"I don't go there myself," he helpfully explained. I can't imagine he meant there was a knitting circle on the first floor but what exactly went on I never learned.

I sat down one day in Kuşadası at a hotel with Carolyn, Charlotte and Sophie to have a drink. I ordered a beer, Carolyn and Sophie ordered Coca Cola and Charlotte a glass of white wine. A waiter brought the drinks. After a couple of sips Charlotte said: "Hey dad, can you taste this? I think it might be off." I drank a little. In fact, it didn't taste of anything.

"I think it has been watered down," I replied. We called the manager and he examined the bottle, then took a sip himself before disappearing. A few minutes later he reappeared with a glass of genuine pinot grigio and an explanation. Apparently, a waiter who has recently left had decanted the wine from about ten bottles and filled them all with water before carefully re-corking them and replacing the metallic cover. Jesus's miracle in reverse.

CHAPTER FOURTEEN

SUMMER HOUSE

Having created living quarters in Number Two it was time to choose our next project. Number One or the ruined barn? We chose the barn and, after speaking to our restaurateur friend Lütfi, we approached Bayram Usta to build it. A quietly spoken man in his late forties, with hands like former Spurs goalkeeper Pat Jennings, he visited the plot and agreed to take on the work for a daily rate. First, we would have to pull down the remaining stones, clear the area and lay foundations. The team that worked on Number Two would do that. We checked at the town hall to ensure that such work would be legal. Accompanied by Levent, I expected to see handwritten plot outlines scrawled in some dusty ledger. Instead we were shown into the office of Tire's building development officer who quickly pulled up a Google Earth type image on a huge flat screen wall-mounted television and, after tapping some details into his keyboard, the outlines of our plot's borders came into sharp focus. Because there had been a building there previously, he confirmed, we were quite entitled to renovate it as long as it was only one storey and didn't exceed the footprint of the original barn.

The crew who worked on Number Two cleared the site in no time and dug out a rectangular trench for the foundations. This was followed by the assembly of metal rod "boxes" that would reinforce the concrete. It was impossible for concrete lorries to gain access to the site. We had been led to believe that there was a man in the area who had some kind of device which could pump the concrete long distances via a tube. But when we tracked him down, he said he was fully booked for months. The concrete would have to be mixed by hand, as before, and poured into the trench via roughly constructed wooden chutes.

The barn/summer house was to be built on the second of the plot's three levels. It was back-breaking work and we couldn't complain when random bits of cement ended up spilling down the nearby retaining wall. At last, the foundation work was finished but I had to water the cement every day to ensure the hardening process. Eventually it was time for Bayram Usta to begin work. He arrived promptly at 8.30am every morning with his helper, who mixed the cement and ferried stone about, and he finished on the dot at 4.30pm. He was able to use a lot of stone that had been salvaged from the ruined barn. But it was clear we would need a lot more. There is stone everywhere around Kaplan and we quickly found two or three suppliers ready to deliver.

The dimensions of the rectangle Bayram Usta was instructed to build were fourteen metres by six metres. The walls would be sixty centimetres thick. The building was to be two rooms, a bedroom and a lounge separated by a shower room/toilet and on the other side of a doorway a small utility room. They would be constructed with one breeze block wall which would be rendered and one stone wall. The rendered wall would be fully tiled but only the shower area of the stone wall would be tiled. With typical ingenuity, Carolyn insisted the bedroom would include a sunken bath. This meant great care would be needed to coordinate the water and sanitation pipes during construction. The shower would be electric but the bath would be fed from the hot water tank on top of the roof of Number Two. I salvaged a one-hundred-year-old old wooden cupboard from Number One and asked Bayram Usta if he could fit it into the wall of the lounge. No problem, he said. He suggested a matching alcove the same size two metres away on the same wall. Prompted by Carolyn, he also agreed to make other smaller alcoves where ornaments could be placed. The lounge was to have its own stone fireplace. But outside there would be another fireplace that could be used in a barbecue area. Each would have its own metal chimney, which would be encased in red brick. The front of the building was to have a glass door and three big doubled glazed picture windows. The two windows in the lounge would slide open.

Bayram Usta completed the stone rectangle, the shower room and the fireplaces at a cost of around £4,000. Our original idea was to have a flat roof and a bridge on to it from the level above. But here we hit a snag. The council insisted that flat roofs require special planning permission and a lengthy inspection process. Anxious to finish the building as soon as possible, we agreed to install a pitched roof instead. Volkan, the metal fabricator who helped on Number Two, was re-engaged to build the skeleton.

While the roof was being built, we turned our attention to the building's flooring and surrounds. We decided to use stone slabs *(kayrak)* for both and began getting quotes. We visited a couple of suppliers and eventually agreed to buy eighteen tonnes of stone from a quarry near Bayindir, a short drive away. The deal was that the delivery truck would stop in Tire and we would meet the driver to lead him up the mountain to Kaplan.

But the vehicle that arrived looked like something out of a transport museum. There was no way it could carry the full heavy load to Kaplan.

Soner, the ex-tea garden manager, was helping me and he summoned a fork-lift truck to take several pallets of stone from the truck. Gingerly, the vehicle began its ascent but had only gone five-hundred metres when you could hear the gearbox screaming. An acrid smell filled the air. Another fork-lift truck was called and a few more pallets were dumped by the roadside. Slowly the driver resumed his climb, going little more than 10-15kph. At last, he reached the outskirts of the village but reconnoitring the road to our house dissipated what little courage he had left. We decided to call a third fork-lift truck and off-load the remaining pallets of stone. The driver of the ancient lorry looked relieved, smiled and turned for home. The final fork-lift driver agreed to return the next day and bring all eighteen pallets from the three different locations to the site.

Soner, his father and another villager Şaban, agreed to lay the stone slabs and to do other landscaping work around the building. Their quote was a bit higher than we might have negotiated. But we figured using local labour would be more reliable than worrying whether or not workers from Tire would turn up. And it was also giving work to the village. The inside of the stone rectangle, of course, was just soil. First that had to be watered and flattened. Then a layer of reinforced concrete plus some damp proofing needed to be put down before the stone slabs were finally fitted. Outside we sketched out two levels of flat terracing and a flight of stairs down to the third level of the garden.

Opposite the outside fireplace we planned for the barbecue area to include some stone seating. We had toyed with the idea of building a small swimming pool. But the quotes came in at around £22,000 and building it in front of Number Two would severely restrict car parking space. We also worried about any children who might wander in when we weren't there and get themselves into trouble. Instead, we opted for a jacuzzi, three metres by two directly, next to the barbecue area outside the summer house, one level down. We had to decide whether to go for a fibre glass or traditional cement and tiles construction and after reviewing several quotes we chose the latter. A company from Kuşadası came to build it. Carolyn also insisted we bought fifty *nazar*, the little blue eyes, to ward off evil spirits and these were cemented into the spaces between the stone paving. When the paving was finished, I gave it two coats with a smelly, white liquid which waterproofed it. The pitch roof was completed in a couple of weeks, finished off in new red tiles.

Inside we opted for white plastic sheeting on the ceiling, a cheaper alternative to wood and at a distance you couldn't really tell the difference. I didn't appreciate the son of one of Volkan's helpers carving his name in the trunk of one of our fig trees. But I didn't make an issue of it. Volkan had also made a metal framed four-poster bed which we erected. Electrician Saygın came to complete the wiring and to plumb in the bath and shower. He brought his two young children with him and they helped to run yards of different coloured wires through the loft space and down into the various rooms. Saygın would often bark orders at them but they were incredibly patient and did as instructed. A junction box was fitted in a space opposite the shower room, where we would later fit an American fridge freezer. We were now able to hang our ornamental lamps, bought in various Istanbul markets.

The huge floor to ceiling windows were delivered and fitted. In the lounge these would slide open. In the bedroom they were fixed. For a few months everything worked perfectly. Then one day I began to get a small electric shock from the shower. There was clearly something amiss with the earthing arrangements. Saygın returned with what looked like a huge medieval longsword. It must have been almost five feet long. He placed it in the garden just outside the summer house and began hammering it into the soil. It was like the Excalibur story in reverse. Instead of rising up out of a lake this lump of metal was heading underground.

He was like a man at a fairground on those machines where you try to raise a hammer to hit a bell by bashing the base with a huge mallet. Knowing how dry the earth gets I couldn't believe for one minute he would manage to drive the metal fully into the soil. But after fifteen minutes of thumping the top was at grass level. Saygın attached a wire from the house, gave it two more blows and that was that. Shocks eliminated.

We certainly made a few mistakes during the renovations. For example, when builder A did a good job at a reasonable price first time around, we would re-employ him for a subsequent phase of construction without demanding to see detailed cost breakdowns in advance. Big mistake. This laissez-faire attitude would often result in bills twice what they should have been. After one such episode, Levent acted as an intermediary as I sat down with one builder, who I won't name, and went through the prices of all the materials he had used. I had earlier been to a builder's merchant and checked everything in his catalogue. The builder came up with a string of lame excuses but eventually handed back £800, which in reality was probably about half the actual excess. On another occasion, I had agreed to pay £200 for a small job but when the work was finished the builder wanted double the fee because of "unexpected problems". Not wanting to get into a legal dispute and knowing the work in the UK would cost twice as much, I paid up.

My old expat pal Chris Chesher's advice is to "stand over the tradesman and check everything he does." But to my mind this is simply not practical with work that can take several weeks. And it also implies from the start that you just don't trust the workman, which makes the relationship awkward. The best way, I believe, is to put everything in writing, secure a quote and get the tradesman to sign it. I do think there's sometimes an element of familiarity breeding contempt. Some shops and restaurants, for example, will give you amazing deals and service on your first visit. But second time around you pay the foreigner premium. I have found a similar situation with certain supposed friendships. More on that later.

Despite a few regrets the summer house looked beautiful and everyone who visited was impressed. Carolyn's vision was rewarded. The transformation from derelict barn was awesome. A man from Tire offered to rent it for a year but we demurred. And Levent suggested using it as a bed and breakfast place. But we decided it was for visiting friends and family only.

CHAPTER FIFTEEN

IT CAME FROM CHY-NAH

The three decades I spent from 1972 as a journalist hold many fond memories. They include going on a bender while interviewing Oliver Reed, being invited into Joan Collins' bedroom and spending a night undercover in a transvestite hotel. PM me for details. But I was more than happy never to commit shorthand to a reporter's notebook ever again. Then one day in 2013, I took a call from Tony, an old friend working in Hong Kong for the Chinese government. He was interested in gathering intelligence about business between China and Turkey and asked if I would cover trade fairs in Istanbul. My scribblings would find a home on a professional website and in a magazine, both designed to inspire Chinese producers and to put buyers and suppliers in touch. It sounded interesting so I agreed. I was soon embroiled in a fascinating world where fortunes could be made and lost and trust and efficiency were prized commodities. With Brexit looming, it was also intriguing to see how business really works at grass roots.

Sitting with a Chinese exhibitor, I would hear people from all over the world ask similar questions: Can you make it? What's the cost? When can you deliver? How long will it take?

Studying Turkey's trade with China also offered a fascinating insight. While the then US President Donald Trump was waging a trade war against China, and the UK was getting nervous about the fate of Hong Kong residents and cold feet about the Huawei 5G deal, China was embarking on a huge project to build closer links to countries like Turkey by reviving the old Silk Road.

China's advantage was, traditionally, that cheaper labour costs meant it could undercut Turkish manufacturers. But there was invariably a catch. Take shoes, for instance. A huge shadow was cast over trade in shoes between the two countries in November 2014 when consignments of toxic shoes from China were smuggled into Turkey. Customers went to hospital with painful rashes and skin empurpling and whenever it rained, others found the polish on their shoes started to bleed. Officials found that nearly twenty-six thousand pairs of shoes containing harmful chemicals were at large. Later Trade Minister Nurettin Canikli confirmed that customs officials had found carcinogenic chemicals in the polish of a further thirty-three thousand pairs of Chinese shoes. Huge numbers of shoes were seized. However, the dodgy goods then went missing while being taken to a disposal site. In response the Turkish government imposed extra import taxes on Chinese footwear.

Sayat Atanasyan had a unique perspective on the Turkey-China shoe business. Eleven years before we met, when he was aged just seventeen, he was sent to China by Turkey's biggest shoe firm Ziylan on quality control duties. His team bought four million pairs of shoes a year, spending millions of US dollars. Now working in Istanbul for a different company, he said: "It was an incredible experience.

"Some of the companies we supervised were so big you needed a golf cart to go from one side to the other. Others were in tiny workshops just five metres square. The Chinese worked twenty hours a day on two ten-hour shifts. But we had to watch them carefully. If we went for lunch, we would return to find lots of mistakes." Two years later he and his colleagues had to flee for their lives in China when Ziylan cancelled an order for twenty thousand pairs of shoes because of quality issues.

"Our interpreter came to our hotel in Guidong at midnight to say the workers were coming with guns to kill us. We left everything, grabbed just our wallets and mobile phones and escaped the city in a hire car." Predictably that story never made it into the Communist government's website or magazine.

Two themes began to emerge as I trawled from industry to industry. First, China's reputation for cheapness was under threat as wages began to rise and second, China was embarking on a huge process of mechanisation. One Turkish shoe factory owner claimed Pakistan was the new low-cost centre where, in 2019, it was easy to find workers at one-hundred US dollars a month. To cut costs a number of Chinese business owners moved production to places such as Cambodia and Vietnam.

"Trading with China has thrown up a few surprises," another Turkish businessman said. "For example, firms will often use individuals' bank accounts rather than a company account. I don't know why. This can create huge problems at customs where officials suspect money laundering."

Really? You don't say.

"Also we once sent around one hundred thousand US dollars for a shipment but realised we had overpaid. Although it took just two days for the money to arrive in China from Turkey, when we asked for the excess to be returned it took two months."

Whichever fair I went to, I was treated with great respect by organisers and exhibitors. Journalists have a far higher standing in Turkey than, for example, in the UK. When you arrive at an exhibition hall there is always a special VIP entrance for the media where you claim your accreditation. And a regiment of Press officers caters for your every request. At an Istanbul fair one of them told me to be certain to be in the Press room at 12.30pm. She said she was arranging lunch on a ferry boat which would travel up and down the Golden Horn, the primary inlet of the Bosphorus linking Topkapı palace with interesting suburbs such as Fener, Balat and Eyüp. During the ninety-minute, three course meal with wine we were royally entertained by a live band.

On individual stands, some bigger than the Centre court at Wimbledon, there was always tea, coffee, cakes, pastries and assorted nuts, served by women who looked like beauty queens or top models. When I covered the shoe fair for a second time, three years later, there was a real upbeat vibe. Alex Zhuang, whose firm Wenzhou Eliyu Footwear which was founded twenty years ago and has a factory employing 280 people, was ebullient. The company supplied a leading German wholesaler and claimed to have strict quality control procedures in place. He said there had been a massive shake-up in China's shoe industry. Around sixty per cent of factories had closed in the last three years because of rising labour costs and because fewer people want to do factory work. The way forward, he argued, was by automation and artificial intelligence.

There was no doubting the work ethic of the Chinese. A Turkish bicycle manufacturer told me the salaries of Turkish and Chinese factory workers were almost identical but in Turkey they work eight-hour shifts to China's eleven hours. But attention to detail was sometimes still lacking.

Arno Logman, a projects manager for Dutch rail specialists Bemo, told me he once ordered six or seven containers of railway lines for a seaport installation. His company had provided the exact specifications and intricate drawings but when the rails arrived the inter-connecting links were wrong.

"The whole lot had to go back," he said.

One of the most interesting fairs was the Jewellery Show of 2013. There I met Payal Shah, the glamorous founder of a company called L'Dezen. Indian-born, Hong Kong-based, Shah's jewellery is worn by celebrities such as Sharon Osbourne, Nicki Minaj and Carmen Electra. L' Dezen is an international brand that offers eighteen karat gold diamond hand-made jewellery, manufactured in house by three hundred workers in Shun De, China. Shah, who has shops in New York, Los Angeles and Istanbul, calls her products "affordable luxury" with pieces selling from two thousand to twenty-two thousand US dollars. She originally trained as an architect but turned to jewellery after her father showed her some diamond slices. She first exhibited in Las Vegas in 2011. The show was a success and she never looked back.

Perhaps the strangest exhibitor I came across was the Ningbo Hookah Artware Company, launched fifteen years ago, selling shisha pipes (*nargile* in Turkish) to Turkey. *Nargile* is from the Persian word for coconut, since the original smoking instrument came from India and was made out of coconut shells. "Shisha" is from the Persian word shishe, or glass. Chief executive Jacky Zhang told me the company sold to eighty-three countries and already had wholesalers in Turkey.

Another weird exhibitor was Ye Jian, selling grow-your-own herb, spice and plant kits. Jian, from the Cangshan District of Fuzhou, majored in English. But after working in a state-owned lighting factory, he set up Fuzhou Premiere Crafts Company in 1988 and employed ten people. All his products, which also include insect "hotels", bird boxes and garden ornaments were exported.

His stand was one of the busiest in the exhibition. As I waved him goodbye, he gave me a sunflower seed in a tin smaller than a can of Coca Cola.

While interviewing Mehmet Demirhan, sales coordinator for Turkey's national broadcaster TRT, at a TV Fair in 2014, I was manhandled away by armed security guards as a Turkish cabinet minister came on to the exhibitor's stand. Some twenty minutes later, when the interview resumed, Demirhan admitted there was little or no exchange of TV content between China and Turkey. But executives were working on it. Demirhan was holding meetings trying to sell dramas such as The Poor Boy and The Rich Girl and TRT's much-praised historical drama *Hürrem Sultan,* about intrigue in the Sultan's palace.

Aside from the fairs, Chinese companies are always trying to break into the European market and avoid tariffs by becoming legal entities based in Turkey. One example was CSUN, bidding to become a major player in solar energy. CSUN became the first Chinese-owned company to establish a manufacturing plant outside China when it opened a six hundred million US dollar factory near Tuzla on the outskirts of Istanbul. I was sent by my Hong Kong friend Tony to check it out. In under two years it moved into profit against a background of over-production and bankruptcies affecting competitors back in China. Moving abroad reduces transport costs, outmanoeuvres crippling anti-dumping legislation and takes advantage of lucrative tax incentives offered by the Ankara government. The plant - the biggest of its kind in Turkey - began operations in January 2013 but officially opened four months later in a ceremony attended by the Turkish Minister of Energy Taner Yildiz, and the Chinese Consul General Zhang Qingyang. It followed an exhaustive feasibility study by CEO Steve Shen, who visited twenty-one locations throughout the country. The five-storey, twenty-two thousand square metre factory employs five hundred local workers in a six-day, twenty-four-hour shift pattern. On Sunday, traditionally a family day for Turks, the factory closes. Mr Shen, originally from Taiwan, was delighted the Turkish gamble had paid off.

Tony in Hong Kong also asked me to write regular updates on China's "One Belt One Road" a massive project to boost China's exports by rebuilding the historic Silk Road. By 2018, sixteen per cent of the European Union's $1,720 billion dollars' worth of imports came from China, making it Europe's largest trade partner. Along this major trade route are most of the world's major economies. However, unlike bygone centuries, ninety-six per cent of exported products now reach Europe by sea because Eurasia lacks land routes. One Belt One Road (OBOR) seeks to address this anomaly. Rail freight volumes from China to Europe increased from fifty-seven thousand to more than three-hundred thousand tonnes between 2013 and 2016.

Getting leading industrialists and senior academics to talk about it was far easier than I anticipated. One telephone call led me straight to the boss of Arzum, one of Turkey's leading suppliers of electrical appliances. Because we hadn't yet moved the telephone from Number One house, now used for storage, I conducted the interview sitting on a plastic chair in a draughty, empty room with mice scurrying about.

China began investing huge sums of money in infrastructure, especially in Turkey. Everyone seemed happy. When China declared 2018 as "Turkey Tourism Year" and Chinese visitors increased sixty per cent to nearly four-hundred thousand, Ankara was delighted. A Chinese minister said he wanted that figure to rise to eight-hundred thousand in the near future. But below the surface all was not well in the relationship. According to figures from 2018, Turkey imported goods from China worth more than nineteen billion US dollars. China was the second largest exporter to Turkey after Russia.

But Turkey's exports to China were worth less than three billion US dollars. A massive deficit. Suddenly, Turkey began to reassess its ties with China. It started buying less from China and China's slowing importation of Turkish goods suggested the friendship between the countries was under strain. They were beginning to haggle.

In May 2019 the website Al-Monitor wrote: "Like the United States, Turkey is irked by Chinese trade domination and has begun to openly express it. Treasury and Finance Minister Berat Albayrak said that the current state of trade with China and South Korea was "not sustainable". Ankara was not specific about economic sanctions on China. But a twenty-five per cent special consumption tax on mobile phones was doubled to fifty per cent. That was a blow as China tops the list of mobile phone exporters to Turkey. Ankara also imposed import restrictions on shoe and textile products. Another favourite ploy is to complicate customs procedures, a regular gripe from exhibitors at the trade fairs.

Politicians, however, faced a difficult balancing act. Turks love their gadgets. The sanitary arrangements in any given house might be medieval but the family has to have every latest gizmo. As Al-Monitor wrote: "Besides mobile phones, the top goods imported from China include audio, visual and other transmission devices, automatic data processing machines and their magnetic or optical readers, synthetic yarn, parts and accessories for road vehicles, electrical transformers, toys, pipes, boilers, tanks, faucets, air and vacuum pumps, gas compressors, fans, monitors, projectors, TV receivers and illuminated signs." Making such things unaffordable was a real vote loser.

Turkey was clearly heavily in hock to China. A Chinese consortium had bought the Yavuz Sultan Selim Bridge over the Bosphorus and its motorway, connecting Istanbul to the new airport. The Industrial and Commercial Bank of China was in talks to refinance loans worth around six billion US dollars for the operation of the new Istanbul airport. Analyst Rupert Stone wrote on the Middleeasteye.net website: "China is involved in Turkey's nuclear development, building its third power plant. On the telecoms front, Chinese tech giant Huawei is constructing a 5G network and has a research and development centre in Istanbul - its second biggest in the world - while ZTE purchased Turkish company Netas several years ago. In the realm of e-commerce, Alibaba bought a stake of Turkey's online retailer, Trendyol, in 2018." China was also providing financing in gas, mining, finance and other key areas.

There was another potential stumbling block to Sino-Turkish relations: the fate of thousands of ethnic Uighurs both in Turkey and China. The Uighurs are Muslims, many who fled persecution in China to avoid being sent to concentration camps. The sanctuary offered to the Uighurs by Turkey angered Beijing. But in yet another twist in 2020 stories began filtering out of Uighurs being rounded up and sent back to China. Then it was discovered that China and Turkey had signed a draft extradition treaty three years before. Ankara, once critical of Uighur persecution, was conspicuous by its silence.

So volatile is the relationship between Turkey and China, it's almost impossible to know what will happen next. We wait and see. Reporting on the trade fairs helped me understand Turkey's unstable economy and showed me a different side of life, the machinations of big business. Always done with a broad smile and a glass of tea, of course.

CHAPTER SIXTEEN

MENS SANA CORPORE SANO

Living in Turkey, as the Latin motto says, ensures a healthy mind in a healthy body. Reasons? Fresh air, plenty of sunshine, no stress and the famous Mediterranean diet, beloved of medics, to name but four. Getting old, however, inevitably brings its issues and one day excruciating pain in my left knee made a trip to the hospital unavoidable. Getting an appointment with an orthopaedic specialist, however, is not always easy. Luckily, Aynur, a nurse we knew, agreed to pull a few strings. But on the day I arrived at A and E where she worked, the doctor's clinic was full.

Some people have private medical insurance and some join a government-run scheme called SGK. Foreigners who are resident are required to have health insurance but bizarrely not if they are over 65. As I'm very rarely ill I had neglected to sign up and, probably foolishly, chose a third option, pay as you go. This time, however, I suspected it would be more complicated. Nurse Aynur shepherded me into a cubicle and said she would give me a pain killing injection to keep me going until the appointment with the specialist. I surmised this would be in the backside and her half smile and nod confirmed it. I saw her hovering with the needle so leaned against the trolley bed and dropped my shorts. Although wearing clean underwear (still following mother's instructions after all these years) this was in fact a breach of protocol. Aynur had expected me simply to lie on the bed and was a little shaken, although I am sure she has seen far worse. I quickly recovered my shorts and my dignity and lay on the bed as instructed. She pulled down the waistband to reveal the necessary expanse of top buttock and in went the needle.

"I'll contact you when I have made your appointment," she said. I had to wait only a couple of days but the pain was worsening. In the day it was not too bad but at night I was in agony. I could not sleep for more than fifteen minutes at a time. In the state hospital system you wait in a reception area as names of the sick are listed on a screen. When it's your turn your name is highlighted in large type. But you have to keep watching the screen because you can suddenly be plucked from the bottom of the list. The screen also confirms whether or not you are "over sixty-five". I am not sure if that is a mark of respect or a sign of increased need of attention.

As a foreigner you are immediately a source of interest. Mainly it's just knowing glances and smiles from fellow sufferers and their supporting family members. Sometimes one will venture a question in Turkish.

"German?"

"No, English."

"Where are you from?" They ask.

"Well, I was born in London but I have lived most of my life near Manchester." Years ago, that revelation would invariably evoke the same response.

"Ah, Manchester, Manchester United, Bobby Charlton, Nobby Sty-lays." Nowadays you more likely to hear something different.

"Ah...my daughter works in a Turkish restaurant in Chorlton." Finally, it was my turn to enter the consulting room. I started to explain to the doctor, Şefik Bey, with carefully pre-prepared vocabulary exactly what the problem was. I knew he spoke no English. But my Turkish was still a bit of a one-way street. I could explain with words I knew. But if someone replied with vocabulary I didn't, I could easily be in trouble. I was only half-way through my first sentence, describing an arthroscopy I'd had twenty-five years before in Buxton, when the doctor snapped at me in Turkish.

"Lie on the bed." Foolishly I kept talking.

"Lie on the bed," he demanded, his face now red and contorted. Sheepishly, I hobbled into the cubicle as his female assistant gestured, I should lie on my back.

"Take your shoes off," the doctor ordered. I flicked my shoes off painfully. The doctor grabbed my left leg and tugged it to and fro for a couple of seconds. I felt a searing pain like someone using a power drill on the joint.

"Put one leg behind the other and squat as if you are on the toilet," he shouted. I thought it an odd request but tried to recreate a kind of lotus position while sitting on the bed.

"No, get off the bed and stand on the floor," he snarled. He meant I should pose as if using a traditional Turkish toilet. Now I was terrified, like some junior ballet dancer at a first audition in front of a maestro. My ultra-slow cross between a curtsy and a pas de deux, seemed to pass muster.

"Put your shoes on," he grunted. I didn't hear him properly. But foolishly decided to try to revive the story about my trimmed meniscus in Derbyshire.

"It's nothing to do with the meniscus," he fumed in his native tongue. "Walk up and down the room." I began to walk.

"No. First, put your shoes on!" The ballet audition was turning into a Gestapo interrogation. My head was spinning. It was an agonising effort to put on my shoes but I somehow managed and began to walk. After two passes, the doctor, now totally exasperated, gestured for me to sit down.

"You need a film," he said putting his hands to his eyes, as if he was holding invisible binoculars or maybe playing charades. I was stupefied. Was I going to watch a video about bad knees? He quickly read the quizzical look on my face.

"Film, film," he jabbered. Then the penny dropped. He meant I needed an X-ray. Why he didn't use *"Rontgen"*, the Turkish word for X-ray, I don't know. His assistant gave us a barcoded piece of paper.

"You pay extra at the cashier's desk," the doctor continued. Cowed, Carolyn and I left the consulting room. After paying £1.20 for the "film" we walked the fifty metres to the X-ray department and entered. A man in a white coat, looking bored, but surrounded by screens like a TV studio gallery shouted in Turkish.

"Wrong door". Still shell shocked from the doctor's consultation, we went back into the corridor where we asked an attendant for the correct entry point.

"Just there, third door on the left." Back we went. I proffered my barcoded paper and the receipt for £1.20. Ignoring them, and without looking up the radiologist asked a question.

"What's the problem?"

"My left knee," I said, holding the offending joint and wincing in a suitably pained manner, like a footballer wanting a free kick.

"Stand over there," he said, pointing at some cream-coloured machinery. At one end was a barrier with a small curvature in the narrow, top edge, like a seat.

"Do I sit?" I asked.

"No," he said, grumpily. He went back into his control room, flicked a lever and I could now detect the camera rising to the level of my knee. Fearing further rebuke, I stood stoically as still as I could. After a few seconds he came back and turned me through ninety degrees to get a sideways shot.

"Finished", he said. I wasn't quite sure whether we had to stay and wait for the traditional X-rays that actors in shows like Casualty throw up against a light box. So, I just stood there with a blank look.

"You can go," said the radiologist. Back we went to cantankerous Dr Şefik's waiting room. A short while later we were in his office again. Miraculously my X-ray was already on his computer. He swivelled the screen to show me.

"You need a full knee replacement operation," he said. I was in such pain I would have readily agreed to an amputation.

"How much will it cost?" I asked

"About 1,500 Euros. But that's a lot, lot cheaper than in Europe," he replied.

Indeed, it was. A check on Google put the cost of a private operation in the UK at £11,400 minimum. I could also have told him that in the UK, if I couldn't afford to go private, as an NHS patient I might wait in pain for a year or more before even a consultant's appointment, let alone surgery. He was already pencilling me in for the op the following week.

"Surgery is on Wednesdays and Fridays," he snapped. "But first you need some tests," he cautioned. "Meanwhile buy yourself a walking stick, it will help." Four days later, stick in hand, we were back at the hospital. I was sent for an electrocardiograph, which passed without incident and then off I limped for urine and no fewer than eight blood tests. No fuss, no more than a five-minute wait, straight in and out. When the results came back Dr Şefik was more circumspect. He perused the print-out carefully.

"There are two readings here and here which are very high," he said. "There seems to be some inflammation or maybe something else. I don't think it's advisable to operate until the figures are much lower. I would like you to see a rheumatologist here in the hospital. Maybe he can fathom what is wrong." He telephoned a colleague and told him he was sending me upstairs. I was now at the back of a very long queue in a different department and this time I had to be patient. We waited nearly two hours before my name flashed up on the screen. But we were in the doctor's room for less than two minutes.

"Ha. I know what this is. Psoriasis," he said, pointing to a rash on my right knee. More specifically he meant psoriatic arthritis.

"You'll need to see a specialist in Izmir." He gave me a name. Now, I always thought psoriasis was merely a cosmetic disfiguration, ugly dead skin and red blotches but no great threat. A quick check of the internet illuminated me. The disease can actually trick your immune system into attacking your joints. A small percentage of people with psoriatic arthritis develop arthritis mutilans, a severe, painful and disabling form of the disease. Over time, it eats into your bones and can totally destroy the small ones in your hands, especially the fingers, leading to permanent deformity and disability. People who have psoriatic arthritis sometimes also develop eye problems such as conjunctivitis or uveitis, which can cause painful, reddened eyes and blurred vision. They are at higher risk of cardiovascular disease. By telephone, we made an appointment with the specialist Nail Hızlı for two days later. It transpired that not only had he previously worked in Tire's state hospital but his brother, a lawyer, actually lived in our village. We had seen his brother several times without, of course, knowing that he had a doctor sibling. Doctor Nail spoke pretty good English and, with my Turklish, we managed to work out a plan of action.

"You'll need to take four types of tablet, two once a week, two every day, twice a day," he said. "If all goes well you probably won't require an operation," he forecast. It was uplifting news. I had already consulted an 80-year-old friend in the UK about knee replacement surgery. He had had the operation only a year earlier and swore it was a "life changer" albeit after six months of terrible pain. I could have kissed doctor Nail. Everyone I spoke to said Dr Şefik was a wonderful surgeon. But if medication could do the trick why opt for being a part Meccano man?

Of course, Turkish villagers try wherever possible to avoid hospitals, pharmacies and synthetic medicines. They often rely on homeopathic remedies, cures passed down through generations. Once when I was ill with flu our neighbour Birgül came around and cut up potatoes into thin slices. I thought she was making a potato gratin. Instead she placed them carefully on my forehead and bandaged them into place. I looked like footballer Terry Butcher in that famous England match but without the blood.

"That's for the fever," she said.

"But I don't have a fever," I protested. "I just feel really grotty." She just smiled. The following morning, I woke up to find my tee-shirt was soaking wet with sweat. I wasn't 100 per cent but I felt a whole lot better. Another village miracle cure is St John's Wort (*kantaron*). Villagers either grow it or pick the wild version. They boil it up for medicinal tea or leave it in olive oil for six months. The golden oil turns red and the ensuing mixture is used as a drink but also to rub on cuts and to treat burns. It produces an amazing plastic like film over any cut. The locals make their own soap, too, from olives, boiling up a steamy cauldron of gloopy mixture. It's meant to be good for your complexion and indeed many elderly villagers have skin that appears far younger than their years. For my bad knee the villagers prescribed eating cow's foot soup and regular rubbing with methanol. But I stuck with Doctor Nail's tablets.

Like everyone, the locals have their aches and pains. But working the land in all weathers seems to keep them pretty fit. One day, however, I looked out from our house and thought one of our neighbours, Ayse, in her eighties, was having a heart attack. She was lying on her back outside her house on a path moving her upper body from side to side. Having done a First Aid course, I ran out expecting to put my CPR training to good use. In fact, Ayse was merely collecting a bunch of sticks which she had tied up with rope like a makeshift rucksack and was wriggling into the shoulder straps. I stopped in my tracks as she heaved the kindling on to her back, quickly stood up and shuffled into her front garden.

Another staple for those in chronic pain is a trip to the thermal baths. We had twice been to Turkey's most famous example in Yalova, where Atatürk himself was a frequent visitor and where he later built a house. Apart from the swimming pools, containing mineral rich water at a temperature of around thirty-six degrees, there are Turkish baths, hot and cold plunge pools, massage rooms and all manner of other therapeutic services. In one public area there is a weird structure about five feet high that looks like one of those air vents you see on ships. You stick your head in and breathe in the sulphur to cure bronchial conditions. There are also public fountains where you can drink the miracle water.

Before a return check-up at Doctor Nail's I had to have my bloods taken again. Back we went to the hospital, where, after paying fifty lira (about £7 at the time) we were assigned to a female doctor called Şerife. We didn't need a consultation, just a computer entry to send to the haematology department upstairs. But there was a long queue. Carolyn marched me straight to the front and, despite my grave misgivings that we committed the most un-British of calumnies, we pushed in. It's actually something the Turks do all the time but I felt terrible. I haven't felt so embarrassed since the special cotton wool pad, impregnated with a sticky menthol solution that I used to wear as a child for a wheezy chest, slipped out on to the stage as my junior school did a dance in front of a thousand people at a top London theatre. A man now behind us pushing his elderly mother in a wheelchair said nothing but I hoped he wasn't carrying a weapon.

Had it been Dr Şefik he would probably have had a thrombosis at our impudence but Dr Şerife simply smiled and, when I told her what was required, she dutifully tapped the relevant information into her keyboard. We had to pay another £3.50 but by the time we reached the blood testing room I was mortified to see the man and his wheelchair-bound mum just ahead of us in the queue. Had the roles been reversed I would probably have given him a withering look. But the man just smiled and made a motion with his arms like footballers do when they are injured and want to be substituted. He was telling me to check the screen and watch for my name.

I was in and out in fifteen minutes. For the results, I had to return to Dr Şerife in the afternoon. When we arrived, her secretary gave me a number. Still racked with guilt from the morning's queue-jumping episode, I decided to wait my turn. It was a grave mistake. Carolyn kept urging me to make my presence known to the doctor but I demurred. At 4.30pm with about five patients still waiting the patient listing screen was switched off and the secretary went home.

"I must be in the system," I told Carolyn. A cleaning lady arrived in a royal blue tunic with a mop and duster and began her duties. Then another woman turned up who was obviously a friend waiting for Dr Şerife to finish. There was just one man ahead of me now. A youngish chap in a suit. The doctor's door opened and would you believe it? Mr Suit wasn't sick at all but a salesman flogging some medical equipment. He was quickly batted away. I looked in to see the doctor putting on her coat. When she saw me she looked a bit sheepish.

"I'm sorry," she said, "surgery is over."

"But, but," I muttered. "I have a number."

"Sorry," she said. "The secretary cannot have entered it into the system and I've shut down my computer now. "If you go to the hospital's information desk, the staff can print out your results." At that point her friend came to my rescue.

"The people at the information desk have gone home," she volunteered. The thought of coming back the next day and queuing all over again did not fill me with joy.

"Dr Recep is still working," said the friend helpfully. Indeed, he was. Dr Şerife knocked on his door. Her colleague was with a patient but soon I heard the two doctors chatting. There was laughter, then silence. Then more laughter. But no sound of a printer whirring. Finally, after about ten minutes, Dr Şerife emerged with two sheets of A4 in her hand and passed them to me.

"Your readings show a big improvement," she said. "The infection is well down." And with that she and her friend walked out leaving Carolyn, me and the cleaning lady to exchange smiles. No operation needed. I was on the mend.

CHAPTER SEVENTEEN

VERY SUPERSTITIOUS

I am sorry but I don't believe in ghosts, the supernatural, miracles, crying plaster Madonnas, UFOs, astrology, demonic possession, angels or levitation. As a journalist I once had to spend a night (well up until 1am) in what was considered the UK's most haunted house, Chingle Hall at Goosnargh, Preston, Lancashire. Absolutely nothing happened. No apparitions, ectoplasm, floating dismembered hands. Zilch. That is apart for some random knocking on the bottom of the floor in opposite corners of the room in which I was standing. The house was home to two elderly ladies whose living room was downstairs and, as I bade them goodnight and left the building, I couldn't help but notice two long handled old fashioned copper bed warmers hanging on the wall exactly below the places where the strange tapping appeared to have come from. What a coincidence.

Another newspaper task that might have shaken my faith in astrology, had I had any, came shortly after the death of comic Les Dawson's wife Margaret in April 1986. In less than a year Les was stepping out with a glamorous barmaid called Tracy, who he eventually married in 1989. My news editor had an idea.

Why couldn't we contact Margaret and ask her (from beyond the grave) what she thought about Les's new romance? Yes, you've guessed, I was working for a red top tabloid at the time. It was a guaranteed page lead either way, whether Margaret scolded Les or gave him her wifely blessing. Of course, getting the interview with a dead woman was the tricky part. I checked my extensive contacts book and began to go through a list of people who claimed to be able to reach the spirit world. The first couple weren't interested but eventually I found a man who sounded promising. His difficulty was that reaching Margaret in the afterlife depended on a strict and specific astrological confluence. Jupiter and Saturn, Uranus and several other planets had to be in the correct orbit or it wouldn't work. I listened patiently as he scribbled something in a book, clearly working out the necessary pattern.

"So, when exactly will the planets be in the optimum assemblage?" I inquired.

"Well," said the medium. "I would say in about two or three months." That was news my boss would not want to hear, I surmised. I put my hand over the telephone mouthpiece and called across to the news editor, who as usual was sucking on his pipe.

"I'm sorry Jeff, the guy says we'll have to wait two or three months." The news editor quickly responded: "Tell him there's £500 for him if he can do it this afternoon." I relayed the offer to the spiritualist. There was a short silence.

"Wait a moment, there's something coming through." Sure enough the piece revealing Margaret's approval of Les's dalliance appeared in a prominent position in the following morning's paper.

Devout Muslims will always take the word of the Koran over any other beliefs. But there is still widespread acceptance of superstitions and old wives' tales in Turkey. Some are the same as in other countries: number thirteen is bad luck, so is breaking a mirror and walking under a ladder. By the way, until writing this book I never knew that a huge number of buildings in the United States have no thirteenth floor, due to superstition. Based on an internal review of records, the Otis Elevators company estimates that eighty-five per cent of the buildings with their elevators do not have a named thirteenth floor.

Did you also know that: A witches' coven consists of thirteen members. There are usually thirteen steps leading to the gallows. There are thirteen coils in a hangman's noose. The guillotine blade traditionally fell thirteen feet. And Princess Diana's car hit the thirteenth pillar at Place De L'Alma Paris France, which led to her death. Spooky or what?

I have my own story about number thirteen. One day I was on a Turkish Airlines flight from Izmir to London. My boarding pass said my seat was 13B. I walked down the aisle ... 9, 10, 11, 12, 14 ... what? There was NO row thirteen. I now realise that many planes ditch row thirteen due to superstition. But this was the first time I had experienced it on a Turkish flight. The plane was almost full and there were five other people who had been allocated a seat in the phantom row thirteen. A harassed cabin crew steward arrived.

"Are you travelling alone?" he asked.

"Yes," I replied.

"Good. You can sit over there. 10E." I found myself sitting between two Russians, man and wife, both in their mid to late sixties and each the size of an Olympic shot putter. I might as well have had handcuffs on. I had my hands in my lap and I couldn't move a muscle. No sooner had the plane taken off than the husband (in the aisle seat) asked his wife for something. She fished in a carry-on bag and handed him a small bottle. To my amazement, he undid his belt and wriggled his trousers to the floor. Then, he took the cap off the bottle to reveal that it contained some kind of foul-smelling liniment which he proceeded to rub into his hips and upper thighs. The stink was making me retch. But he rubbed all the more. It was like spending three and a half hours in a straitjacket on the physio's table in a Rugby League team's dressing room.

In Turkey the list of superstitions is much longer than elsewhere. Nazar, the evil eye, is much more than just a pretty blue charm that you can buy all over Turkey. It supposedly carries great power. The story goes that there was once a massive rock by the sea that, even with the force of a hundred men and a lot of dynamite, couldn't be moved or cracked. In this seaside town lived a man known to carry the evil eye. The townspeople persuaded the man to inspect the rock, and upon looking at it he said, "My God! What a big rock." The instant he said it, there was a rip, roar and crack and the unbreakable rock split in two. Part of the superstition is the idea that when someone feels envy, they cause bad luck. Many Turks therefore prefer not to talk too much about their success or happiness in order not to draw increased attention and thereby misfortune.

On an expat message board in Turkey I read a story about an American woman who was sent a package containing an evil eye charm by her Turkish in-laws when her first child was born. She didn't use them on the baby's clothing. When her son was diagnosed with cerebral palsy her mother-in-law's first comment was....."Well, you didn't pin the evil eye on him, what do you expect". The woman decided to get a tattoo of the evil eye motif and later moved to Turkey where she experienced more superstitions. Neighbours would melt lead, then prepare a separate pan of water containing bits of bread, onion, lettuce. They would put a towel over her head and hold the pan of water above the towel. Then they would dump the hot lead, which had turned into a liquid, into the pan of water. It would sputter and crack as the neighbours told her whether someone's "eye" was on her. The whole rigmarole would then be repeated on her tummy area, then on her legs.

In Turkey you should never button up your coat while facing someone because it's believed that this will shut out that person's good luck. Similarly opening a lock above someone's head with a prayer is believed to open that person's good fortune. If you are the first customer of the day in a shop when you hand over your money, don't be surprised if the shopkeeper throws it on the floor. This is considered good luck. He may also utter the words bereket versin. It means may it give abundance or more simply good luck. You should reply *"bereketine gör"* which means see your blessings.

On a holiday in the 1980s I read a tale in a Turkish newspaper that touched the heart of my grizzled news editor when I returned to work in England. It involved a teenage girl who had been bed-ridden for months with a stomach complaint. The family, based in a dirt-poor village in Anatolia, could not afford medical treatment and had instead turned to a kind of shaman or medicine man who put an allegedly magic amulet under the girl's bed, sadly without effect. My national newspaper paid for the girl to be sent to a top hospital and she was found to have a two-foot long "water snake" in her intestine. After it was removed, she made a complete recovery.

One of the best examples of superstition is the belief that gifted people can read your fortune from the grounds in your Turkish coffee cup. Levent's mum is a firm believer and has often read the cups for us. On another message board a woman wrote how twenty years earlier she was in Alanya on the beach when a gypsy woman came up and insisted on reading her fortune. The woman wasn't particularly impressed but was slightly intrigued when the gypsy told her she would meet and marry a handsome man with green eyes. About one hour later a very handsome Turkish man with wonderful green eyes came up to her and asked to chat. They quickly became friends but on their second date she learned that he had bribed the gypsy to "foresee" their initial meeting.

The same website had a spookier tale from a British restaurant owner. She told how two Swedish women came in one day and a waiter called Salman read their fortunes in a coffee cup. The first woman's reading was straightforward but Salman advised the second woman to see a doctor when she got home. A year later the woman returned and asked if Salman was still there. She had acted on his advice and a mammogram showed early signs of cancer for which she was still receiving treatment. Make of that what you will.

The history of fortune-telling and astrology goes back at least to the Seljuk Empire and the time of Tuğrul and Çağrı Bey in 1028. By the fifteenth century, the müneccimbaşı, or chief astrologer/astronomer was a recognised position in the Ottoman Palace. One of the Ottoman Empire's most celebrated was Taqi al-Din Takiyüddin who, before his death in 1585, built a huge observatory in Istanbul. Months later a comet appeared in the sky and Taqi al-Din interpreted it as bringing success to Sultan Murad III.

Nowadays in Istanbul you can have your coffee grounds fortune read in scores of cafes. One of the most famous is Melekler Kahvesi in Taksim, founded in 2001. There is actually a very set procedure for the activity. The Turkish coffee used in fortune telling should be prepared in a small copper pot (*cezve*). Only one cup is brewed and should contain a little sugar to help distribute the grounds and make the read easier. After the person whose fortune is to be read finishes the drink, the saucer is placed on the top of the cup which is then swirled around. The cup is left to cool. Some people place a coin on the cup as it's cooling to dispel negative energy. The reader interprets the grounds with the handle facing towards him or her. The right side of the cup represents the present and the left side the future. The handle area represents family and social relations. For around £22 you can even learn the art yourself during an hour-long demonstration in Istanbul's Beyoğlu district.

So, what are the other superstitions in Turkey? When someone is leaving on a journey it's extremely common to pour a glass of water over a mirror or on to the road behind them as they leave. The idea is that the person's journey will be smooth like water and that they will return in good health. Turkish people believe that some activities should start with the right hand or the right foot. For example, while entering a house, a person should enter with right foot first. When having breakfast, lunch or dinner, the right hand should be used first. In the same way you should board a plane with your right foot or get out of bed from the right side. Similarly, you should not eat a meal while having one foot over the other. It shows disrespect to others at the table and it is considered as the sign of famine.

There are many more. Itching of the right hand means unexpected money will arrive in the near future. However, itching of the left hand means you could be in for a sudden loss of money. Whereas if British people feel their ears are hot, it's said someone is talking about you, in Turkey it's when you have a ringing sensation in your ears. If the ringing is on the left side someone is saying negatives things about you, if the ringing is on the right side, it's more positive. Similarly, if your eye twitches it means someone is coming to visit you soon. There are literally hundreds of these shibboleths.

Bad luck: a rabbit running in front of your car, crows flying around a house. Bad weather: if the quince harvest is good the winter will be heavy. Laundry: should never be done on Saturdays and Tuesdays. Children: if you have to leave them alone place a broom beside them. If you jump over a child, he/she remains short. Boys: A lock of hair from a boy's first hair cut is put in his father's pocket to bring good luck. Afterlife: It is considered the sign of death when an owl sings in the eaves of a house. Graves: You must not point at a grave or a graveyard. If you do, the finger must be bitten and put under the foot.

In Istanbul there used to be a man called Sahan who read your fortune using three rabbits. Their names were Bonçuk, Siri, and Pamuk. Having crossed his palm with silver you gave your name to one of the rabbits who promptly picked out one folded-up piece of paper (like a fortune cookie) from a pile. The paper had a number on it and Sahan would then punch the number into a voice recording machine which would recite your fortune in English. He had a few imitators who didn't bother with the machine but simply let you take the fortune cookie the rabbit had selected.

Carolyn, who believes in most things supernatural from ghosts to ouija boards, was enthralled by coffee cup fortune tellers. So, one day in Şile I decided to play a prank on her. I had come to the beach early and asked the woman in the bar if she ever practised clairvoyance. She said "sometimes" so I gave her some detailed information about Carolyn and arranged that, when she arrived, I would order some Turkish coffee and ask for a reading. About an hour later Carolyn joined us.

"You'll never guess," I said. "This lady is an expert fortune-teller. Why don't we have some Turkish coffee and hear her predictions," I said. Carolyn readily agreed. A few minutes later the woman was staring into the porcelain with all the authenticity of Gypsy Rose Lee.

"Ah, I see a metallic blue car," she said. Carolyn, who drove a blue Peugeot, looked stunned.

"And look here, there's a shape that indicates a black dog." Carolyn's eyes were on stalks.

"You have a sister and she has three children," the faux oracle continued.

"That's ridiculous," gasped Carolyn. "How could she possibly know that? So, what about the future," Carolyn asked. The woman, warming to her task, peered deeper into cup.

"Yes, I see wealth, you are very lucky. You will be rich." There were other predictions about foreign travel and how our daughters' lives would shape up. Carolyn was so taken I didn't have the heart to reveal it was all a hoax. In fact, I didn't tell her for two years. She was fuming when she learned the truth and I was lucky to get any tea that night.

CHAPTER EIGHTEEN

KIDS AND CAMELS

As in many other countries, including the UK, working the land is a tough way of life. So, in Turkey members of the younger generation usually prefer jobs in factories, restaurants and offices rather than toiling in the fields or large allotments. The demographic of villages, certainly near large conurbations, is rapidly changing and the average age is rising.

In Kaplan, we have only two children. The village school, with Atatürk's golden bust still resplendent above one of his classic sayings *Ne mutlu Turkum diyene* (how happy is the one who can say 'I am a Turk'), has been empty for many years. The kids, Ahmet Can and Batuan belong to Soner, the man who grabbed the murderer's knife in the tea garden, are bussed to classes every day in Tire. But in the evenings or holidays, they too help out rounding up and grazing the animals and performing menial chores. We decided to give them a treat one day by suggesting a trip to the council swimming pool.

"Can you both swim?" I asked Ahmet Can, then eleven.

"Of course," he replied. So we agreed with their parents to pick them up the following day. There are actually four swimming pools in Tire. Two are in the newly-built Ramada

Hotel. There is a council-run pool and another is among a group of restaurants near the town centre. That one is empty and unused. The Olympic-sized pool was built years ago for a major sporting event but, not long after its official opening, a child drowned with no lifeguard in attendance. The council decreed it should immediately close and to this day it remains a forlorn monument to the tragedy. The other civic pool, near the local state hospital, is clean and well kept. Everyone has to wear a swimming cap or *bone* (pronounced bon-ey, from the French bonnet). It's a magnet for children in the school holidays and attendants periodically have fun splashing customers with giant hoses.

Inevitably, as a foreigner, a trip to the pool quickly turns into an al fresco English lesson. The questions soon fly.

"Where are you from?"

"What is your name?"

"What are you doing here?"

"What is your job?"

"Ah, you speak Turkish?"

"Do you like Turkey?" I took the kids to get changed and brought them to the side of the pool.

"Now you are sure you can swim?" I asked again. Confident nodding was the reply. Then without further ado the younger boy Batuan, then seven, jumped into the deep end and sank like an anchor straight to the bottom.

"Oh my God!" cried Carolyn and dived in. She was a regional swimming champion back in the day and also an instructor. Within seconds she emerged holding Batuan's head above the water line and bringing him to the side of the pool. I knelt down and dragged him on to the travertine.

"You have never been in water before have you?" I asked.

"No," he replied with a remorseful look. Just then his brother leapt in too and began thrashing about like someone being attacked by a swarm of invisible piranhas.

"You had better get him out as well," I said to Carolyn, who was already in rescue mode. A minute later both boys were sitting on a sun lounger, wrapped in towels, while I read the Riot Act.

"Look the water is very dangerous, if you don't know what you are doing," I said sternly in Turkish. But I knew they were eager to get back in. The teaching of swimming in pools is very patchy in Turkey to say the least. Even Ramzi, the man in charge of the civic pool admitted he could not swim, despite working for six years as a barman on a cruise ship touring the Caribbean. Carolyn, meanwhile, had walked to the pool's small cafe and returned clutching an assortment of garishly coloured flotation aids, including long, thick lengths of plastic which the Turks call *makarna* (pasta).

"Now, if you go into the water you must use these," I admonished the boys. They were quickly back in, with Carolyn and me trying to show them basic swimming techniques. It wasn't very successful. They were about as co-ordinated as someone who has just grabbed a live electrical cable. We agreed to take the boys back to the pool the following Thursday. But when we arrived, we realised that was a day reserved exclusively for women. The boys looked crestfallen. Carolyn and I had a quick re-think and wondered if we might take them to the seaside instead. A quick telephone call was made to their parents and the plan approved.

The ride to Pamucak took just forty minutes. They took to the sea like ducks to an abattoir.

"Urgh," they moaned. "It's full of salt. Awful." But they loved the sand and immediately began in turns to bury each other up to the neck. They seemed to be having fun so Carolyn and I decided to take a dip ourselves. Our backs had not been turned for a couple of minutes when we noticed the rascals had found a quad bike and were trying to hot wire it. When that failed, they attempted to jump start it with the older boy pushing and the younger one sitting in the driver's seat.

"Hey," I shouted. "Get off that." Undeterred by the swimming experiences, we decided soon after to take the boys on another treat when the circus came to town. By comparison to the Mongolian circus, mentioned in an earlier chapter, the troupe that came to Tire was quite tame. The highlight was a high wire act featuring a man shuffling along a metal rope while standing in a tin can. That certainly was impressive. Nothing went awry and no one's prospects of fathering children were jeopardised. There was one worrying moment when one of our charges volunteered to enter the big top's ring but it was only to be made fun of by a clown with a balloon, not the target of an axe throwing routine. The clown had Batuan standing opposite him on the outer ring and repeatedly came towards him as if to hand over a giant balloon. Each time the clown would accidentally burst the balloon before the kid had a chance to grab it. But in the end, before Batuan was exasperated enough to punch him on his big red nose, always a possibility, the jester delivered the balloon intact to a round of applause from the audience. Outside, after the show, we asked the clown to pose for photographs with the boys.

We decided to treat the kids to a Burger King meal. I went to the counter and asked if they had a children's menu but before the girl assistant could answer, Ahmet Can ordered a Double Whopper and large fries plus a portion of onion rings from the adult list. Batuan said he'd have the same. The pair ate as if they had been stranded on a desert island for a month. A few days later our good deeds earned us an invitation to Batuan's birthday party at Soner's house. It lies on a corner up a steepish hill just above the village square. The building is a single storey, flat roof structure. But Soner had hired a disc jockey with an impressive deck and an array of powerful speakers and installed the sound system on the roof. This would double as a dance area, guests throwing their shapes around a one and a half metre-high chimney pot camouflaged with a black bin liner. I had visions of the DJ playing some kind of pogo dance song by the Sex Pistols and the entire gathering crashing through the roof into Soner's living room. But fortunately, the gyrating was relatively reserved and the masonry held firm. I noticed all the women, in headscarves, were congregated in one corner of the roof space. If there was any alcoholic beverage it was well hidden. I had taken the precaution of bringing four cans of beer and, sitting in the corner opposite the village women, I shared my stash with two men I knew from the tea garden. Carolyn and I stayed until after the ceremonial cutting of a huge cake and then we made our excuses and drove home. We often see the kids in the village and definitely on special holidays when true to tradition they knock on neighbours' doors for some pocket money.

Not long after we arrived in Kaplan Soner approched me with a grin which suggested he had more toes than teeth.

"Hey George, there's a camel wrestling event in Tire tomorrow. Do you want to go?" he said.

"Sure," I replied.

"Then meet me in the village square at 9.30am and we'll go together." I reported the following morning but Soner looked bewildered.

"Where's your car?" he asked.

"I don't have one. We haven't bought one yet," I replied.

"No matter," he responded and motioned for me to mount the back of his motorbike. We headed off to town, neither of us wearing a helmet. The camel wrestling was held on a strip of land near the civic pool, which the rest of the year doubled as a lorry park. It was a very colourful and atmospheric occasion. We arrived at 10am to find a few thousand supporters already sitting on a tiered grassy bank where plastic tables and chairs had been carefully positioned. There were very few women in the crowd. I guess they were outnumbered fifty to one. As we walked through the entrance my nostrils were alerted to a strange combination of smells from the aroma of grilled meat to camel dung. Around the fenced-off camel fighting arena were stalls selling food, soft drinks and souvenirs, especially the famous orange scarfs embroidered with camel motifs, worn by aficionados of the sport. I passed a man hovering over a two-metre long barbecue. Above his head was a sign saying: "Grilled sausages - all certified one-hundred per cent camel meat." Nothing like incentivising the competitors.

As we walked through the throng, a friendly voice shouted us over and there at one table were seven or eight Kaplan villagers already drinking beer and *rakı*.

"Come, sit," ordered one of the men, thrusting a bottle of beer in front of me. I had no sooner finished it than its place was taken by a glass of *rakı*. It was as if I had wandered into the perfect pub, live sport, free drinks and bonhomie. Not wishing to appear a cheapskate, after an hour I wriggled out and bought a bottle of *rakı* from one of the stalls.

The sport, which some people might find cruel, involves two male camels tussling in a seemingly endless headlock. But experts will tell you the camels have a number of moves, including single, scissors, hook, fling, fork, leg put and leg lift. A camel can usually only learn one of these tricks, two at most.

The board of referees pays close attention to the type of trick the camel performs to guide them when they pair the animals for a match. Referees usually put together two camels who perform the same trick.

Camels fight by weight. Previously there were four classes *ayak* (lightweight), *orta* (middleweight), *basalti* (light heavyweight), and *bas* (heavyweight). Recently this has been changed and now the camels are usually categorized into three group, *orta* being excluded. Only camels older than twelve can wrestle in the heavyweight category. The camel who can force its opponent's neck virtually on to the floor - called overthrowing - is the winner. This is the most common form of victory. At that point two sets of men, each team dressed in an individual coloured shirt, rush in to pull the camels apart. But there are two other ways of winning, *bagirtarak* (screaming) and *kacirtarak* (bolting), the complexities of which are about ten times more obtuse than explaining leg before wicket in cricket to a Turk. Sometimes contests even end in a draw. When this happened in 2013, at an event in Selçuk, a fight between the owners of the competing camels broke out. The two teams usually employed to keep rutting camels apart had to swiftly move in to separate the belligerent men.

Referees are on hand to prevent biting and other non-regulation violence. Serious injuries are rare, since camels can usually only harm each other with their teeth and during fights they are muzzled. When muzzles fall off or camels prove especially aggressive, however, damage can be done. As the victor is confirmed, the crowd bays with delight. The events are routinely televised, some of them live. A cacophonous public address system offers a running commentary. The combatants, some weighing half a tonne, and carrying names like Thunderbolt, Falcon, Destiny, Black Ali and Jackal, are often egged on by the introduction of a female camel on heat. During the bout their mouths are usually dripping with foamy spit.

Camel fighting is said to have originated among ancient Turkic tribes around two and a half millennia ago. After Atatürk founded the Republic, it fell out of favour and the government condemned it as an unsophisticated, rather backward pastime. But in the 1980s it was rediscovered, government advisers deeming it was an important part of Turkey's culture and doubtless a potentially lucrative tourist attraction.

Most camel wrestling festivals are held in the Aegean region from November to March. Around one hundred fighting camels take part, with each camel competing in approximately ten matches. Some festivals attract as many as 20,000 spectators. It's quite a spectacle as the gaudily-attired camels strut around with their ornate saddles, tinkling cow bells, mirrored blankets and other colourful apparel. Most fighting camels are imported from Iran and Afghanistan, aged seven or eight, and are kept until they reach wrestling age of twelve or thirteen. While waiting to compete the camels are tethered in one area and spectators are free to view them and pose for photographs. The owners are incredibly proud of their animals and will often encourage foreigners to take a picture of them standing together. This is sometimes the prelude to an old trick on visitors from abroad when the owner tells you to rub camel spit all over your face because it is good for your complexion. Beware of that one.

Among the crowd wandered several men dressed up in the traditional costume of the Efe, a kind of swashbuckling mercenary fighter, complete with bandolier of bullets, gun and sword. You don't get that at the Horse of the Year Show. Also weaving through the crowd are groups of musicians playing lively traditional songs, sometimes directly into your face, touting for private performances that will earn them extra tips.

The camels themselves are celebrities and their value can rise to seventy thousand pounds or more. How long the sport can survive in an era of increasing animal rights sensitivities remains to be seen. In 2020 that national British treasure Sir Trevor McDonald was plunged into an animal cruelty row when he attended a camel wrestling event while making a programme for ITV. Campaigners slammed the broadcaster for "legitimising" cruelty. Viewer Catherine Joy was quoted in a national newspaper as saying: "I'm utterly horrified to see camel wrestling. This 'sport' should not be on our screens." Saying that, powerful voices in Turkey are trying to secure for the sport a coveted place on the UNESCO list recognising intangible cultural heritage. According to a university thesis from 2015, there are only around one thousand fighting camels left in Turkey.

Even if animal rights protesters eventually get their way there's already a possible plan B. In 2011 Ismail Egilmez celebrated when his beloved beast won the first-ever camel beauty pageant in Selçuk.

"I love that camel exactly as much as I love my family. It's as precious as my kids," he gushed. Necidet Durmaz, one the judges of the beauty pageant, insisted that wrestling camels are naturals as contestants in a beauty contest.

"The camels have much deeper feelings than all the other animals. They do all the right moves to please the crowd. They love it," he said. Who knew?

CHAPTER NINETEEN

ANNOYING HABITS

Throughout this book I rightly sing the praise of Turks for their innate and fulsome generosity. But it's fair to say they do have some rather annoying habits. Driving etiquette, for example, leaves a lot to be desired. To Turks a "one-way street" sign is merely advisory. And many a time I have pulled over to let an oncoming car pass only for a Turk to overtake me and block the entire road for several minutes. Anyone who has taken a British driving test will be familiar with the phrase mirror-signal-manoeuvre. Such niceties are completely alien in Turkey. The vast majority of vehicles do not appear to have been fitted with indicators. If such devices really have been installed, they must have rusted and perished through lack of use.

If a driver's side indicator (on the left in Turkey if you are behind) should ever begin to flash, it is by no means a sign that the vehicle is about to turn left. In fact, I would say in all but a few cases this, by contrast, warns that the driver is going to pull over to the kerb (on the right). That is because the driver's side blinker also operates an invitation for the vehicle behind to overtake. The driver in front is telling you the road is clear. Well, by clear, he or she means there is a few seconds available, if you are brave or foolhardy enough, to attempt the manoeuvre before the articulated lorry coming the other way at high speed will reduce your car to a thousand pieces.

As Billy Sevki Hasirci, author of the hilarious blog Arse About Fez, puts it so eloquently: "Overtaking in Turkey is equivalent to sliding three bullets into a six-shooter and sucking on the barrel." At night you might want to add another couple of bullets. While overtaking and straddling the central white line you suddenly realise that the oncoming moped is in fact a 48-seater coach with only one working headlight. Or the scooter in front, that you are just about to pass, is actually a lorry full of tomatoes with only the nearside red tail-light functioning. Once in daytime on a two-lane road I went to overtake a tractor and trailer with its right-hand indicator flashing. I was almost alongside when the driver, without signalling or checking his rear-view mirror (redundant in Turkey unless reversing at high speed), suddenly turned left. I avoided a collision by a whisker.

Speed is something most Turks seem to live for. Or should that be die for? Unlike in the UK, speed cameras, though they exist, are few and far between in Turkey. It's bad enough being passed by an oncoming vehicle going so quickly you can almost feel the G-force comforting your face. Far worse is when you are aware of someone behind you flashing their headlights. You look in your rear-view mirror to see the driver is so close you can count his fillings and read the brand name of his sunglasses. This impatience is most acutely seen at traffic lights. Turkish cartoonists explain the traffic light sequence as green, then flashing green, then red, then amber with a trumpet. Unless you are in gear, tyres smoking and ready to move off like Lewis Hamilton on the F1 grid, the split second that the amber light illuminates you can expect an extravagant blast on the horn of the vehicle behind. Once in Izmir, I stopped at a traffic light on red only for the taxi driver behind me to sound his hooter anyway, then get out of his cab and shake his fist at me for not simply ignoring the warning light.

Getting cut up is a daily occurrence. In one of the closest near misses I ever had in Selçuk, I was semi-amused to see the company name painted on the back of the van that had just lurched dangerously in front of me was FUKA. Then there is the unfathomable roundabout protocol. Until around 2019, when some new signage came into force on certain roads, the Turkish system was that on approaching a roundabout you had every right to go for any perceived gap. The amount of whiplash cases this causes would (if in the UK) keep Claims Direct in business for a thousand years. Then some local authorities tried to change the rules. If you were already on the roundabout you had right of way, as in the UK. Turks, as you might imagine, are not given to obeying rules, especially rules that are suddenly changed. In the UK, of course, in general, if a vehicle collides with the back of your own its driver is at fault. But I got dog's abuse one day on a roundabout in Torbalı when I had to brake hard as a car shot in front of me from an access road. The *dolmuş* (minibus taxi) behind missed going into me by the thickness of the driver's moustache. He wound his window down and questioned my parentage for not just ploughing on and forcing the infiltrator to brake.

So driving in Turkey is a constant game of "chicken" and driving carefully can therefore prove to be quite dangerous. If the other driver feels you might hesitate instead of putting your foot down, he'll attempt to join the traffic. Nowhere is this more heart-stopping than when approaching an inter-section with a narrower road. You are on a main thoroughfare when you spot a car or a motorbike approaching from a road on the right but at an irresponsibly high speed. Is he going to stop? You are not sure. To complicate matters, often the motorbike is carrying father, mother, two small children and sometimes a live animal, too. Or the biker has a pair of stepladders under his arm. Or his pillion passenger is holding a door. No matter, he still maintains his speed. You simply have to act like a Turk and brazen it out. Just keep going, even when the front of the vehicle or bike is a metre or more over the white line. He will stop. Just believe. And pray. Reading your mind, he finally stamps on the brake just in time, showing neither the slightest glimmer of road rage nor contrition as you hurtle past.

In 2018, Turkish man Abdulkadir Erdoğan shared a video on social media showing himself driving a car with his feet while eating from a basket of fruit. If you Google 'Hurriyet Daily News' and 'man driving with feet', you should be able to watch the video. There was a public outcry but Abdulkadir insisted he had committed no crime, claiming he was only indulging in "relaxed" driving around thirty-five km per hour on a side street. He was released, pending further inquiries, then posted another video showing him driving while smoking a shisha pipe. He was eventually jailed for eighteen months.

The kicker to all this is that the wearing of seat belts, though mandatory, is regarded as optional throughout Turkey. Abdulkadir was not wearing his as he imitated a Roman Emperor while driving. The feeling is you are a bit of a wuss if you put it on. Your taxi driver will only put his own belt on when passing a police checkpoint, for example in an airport. After all, Turks reckon they don't need it. They already have the blue trinket thingy *(nazar)* hanging from the rear-view mirror to ward off evil spirits and bad luck. And if that doesn't work there's probably a sticker on the back too saying *Allah korusun* (may God protect).

Talking of Turkish taxi drivers brings us to the second annoying habit: overcharging Johnny Foreigner. Because securing a taxi licence can cost the equivalent of tens of thousands of pounds a few unscrupulous drivers will resort to tricking customers to recoup their outlay. The golden rule is to check that the car has a working meter when you get in. If it doesn't, get out. Or if the driver has turned the meter off during the journey, refuse to pay until he states the correct price. Don't let the driver give you a price for the complete journey beforehand unless you've done the trip many times before and know the going rate. Sometimes there are bargains to be had because the driver might go "off the books". I've had a cabbie drive to his house with me in the back, park up and continue the journey in his own car. It was a good deal, a win-win situation. But you have to be experienced and streetwise. Then again, in Istanbul some have been known to cross the Bosphorus and back to add extra miles to a journey. Keep an eye on the meter and try to have the correct fare ready when you stop. Tipping is not expected. But if, say, you give a fifty lira note for a forty lira ride the driver will often not give you the change unless you specifically ask for it.

Always remember the denomination of the note you hand over. Some drivers will insist you passed over a fifty lira note when you actually gave a one-hundred lira note. I heard of a driver who kept a five lira note up his sleeve and would insist you gave it to him instead of the fifty lira note you actually handed over.

Duping foreigners, of course, happens everywhere in the world. But because Turks assume all foreigners are rich, some perceive they are fair game. Another trick, I am sorry to admit I fell for, was the shoeshine man's dropped brush. It goes like this. You are walking along a street behind a shoe cleaner carrying his wooden box of polish and creams. Suddenly you notice he has dropped a brush. You pick it up, run towards him and alert him to the mishap. He thanks you profusely and offers to clean your shoes "for free". You try to dissuade him but he's adamant he must repay your good deed. Half-way through the shine he begins to tell you about his sick wife who is dying of cancer and his son who was born with cerebral palsy. Now thoroughly ashamed that you are making this ill-fated man work for nothing, you begin fishing in your wallet for a note as the man dips in and helps himself to forty lira, several times the going rate for a quick brushup.

Years after I was duped, I was walking to my hotel through the Sultanahmet district when a shoeshine man, sitting on the pavement this time, appeared to drop his brush. I kicked it as far as I could down the road. My hotel was only a few yards away and, when I told the manager about the incident, he rushed out and, with fist clenched, told the man to "clear off".

In her book Yabanci (foreigner) Dutch author Ellis Flipse tells how a notary's fee for a fairly routine job dropped from one thousand five hundred Euros to one hundred and seventy-five in twenty-four hours after a Turkish friend interceded on her behalf. On a far grander scale, Alev Scott in her wonderful book Turkish Awakening describes property scams on naive tourists that have netted Turks millions of euros. They often involve a whole network of dodgy estate agents, lawyers and notaries. Most Turks would, quite rightly, view such behaviour as shameful. But a few would argue the tourists deserved all they got.

A man from Kent, who wanted to move to Turkey, told a sorry tale on a message board. He bought a house off plan and made a twelve-thousand-pound deposit. The finished house cost one hundred and twenty thousand pounds. Then on one trip he found dozens of footings had been made beside the villa where an olive grove once stood in an area the builder promised would never be developed. The businessman couldn't sell the new villas and the family from Kent ended up living next to a ghost town of half-built homes. The builder then remortgaged every villa without a *tapu* (title deed) to raise funds despite the owners having paid in full. Several owners lost everything. Management charges doubled then trebled, *Burası Türkiye*, this is Turkey, anything goes.

I have learned another lesson: never lend money to a Turk. He will come up with a sob story, ask to borrow some money and never give it back. I was especially disappointed in one English teacher at the college where I worked, who asked to borrow three hundred and fifty pounds, claiming he was in dire financial straits. Months after, having moved to a new job, he made a string of excuses when asked to repay the loan and never did. Worse was someone from our village, who asked to borrow two hundred and fifty pounds after an alleged car accident and never repaid it. We had given him work but now we don't speak any more. That's difficult when you pass the guy two or three times a week in the village. You would think your reputation was worth more than that. But apparently not. Obviously, he has never read Socrates who said: "Regard your good name as the richest jewel you can possibly be possessed of." When I told the story to a Turkish acquaintance he said: "Turks don't look at such things as a loan but as a donation".

Plain speaking can be another irritant. Turks are nothing if not blunt. "You've put on a lot of weight," they'll say. Or "phew, have you been eating garlic? Your breath stinks." Or "how much did you pay for your new roof? What? You were robbed". One expat even claimed a Turk asked if her husband was circumcised. Once, when Carolyn made Chinese food for a

Turkish couple who had become good friends, the wife took one mouthful and spat it back out on to the plate.

Litter, too, is another major bone of contention. It's especially worrying when you have dogs and thoughtless Turks, during a picnic, have deliberately smashed dozens of beer bottles at the scene. Some idiots even dropped broken glass into the fountain on the mountain top where our dogs jump in for a drink after their walk. The tonnes of litter left on the country's beautiful beaches is criminal. You'll find everything from soiled nappies to half-eaten food and, of course, scores of empty bottles. My public-spirited American language teacher friend Bill Rocap often goes beachcombing for litter near Bodrum. He once actually collected rubbish discarded by a man who was still lying on his beach towel. The man's wife gave her husband a nudge as if to say: "Hey, there's a foreigner here cleaning up your mess." But far from apologising the Turk looked insulted and claimed he was entitled to soil the surroundings because he was on holiday.

"I live here," said Bill, with a withering look. In her book Yabanci Ellis Flipse recounts how two English friends, who were running a hotel in Dalyan, had a lot of building rubble left over from renovations. Public spiritedly they found a tractor driver who agreed to take it away for a fee. But a few minutes after the man disappeared, they discovered to their horror that he had simply dumped the debris on an open stretch of land not fifty metres away. With our own building work most of the tradesmen just left the rubbish for us to clean up. When I complained to Volkan, after he had done the internal roofing work, he tried to burn the off-cuts of plastic sheeting, sending toxic fumes everywhere.

At the summit of the mountain above Kaplan, where we walk the dogs, there are numerous wind turbines. But as you hike to the top you can see, on the beautiful wooded slopes, a huge pile of thousands of polystyrene food trays obviously used by the workers who erected the windmills and then dumped. I took photographs and informed my friend Murat, a senior council official at the time, but nothing was done. In another spot someone had fly tipped a truckload of builder's waste, including old doors, window frames and linoleum.

Employees of the Izmir big city authority were equally guilty when erecting warning road signs on the route from Kaplan up the mountain every twenty metres. The signs arrived with a protective plastic coating. These were simply peeled off and discarded on the roadside. The whole road safety exercise was itself a bit of a farce. The signs must have been a job lot from another undertaking because they included warnings to "beware of deer" - an animal no one has ever seen in the area. A few months later council officials decided to resurface the road. The heavy JCBs and steamrollers knocked down twenty-five per cent of the newly installed signs, which now lay twisted and mangled at the roadside.

There was another example of muddled thinking in the autumn of 2019. Around eleven million trees were planted in a single day all across Turkey in a massive government-backed initiative to improve the environment and to get into the Guinness Book of World Records. But a few months later an official claimed up to ninety per cent of the trees may already have died. The head of the country's forestry union said the failure rate was three times what it should normally be because many of the hundreds of thousands of volunteers, who helped in the planting on November 11, 2019, were "not experts". He said it was wrong to run the campaign in a period without adequate rainfall.

As in many countries, red tape and officialdom can also be a nightmare. Who knows how many follicles have been forcibly torn from the scalps of foreigners applying for a resident's permit (*kimlik*). The process begins online but the government website is always crashing or malfunctioning. Often it will work in Turkish but not in English. So you have to use a dictionary and take your time. Sometimes you just have to put in deliberately inaccurate information in order to move to the end. The "errors" can be corrected later when you go for your face-to-face interview.

You should be able to complete an online application in twenty minutes but it has sometimes taken me nine or ten hours over four days. The interview stage, for which I have to travel around ninety minutes to Izmir, has its own traps. You need to ensure you have all the necessary documents, such as health insurance, four passport photographs and proof of money in the bank, if requested. Once the website gave me an appointment for 12.30pm. I arrived at 12.20pm to find half a dozen people waiting. Then at 12.30pm a guard emptied the waiting room and began bringing down the roller shutter doors. Silly me. Of course, 12.30pm to 1.30pm is lunch. I returned at 1.15pm to find a least two dozen people waiting in front of the shutters. I deliberately don't use the word "queueing" because in these circumstances the concept doesn't apply. Like a Primark sale in the UK, as soon as the doors opened the throng barged inside and each person was given a number. Finally, I was in a genuine queue. I sat next to a young Dutch musician. When his number was called, he skipped happily into the adjoining room where a row of officials awaited. About fifteen minutes later he emerged dismayed. He was missing a certain document and would have to begin the process all over again, starting online. Nightmare.

The *Göç İdaresi* office deals with every issue involving foreigners, not just residency. One day, after my number had been called, I was sitting opposite a pleasant and experienced clerk who was painstakingly checking my online application. Suddenly, two desks away, a huge row erupted. A female official had obviously refused some kind of permission to a man from Uzbekistan. It all kicked off and the disgruntled applicant began waving his arms and shouting. Undeterred, the woman shouted back even louder, throwing papers and documents at the man. After a couple of minutes, the official handling my case rose to his feet and went to the aid of his colleague. He, too, began shouting. The commotion continued for a good ten minutes, with two other clerks joining from another room. Eventually the foreigner trooped away, tears in his eyes.

Previously resident's permit applications had to be made every year. Then the system changed and a two-year permit was granted. However, having done everything asked of me and having paid for a two-year permit, when my credit card size *kimlik* arrived it was only for twelve months. I searched Google and found a telephone number for the Izmir office. When I rang it, a recorded message said I had to phone Ankara. And when I phoned Ankara a call-handler said he couldn't help, I would have to go back to Izmir in person. Surely not. I searched for an e-mail address. Eureka, I found two, one for Izmir and one for Ankara. I sent an e-mail to each outlining my plight. No reply. Three days later I wrote again. No reply.

I contacted an English guy called "Doc" Martin Redman who runs a brilliant website for solving expats' problems. He advised that an e-mail was useless. As the Ankara call handler advised, I would have to go again in person. Despite that I let three more days pass and I wrote another e-mail. I also wrote two letters and mailed them to Izmir and Ankara. Nothing came of the letters. Then bingo. I got an e-mailed reply from Izmir.

"After checking your application, it is understood there had been an error in our system," the e-mail admitted. Your new two-year *kimlik* will be posted to your address." Marvellous. Except two weeks passed and nothing came. I concluded Doc Martin was right and drove to Izmir. Fortunately, after explaining my predicament in my primitive Turkish, I was guided to the boss's office, bypassing the familiar row of clerks. But when I told my story to the top brass, he was less interested in the mistake than in the e-mail I had received.

"Who wrote it?" he asked.

"I don't know. It was unsigned. But it came from this office," I replied.

"Do you have a copy?" the official questioned. Then, using his own mobile phone, he took a photograph of the e-mail on my phone.

"I will look into this," he promised. I asked for and took down his personal e-mail address. A week passed. No news. I wrote him an e-mail. Eight days later the official said a new card was on its way. And after a further delay of ten days (and two months after it should have arrived) the two-year permit was finally delivered. I've heard a story about a residency permit being delivered to the wrong address and the applicant being unable to retrieve it. He was told: "You'll just have to start again." He would have to claim back any costs incurred from the post office, he was told. Good luck with that.

Once you have your *kimlik* things can still go wrong. Until I got around to putting my ID card in a special plastic folder, I simply had it in a wallet with my credit cards. One year the writing on one side of it completely rubbed off. You could see by looking at the reverse side that it was in date. But my name, date of birth, country of origin and the serial number of the card had vanished. I was due to apply for a new card in about three or four months and did not want to go through the rigmarole of a trip to Izmir and a lot of form filling to get a replacement. But the two trips I made to the UK and back during this time were interesting. Each time at passport control I was escorted to a senior official's office where a man with some serious metalwork on the shoulder of his uniform would sign into a computer and check my record.

There was the usual exasperation in 2019 when the government introduced a rule about the registration of mobile phones. Subscribers had to provide answers to a list of questions confirming things such as date of birth and resident's permit number. A helpful link to an online form was sent via SMS message. Despite filling in the details at least six times each Carolyn's phone and mine - each registered with Vodafone - were both cut off. We went into a Vodafone shop in Tire and gave our details to an assistant. She typed them into a company website. But we had to return two or three times each before my phone was reconnected. Carolyn's never was and, losing patience, we were forced to change to a different provider Turkcell. But there was a further delay because the switch had to be approved by the company you were moving from and an "exit fee" had to be paid.

The normal Turkish explanation for situations like this is a shrug of the shoulders and the phrase *Burası Türkiye*. This is Turkey. This is why I have avoided applying for a Turkish driving licence. You have to begin with an online application. But the system is invariably down or not working properly. If you do get an appointment at the relevant office, officials may want a notarised copy of your UK driving licence first to send off to the issuing authority and have it checked before starting the exchange process. If all goes well, you'll get a phone call (which could take as long as six months). This confirms the Turkish end has heard back from the DVLA. Documents you will now require include a photocopy of your resident's permit card, a notarised translation of an education certificate, a doctor's report which may include a hearing and eye test if you are over 65, a card showing your blood type, a criminal record check from your local Turkish court, receipts of various taxes and proof of address.

Many expats have done it and say it's not too gruelling. But many have also fallen foul on not being able to provide a relevant school certificate. Given the Wild West nature of driving on Turkey's roads, it's hard to see the relevance of being able to prove you got a GCSE in woodworking or whatever. But rules are rules. You can drive in the UK for up to twelve months legally on a Turkish licence. But there can be cost implications for your insurance and also some car hire firms are reluctant to hire to Turkish driving licence holders. And after twelve months you'll need to apply for a provisional licence and pass the theory and practical driving tests to drive in Great Britain.

Thankfully, there is a Plan B. If you leave the country at least once every six months, the clock is reset and you can drive on your English driving licence for a further six months. I have many other examples of institutional incompetence and tedious red tape but the re-telling is understandably dull. However, I will briefly convey two more episodes. When I first tried to register a foreign mobile phone for use in Turkey the woman at the government tax office where I had to pay my fee brazenly told me: "It's impossible. It cannot be done." I knew she was wrong because an American friend called Susie had given me a step-by-step guide. As soon as I mentioned her name the clerk's mood changed.

"Ah, you are a friend of Susie. OK you need to pay 128 lira." Moments later my phone was legal. Whether the idea of customer service is in its infancy, whether training is below par or whether many desk jobs interacting with foreigners are just crushingly boring, I have no idea. But most expats have experienced being given the run around in pursuit of some piece or paper they desperately need. Finally, there's the frustration of having your water, electricity or telephone cut off. Interrupted supplies are far more prevalent than in the UK. And repairs far slower. In May 2019 when the water company, putting in a pipeline, severed our telephone and internet cable in five places in one calamitous action, redress took almost nine months. It wasn't just us, the whole village was cut off. To add insult to injury the phone company Turk Telekom insisted on taking monthly direct debits from my bank account despite delivering no service. When I queried this, I was advised not to stop the payments because it could lead to a complete termination of supply and a heavy fine. The cessation caused no end of problems. Because the mobile phone signal was so weak, to check e-mail we had to drive to Tire and use the wifi in different cafes and restaurants. I must have rung the Turk Telekom customer helpline twenty times. Each time a call handler promised the fault would be repaired "by the end of the month".

Levent even went to the regional office in Ödemiş where a totally unhelpful official said the repair was very expensive and they didn't have any budget for it. That, despite a law that says supply has to be restored as soon as possible. The severed phone line was especially annoying for our friend Lütfi, as all calls to his restaurant had to come through to his personal mobile phone. After almost nine months the line was repaired with no apology. Some credit was accrued for the direct debit payments made during the intermission but it wasn't complete.

In the not too distant past in Turkish villages water used to be free. And many villagers think it still should be. In some places (not Kaplan) they simply refuse to pay the bills. So the frustrated *Muhtar* (head man) resorts to turning off the supply every day for a few hours forcing the disgruntled villagers to cough up. In one village the stand-off continued so long that the Muhtar's solution was to double the price of water. The villagers who paid simply subsidised the ones who didn't.

Burası Türkiye.

CHAPTER TWENTY

KIND HEARTS AND HOSPITALITY

We entered a small tailor's shop in Tire, no bigger than two telephone kiosks knocked together, and asked if the owner would sew up a seam on one Carolyn's dresses. He immediately stopped what he was working on, put her dress on his machine and sewed the seam.

"How much?" I asked. He threw his head back and made the strange clicking sound with his tongue, the traditional way of saying no or nothing. We had an even more bizarre experience on a tram in Istanbul once when Carolyn realised the seam of the dress she was wearing had come apart. A woman sitting next to her spotted her concern, rummaged in her bag for a needle and thread and sewed up the dress as we trundled along from the airport to Sultanahmet. These are just two of countless examples of Turkish kindness and hospitality.

That is not to say Turkey doesn't have its darker side. Once while waiting for a bus in Selçuk, a renowned tourist area, Carolyn realised her watch had been stolen. There could only really have been one culprit, a seller of wooden flutes, but he denied all knowledge, when she confronted him. A few months later we were back in Selçuk sightseeing. Carolyn had popped into a shop and I was walking ahead, towards an historical building, when a man approached me.

"Do you know the history of Selçuk?" he asked in rather good English.

"Well a bit," I replied.

"For instance, do you know about the wonderful architecture over there," he said, pointing vaguely into the distance at a mosque. I was squinting at the skyline when I suddenly heard a commotion. Carolyn was running towards us.

"Stop, stop," she shouted. Then she pointed at the man.

"It's him, it's a trick. He did the same to me." I then realised the man was selling wooden flutes and put two and two together.

"He's a con man. He'll have the watch off your wrist as soon as look at you," Carolyn continued. The flute seller looked slightly shocked but did his best to maintain his cool.

"What are you talking about?"

"You," accused Carolyn. "You stole my watch."

"I don't know what you are talking about," he said. Then he added with a hint of a smirk: "I must have a double." His demeanour and body language were defensive rather than aggrieved or angry, which is what you might have expected from a proud Turk, accused of theft. But he knew we had no evidence and even though Carolyn had reported the stolen watch to the police there was nothing they could do.

Set against the hundreds of good deeds done to us over the years by Turks, the watch affair was a minor blemish on the country's integrity and fulsome generosity of spirit. Even in warfare this inherent humanity was often shown. You only have to look through the archives of the Gallipoli campaign, for example. During negotiated pauses in the fighting, it was customary for Turkish soldiers to swap cigarettes and photographs with the English, Australian and New Zealand troops as they dug graves. Foreign journalists reporting on events in 1915 praised the way Ottoman troops treated British, Australian and New Zealand prisoners of war.

Charles Suckling, a submariner in the Royal Australian Navy, was captured and brought to Istanbul. In a journal he wrote: "After getting off the ship we were brought to a place that I believe was a military barracks. As we walked on the streets it seemed that all the people in Istanbul were standing on both sides of the road just to see us. They did not show us any hostility. When we arrived at the military barracks, we were given Turkish navy soldiers' attire, jackets, slippers and a fez. With the help of a translator, the Ottoman commander said we should not consider ourselves as prisoners but guests of the Turkish state. We were to ask him if we wanted something and he would do everything he could to make it happen."

Compare this to the treatment of Allied troops by the Japanese in World War Two, for example. Lt John Pitt Cary, another Pow, also wrote of his captivity.

"I shared a house with other officers. During my time in Afyonkarahisar I drew and painted with oil paint. I fed one of the turtles I found in the garden as if it was a pet and organised betting games. I enjoyed racing my turtle."

Life was possibly a lot harsher for some other PoWs. But there appears to have been a genuine respect for most of the allied troops. Anzac Day on April 25 is a solemnly observed national day of remembrance in Turkey to honour troops of every nationality who fought at Gallipoli.

Mustafa Kemal Atatürk himself wrote:

"Those heroes that shed their blood and lost their lives.
You are now lying in the soil of a friendly country. Therefore,

rest in peace.

There is no difference between the Johnnies and the Mehmets to us where they lie side by side here in this country of ours.

You the mothers who sent their sons from far away countries wipe away your tears. Your sons are now living in our bosom and are in peace.

Having lost their lives on this land they have become our sons as well"

I have benefited from many other acts of generosity. One day, for example, crossing the Bosphorus in Istanbul with Carolyn, daughters Charlotte and Sophie and a couple of friends, newly arrived from the UK and laden with bags, I accidentally left a plastic bag at the ferry station on the European side. I realised only when we reached the Asian side. There was nothing of real value in the bag. No credit cards and such. But it held my dearly loved Tilley hat, some blood pressure pills, sunglasses and several books. I went to the kiosk at the landing point and knocked on the window. A man opened it two or three inches and peered out.

"I'm sorry. Can you help? I have left a bag on the other side," I explained in Turkish.

"Wait a moment," he said and shut the window, about ten minutes passed and I was just about to give up, especially as Carolyn and the rest of our party were anxious to catch a bus. Finally, the window opened again.

"Wait there. It will be on the next ferry, arriving in about ten minutes. A man called Ahmet will hand it to you," he said.

"Fantastic," I said and waved a twenty Turkish Lira note in his direction.

"That's ok," he said and closed the window. As he completed his mission, Ahmet did exactly the same when offered a financial reward for his kindness. Sometimes there's an ulterior motive behind the hospitality. One day when Levent lived in Yalıkavak, near Bodrum, we paid a visit to an abandoned village called Sandıma. It's on a hill and is famous for a number of old, white, stone houses that stand empty and crumbling on the rocky escarpment overlooking the bay. The story goes that the villagers abandoned Sandima because they couldn't make a living and were encouraged to exchange farming for the better paid trade of sponge diving. This is how Yalıkavak was founded. Nowadays, of course, the sponge diving has been replaced by tourism. Sandıma is empty but for one house owned by İsmail Erkoca, a sculptor, and his wife, Nurten Değirmeci, an artist, who came from Istanbul in 2004. They set up a studio there. You can't miss their home as you wander around and we were invited to have a cup of tea and a look round. It was like touring a museum. The house was packed with paintings, sculptures, weavings and other artefacts. At the end of our visit Ismail, who looked like Jesus, thin and gaunt in a simple white shirt, with a long mane of grey hair, kissed me on both cheeks and Carolyn on her right hand before bringing her hand to his forehead.

"You," he said to me earnestly, "you are Romeo." He turning to Carolyn.

"And you, you are Juliet." It was corny but after that farewell we couldn't leave without buying something. We handed over about £15 in Turkish lira for an oil painting of three whirling dervishes.

The Turkish sense of hospitality continued when we pitched up in Kaplan. No sooner had we arrived than restaurant owner Lütfi offered to drive us to town and back every day until we bought a car. At other times Ibo, the friendly taxi driver we found, was always just a phone call away, whatever the predicament. We were still exploring Tire when one Saturday we wondered if any tea houses of cafes were showing Premier League football live. We wanted to watch our beloved Tottenham Hotspur. We asked two teenage boys passing in the street and they suggested a place about fifteen minutes' walk away. Instead of simply giving us directions they insisted on escorting us there, asked the cafe owner to change the TV channel and then bought us several teas before they left at half time.

On another occasion, in a different tea house in Tire where we were watching football, we went to pay and the boss said our waiter had already paid for our teas and mineral waters before finishing his shift and had gone home. Carolyn and I were shopping in Migros supermarket one day when a worker said the female manager wanted to see us. We looked at each other and wondered why. Had we done something wrong? Had we not paid the correct amount on our last visit? Had our debit card payment been declined? We went to the manager's office like naughty pupils entering the headmistress's study. By contrast, she came out smiling and handed us a large brown envelope. We opened it and to our astonishment we had been awarded a "Customer of the Year" certificate.

"Thank you for shopping with us," she said. We were stunned. Another time Carolyn was at the hairdresser's in Tire when she complained about a pain in her foot. A couple of days earlier on a dog walk she had trodden on a stone and heard something click. She had been hobbling ever since. Demet, the shop owner was adamant.

"We need to get this fixed," she said. She shut the shop and used her own car to drive Carolyn across town to a metal workshop. The man there stopped what he was doing and listened patiently as Demet retold the story. Then he produced a piece of wood about 40cms square with what appeared to be a wooden ball underneath. He told Carolyn to put her foot on the board. But just as she did so he grabbed her foot and twisted it hard. There was a loud clicking sound and immediately the pain in Carolyn's foot disappeared.

"Wow," she exclaimed. "It's a miracle. No pain." Apparently, the man's father had been a part time chiropractor and had passed on his talents to his son. The fee? About £2. The bone magician refused to take more. And Demet drove Carolyn back to the salon to finish off her hair.

If there's one thing a Turkish village does not need it's a Neighbourhood Watch group. Knowing everyone else's business is an integral part of village life, which I find reassuring. Neighbours, realising you are away for a couple of days, will come in and water your plants. Go to the communal bins with some rubbish and a neighbour will ask: "What are you doing?" Get into your car and they will inquire: "Where are you going?" Arrive home and someone will say: "Where have you been?" As we drive in and out of the village, we often spot a face behind a twitching curtain. Some foreigners might find this annoying. But for me it's a sign that someone is safeguarding your interests. Indeed, the Turkish word for friend, *arkadaş*, literally means "someone who watches your back."

In 2018 I decided to go skiing for a week in Turkey. Carolyn didn't fancy it and stayed in Kaplan. I was a late adopter to skiing. Back in the day, every winter many friends begged me to join them on the slopes. But my sport was amateur football. I played Saturday afternoon and Sunday morning and I was always reluctant to let teammates down by swanning off skiing mid-season. But one year, when working on a national newspaper, I was offered a "freebie" holiday to the Spanish ski resort of Formigal in return for writing a travel report. I joined a ski school class of three, the other learners being an English brother and sister aged eleven and twelve who, naturally, ended the week far more adept than me. But a passion skiing had begun and in subsequent years I organised annual trips for my friends that saw us travel to wonderful slopes in Austria, Italy and France.

The largest group I managed was twenty-three. I would collect the money, make the booking and arrange the meeting point. For every ten places the tour operator generally offered a substantial discount. I would spend the rebate on "lucky bags" for the group that contained exclusively designed sweat-shirts, sweets and other bits and pieces. The trips were generally for two weeks. But some friends could only sign up for one week. In that case we would arrange for the seven-dayers to join for the second week and on the first night after their arrival we would always hold a fancy-dress party.

There were always crazy pranks. I remember one year, just before pal Brendan and his wife - seven-dayers - arrived at our hotel, we prised the door number off their room and stuck it on to a broom cupboard. As we "helpfully" led them up the stairs to their accommodation and opened the door Brendan famously remarked: "It's a bit small isn't it." It was probably an error on my part, one year, to include a water pistol in the lucky bag. One of our party was busy squirting anyone who came within firing range in our Austrian hotel when a stern looking man in a dark suit advanced.

"I am ze manager of zis otel and if you do not stop wiz this vater pistol I will have you ejected!" he boomed. Nonplussed the reveller, who wishes not to be named, replied: "If you are the manager, I'm Donald Duck" and promptly emptied half a pint of water all over the man's face. I can't recall what happened next. But I don't think he was expelled. Another perennial was to mark the end of the holiday by collecting small (foreign) change – nicknamed "dross" - from everyone and buying the so-called dross tree, some kind of plant. This would be presented to the manager of the establishment where we had been staying by way of an apology for our boorish behaviour. Looking back, I don't believe we ever did anything really terrible but the staff were probably delighted when our transfer bus finally pulled away from the forecourt.

There are forty-one places to ski in Turkey. I flew to Kayseri and a service bus took me to the modest hotel in the resort of Erciyes. The ski area opened in 2012 and the highest point is around 3,000 metres above sea level. There are fifty-five kilometres of piste and fourteen ski lifts. It sits in a highly conservative area of Anatolia and there is a huge and beautiful mosque on the edge of the main piste. Tourism advisers and ski instructors were imported from Austria and the lift system was excellently designed. My hotel was basic but friendly on the edge of the resort. A ski hire shop was just a few yards from the front door and nearby was the entrance to a major lift. Very convenient. Unfortunately, high winds meant that only one longish run was available to me. The lifts that linked the summit of the run to the rest of the resort were temporarily closed. I spent the first day getting my body used to the sport again. It must have been twenty years since I had worn skis. But I soon found my rhythm. The run next to my hotel was partly red, partly blue. Not too difficult. But I chose to go in early January and the near freezing temperatures meant the piste was hard and in places icy.

I am quite a defensive skier, not a thrill seeker. I'm just happy to enjoy the views and get down in one piece. Unlike resorts in Europe, there were no bars and cafes on the piste I was using. So there was no opportunity for a coffee or a hot wine and a chat with fellow enthusiasts. It was straight up on the lift and back down, with the occasional stop for a breather. I nipped back to the hotel for a spot of lunch and then resumed my solitary exercise until fatigue started to kick in around 4pm. That evening, when I mentioned the issue to the hotel manager Timo, he said: "No problem.

"Tomorrow I'll take you by road to the main skiing area and bring you back at the end of the day." Next day, as good as his word, Timo dropped me off outside a huge gondola station.

"Meet me in that five-star hotel over there at around 4pm," he said, pointing across to the Magna, a building that looked like a palace. After an exhilarating day exploring the slopes, I made my way to the meeting point. I left my skis and poles outside and clomped my way into the luxurious bar area. I spotted Timo talking to a younger man and he waved me over.

"Hi George, meet my friend. He's the owner of this hotel," he said. The suave, handsome friend looked only about thirty years old, surely a little young to be running such a high-class hotel, where rooms were around £250 a night. He and Timo spoke perfect English and soon the three of us were engrossed in chat. So much so, none of us noted the huge snowstorm that had begun outside. Timo took a phone call and suddenly I saw his expression change. When he returned he looked glum.

"My driver cannot get here to collect us. All the roads are closed. We are snowed in. The police have decreed that we stay put." Still wearing my ski jacket, salopettes and boots and realising I had only about £10 in Turkish lira on me, I pondered what to do.

"Have another drink," said Timo, as his boss pal asked if I would like some food.

"How about a beef sandwich and French fries," he asked.

"Sounds wonderful," I replied. My mouth salivating. After the meal, came more drinks and more chat and without spending a lira, I was asked if I wanted to go to my room. I was handed a key card, a hotel porter escorted me upstairs and we entered probably the biggest and most sumptuous hotel room I have ever stayed in.

I stripped off my ski gear and stepped into the shower. Unlike some Turkish hotels where you wait ten minutes for hot water here it was instant. A few minutes later, towelling myself dry, there was a knock at the door. I opened it to find a waiter holding a huge tray of fresh fruit the diameter of a regimental drum.

"Er, thank you very much," I stammered. The following morning, I joined Timo for breakfast.

"What's the weather forecast?" I inquired, hoping for another large dump of snow.

"Not good," he answered.

"The police say the roads are still not passable." What a shame. It was about 1.30pm when snow ploughs finally carved out an escape route. Timo and I thanked his hotel owner friend profusely and waved him a fond goodbye. I had already asked Timo what we should do about the bill.

"What bill?" He said. "Don't worry about it."

In 2019 daughter Sophie and husband William visited but had to travel to Bodrum for a friend's very expensive and high-profile wedding, with hundreds of guests. The best way was by bus from Aydin, about an hour's drive away from our village, and I volunteered to take them. Carolyn joined us. I did my research and checked where the bus station was in Aydin and to be safe printed out the details from Google maps. We arrived at the bus station which was pretty deserted about twenty minutes before Sophie's bus was due to leave and decided to kill time by having a tea in a cafe. After about fifteen minutes an empty bus pulled up and, to be on the safe side, I decided to check with the driver to ensure the Bodrum bus was on time.

"Excuse me," I said in my best Turkish.

"Can you tell me when the Bodrum bus leaves?" The driver, whose name was Mehmet and in his late fifties, looked at me quizzically.

"You're going to Bodrum?"

"Yes, well no, not me, my daughter and her husband."

"But my friend," Mehmet continued. "You're in the wrong place. This is the old bus station. They built a new one a couple of years ago and it's about five kilometres away." My heart sank. There was only one bus a day and now Sophie and William were certain to miss it. They would also miss the glittering pre-wedding reception with all their friends and, if they caught the same bus the next day, they would arrive in the middle of the wedding ceremony. I pondered the options. There was no choice. I would have to drive them all the way to Bodrum myself. It's around 155 kilometres and about a two-hour drive. Bus driver Mehmet realised that my brain was whirring. But he seemed very calm.

"Come, finish your tea." Then he took out his mobile phone and rang the new bus station to tell them to hold the bus.

"I don't believe it," I said to Sophie and William. Royalty wouldn't get this treatment. As we finished our tea, I asked the driver for directions. He started describing the route.

"Well, turn out of the car park, drive to the roundabout and go completely around because you need to be on the other side of the dual carriageway. Then take the third turn … oh don't worry. Where is your car? I'll show you." He jumped into the front seat of my Duster while Carolyn, Sophie and William squeezed in the back and off we went. I think the swanky new bus station was less than five kilometres away. But it was a ten-minute drive in heavy traffic. When we arrived, there was a one way system to a "drop off" point but a sign saying "no waiting".

"Ignore that," said Mehmet. "Just leave your car here."

"But won't I get a ticket?" I asked.

"Come on," he said waving his arm like an underarm bowler. Together we went into the station forecourt and up to the ticket office where I bought two tickets to Bodrum. Carolyn, Sophie and William were not far behind with their luggage. A man with a high visibility jacket and a walkie-talkie was eyeing my car.

"Leave it," Mehmet told him. "This man is my friend."

We handed Sophie and William the tickets and escorted them to the bus, which was on the stand with its engine running. Fortunately, the other passengers were not glaring or waving fists. They seemed quite relaxed.

"Thank you, thank you," I said to Mehmet.

"You're welcome. Now let's go and have another cup of tea." We drove back to the old bus station where it turned out that Mehmet owned the cafe we had been using and the waitress who had served us was his wife. He ordered another round of teas. Then Mehmet told us how about twenty years earlier he had been out of work and struggling. An elderly English woman he knew loaned him £400 and he used it to rent a minibus and start his own business. The venture went from strength to strength and now he now had five buses and ten employees, plus the cafe.

"I tried to give the money back to the English woman but she would not accept it." Maybe his good turn to us was in part a bid to balance his debt to the old woman. But I prefer to believe he would have done it anyway.

CHAPTER TWENTY ONE

FATE

My whole world turned upside down shortly before 10am on November 25, 2019, when Carolyn had a sudden cardiac arrest and died. She was 58. She fell in the bathroom of Number Two and I couldn't revive her. Soon the house was full of paramedics and Jandarma officers. It's hard to describe my feelings at the time. I'm rather ashamed to say I wasn't tearful. I blame that on my boarding school upbringing that taught me to shield my emotions. I was also in shock. I just stood there watching as the medical people, police and forensic team did what they had to do.

Levent was with me most of the time, explaining the procedures. Who knows how any of us will behave in extreme circumstances? I had to attend the local police station to give a statement, Levent and neighbour Aytekin came with me. Normally they would insist on an interpreter but, with my basic knowledge of Turkish and Levent's English, we were good to go. The officer began typing into a computer while simultaneously asking questions. Either Levent or I would answer. While tapping the keys he would break off to reminisce about previous cases.

"Yes, I remember one case. A woman had fallen downstairs and broken her neck. Or so it appeared. On the face of it there was no reason to suspect foul play. But we weren't quite happy with her husband's account of what happened. We made some investigations and eventually it emerged, after the post-mortem, that he had struck her and deliberately pushed her. He's serving a life sentence now." The officer carried on with his two fingered typing. His form was titled "suspicious death". The formalities over, I walked out of the police station still in a daze. We were given a document that would allow us to bury Carolyn but first there would have to be an autopsy.

A special vehicle took Carolyn to the Tire hospital's mortuary. But the lone driver needed help to bring her inside. So Levent, me, Lütfi and his son Serkan lifted her body bag and took it inside. The mortuary attendant opened one of the compartments but unfortunately it already had a resident. So did his second choice. On the third try he selected an empty compartment and Carolyn was laid to partial rest. The following day we had to return to help move her into another vehicle to be taken to Izmir for the autopsy. Arrangements at the Izmir hospital were better and a team of helpers was on hand to take her inside. But the following day our volunteers had to be back in position at Tire hospital to return Carolyn to the local mortuary. This time the group of friends insisted that I waited outside while they transferred Carolyn back into the metal compartment. The results of the post-mortem, I was told, would be communicated in three months.

Normally Turks are buried within twenty-four hours. Our time frame would be longer, about ten days. We had to speak to the head man of the village (*muhtar*). He was very sympathetic and said a place would be reserved for Carolyn in the local graveyard.

"We'll make the plot wide enough so eventually you can go alongside," he added helpfully. I appreciated that.

Hüseyin, neighbour Birgül's son, and a friend would dig the grave, it was agreed. I looked for someone who could conduct a ceremony and came across Gordy, aka Gordon Copsey, a lay preacher from Norfolk living in Kuşadası Over the phone I thought he was from the West Country. He sounded a lot like the comic Jethro.

"Do you want the robes?" he asked when I phoned.

"Yes, most certainly," I replied.

"Oh, and can I bring my wife?" he added.

"Of course." I arranged for our taxi driver pal Ibo to collect them from Kuşadası. Helped by daughters Charlotte and Sophie, I organised a two-sided funeral card. On the front was a lovely picture of Carolyn and our first granddaughter Emmy. At Charlotte's suggestion we also included a Turkish flag motif. On the back were the lyrics of the song The Hills are Alive with the Sound of Music. It was a song Carolyn loved and one she had performed many times in amateur dramatic productions and at family gatherings. On the day of the funeral Carolyn, true to Turkish tradition, had to be washed and placed in a special white shroud. This was performed in a building at a large cemetery in Tire. I went with Lütfi to oversee the arrangements and paid the woman whose job it was. Turks don't usually use a coffin, except sometimes to take the deceased to the cemetery. Any ostentation is frowned upon. The sentiment appears to be that the money is better spent on the living. We had been waiting a few minutes when Lütfi, turned to me.

"Come with me." He took me to what looked like a corner shop. I thought he was going to buy cigarettes. But because of its location the shop had three special lines, a reed matting which goes over the body in the grave, two carved sticks which mark the head and the foot of the grave and a clay water urn which is traditionally placed by the side of the grave following burial.

Muslims usually take the deceased to a mosque for prayers and there follows a ceremonial procession to the graveyard. Instead, we had arranged for a special vehicle. Many years before in Marmaris while sitting in a *dolmuş* I remember seeing a funeral procession pass by. I tried to take a photograph from a window as the body was being carried through the town. The driver stopped the minibus, jumped out and told the fifty or so mourners there was an English guy who wanted a snap. They happily posed for me as I shuffled, rather embarrassed, in front of them. At Carolyn's funeral I did not take a camera but noticed Levent taking photographs to record the event.

In the flesh, Gordy was every bit as crazy and funny as Jethro, white-haired, red-faced, with a dry wit and calling everyone "pard'ner" He got changed at our house but the ten-minute walk to the cemetery was all uphill and he was panting and more flushed than ever when he arrived. Levent had organised for the funeral to be advertised over the town's public address system and almost the whole village turned up, along with most of the parents of the English language pupils I was teaching. In the past women were not allowed to attend Muslim funerals. Times have changed. But I noticed most of the village women were huddled away in one group at the back of the congregation. Also present from England were Charlotte, husband Alistair and baby Emmy, Sophie and husband William, Carolyn's sister Melanie, her son James and Carolyn's best friend Kathryn.

The *muhtar* had chosen a prime spot near the road. But Gordy had to give his address standing nearby on a narrow cemetery wall. Wobbling ominously, he delivered his own version of the brief synopsis of Carolyn's life that I had prepared and then asked the congregation to join him in the Lord's Prayer, which seemed vastly different from the one I learned at school. Lord's Prayer Lite, we all agreed. Then Gordy seemed to sway in the wind and a couple of Turks grabbed him to stop him from joining Carolyn in the grave. Next up was a *hoca* (religious teacher) who was also part of the family who had previously owned our house. It hadn't been arranged but I was thankful for his intervention. It showed how much we respected Islam and how grateful we were for the kindness of the villagers and especially the *muhtar*. The *hoca* said prayers in Turkish. I couldn't catch exactly what he said but traditionally such prayers are designed to help the deceased on the other side. After that, the protocol is for the family to lower their loved one into the grave. After an earlier family discussion, we had agreed we weren't comfortable with that and Birgül's husband Yalçın organised a group of villagers to undertake the task. Afterwards we were invited to throw in soil and flowers. Zeki, the English language camp organiser, sent a huge six-foot flower arrangement. Hüseyin and his chum filled in the grave and we decorated it with more flowers.

In Turkish culture the dead person is remembered on the third, seventh, fortieth and fifty-second days after death with religious ceremonies and meals. People tend to visit graves on religious festivals or on the day before them. During these visits they pray in front of the graves, burn incense and candles and distribute money, sugar, sweets and foodstuffs prepared at home. Carolyn and I had been in the village tea garden one time when neighbour Fadime was remembering the death of her husband. Food and milky yoghurt were distributed to anyone who was there. We tucked in. Sometimes a special van is commissioned to cook and hand out a sweet fried doughnut called *lokma*.

After the funeral ceremony, everyone was invited back to a private room at the back of the village tea garden for a teetotal wake but only a handful of non-family members took up the offer. I had prepared a selection of photographs of Carolyn charting her life. We shared many happy memories. This was a moment for remembering the fun times: like the skiing holiday fancy dress party where she went as a gin and tonic and the day, she bought a Christmas tree so huge three men had to carry it up four floors to our flat in a converted mill in Derbyshire. The following December when we drove into the farm where she had bought it everyone ran away and hid. Then there was the time she insisted on buying a huge turkey in England and bringing it back for Christmas dinner in Kaplan.

"You can't get them over there," she said. When we later went to the supermarket in Tire they were selling dozens of them at a third of the UK price.

Carolyn was incredible at a variety of jobs, interior design, flower arranging and planning out a garden. She once earned a tidy side income buying women's dresses on eBay, re-photographing them on a mannequin and re-selling them at a substantial profit. Wherever she worked, usually in sales, she was invariably top of the leader board. Once, she was tasked by a major insurance company to tell customers that their premiums had been wrongly calibrated for several years and that they would rise by more than 200 per cent. Her retention rate was a staggering seventy-eight per cent, when most colleagues were struggling to reach double figures. She was also brilliant at team building, spending hours making stuff to decorate offices for events such as Halloween or the World Cup Finals.

"Every office needs a Carolyn," one of her bosses famously said. We both agreed that our greatest achievement was producing two beautiful and talented daughters who, through their hard work and self-motivation, had carved out excellent careers. When the tea, cake and chatter was over we summoned a taxi to take Gordy and his lovely wife Rosemary home to their seaside flat and we walked back to the summer house.

We were still reminiscing when our dentist friend Cem, his wife Zeynep and son Cem Kaan, arrived. Although we had kept in touch via WhatsApp and the odd phone call, we hadn't seen the family in person for more than a year so their visit was a pleasant surprise. Cem Kaan explained how he had really enjoyed his ten months in England and confirmed his proficiency in the English language with some colourful swear words.

The Turks have a phlegmatic view on death. They will often use the word *kader* (destiny). Muslims fundamentally believe that this life is merely a trial for the after-life. Hopefully your loved one is now on his or her way to "the garden" there to wait for Judgement Day. That evening our family and close friend Kathryn went to the *Dağ* restaurant for a meal. Despite the circumstances, it wasn't a sombre occasion and the food was excellent. True to form, owner Lütfi refused to take any payment. Melanie, James and Kathryn were staying at the newly-built Ramada Hotel in Tire. Carolyn and I had called in five or six times asking when the indoor swimming pool would be ready, as she wanted to buy a season ticket to use it. She loved her swimming but sadly the hotel's new pool was an experience she never lived to enjoy.

As promised the autopsy results arrived three months later. The two-page report blamed a build-up of material in Carolyn's arteries. I was formally absolved of any blame and discharged from any threat of criminal prosecution. A few weeks after Carolyn's funeral I bought a headstone and fitted it myself. By Turkish custom I should really have waited a year. But I wanted to finish it and to show Charlotte and Sophie. As the Turks say: *"Hayat devam ediyor"* ... Life goes on.

CHAPTER TWENTY TWO

MOVING ON

Levent stretched across the dining room table and poured me a tea. "What will you do now? Will you go back to England?" I looked out of the window and watched a villager leading a flock of sheep down the hill. As he noticed me he raised a calloused hand, waved and smiled. I dropped a sugar cube into the tulip-shaped tea glass and swirled the brown boiling hot liquid with a tiny spoon. The decision was pretty straightforward. The lifestyle, the weather, the hospitality, the food and much more were compelling me to stay. It was not going to be easy to live alone after sharing a life for nearly forty years. But growing up as an only child, including many hours spent playing table football with myself and boarding school where I had to be emotionally strong and independent to survive, reassured me. Thanks to technology, video chats to family and friends were only a computer click or two away. Then there was Darcy and Willow. I did not want to uproot them and send them 2,000 miles to a strange environment.

"No, I think I will stay in Turkey," I said to Levent.

"Good. If you are happy here, why not?" he replied. I joined a social network called Inter Nations which held events and get togethers. On a visit to a winery near Izmir airport, I was amazed to learn Turkey had a nearby training centre for astronauts. On the wall of the winery's restaurant were framed photographs of famous American spacemen and women who had visited while lecturing at the facility. And via an expats' Facebook group I made some new friends in Kuşadası. Two of them, Alan and Ann Kennedy, ran an animal charity and I donated Carolyn's clothes to raise money for vets' bills. The couple also hosted a weekly trip to local restaurants for up to ten people and I joined in the soirées. Two months before she died, Carolyn and I had rented a house by the seaside at Yoncaköy in Aydin province about twenty minutes' drive from Kuşadası. The dogs loved romping on the beach and we loved feeding the strays. So I would leave Darcy and Willow there for a few hours on their own during the Tuesday night outings.

Of course, I had no idea that the coronavirus pandemic that rocked the world from early in 2020 would soon impose an extra layer of isolation. The Inter Nations events went online and the Kuşadası dining stopped altogether. The government, as elsewhere in the world, imposed severe restrictions. For three months I could no longer travel to the seaside house because journeys between provinces were banned. At its height people my age in Izmir province were allowed out only between 10am and 1pm and not at all at weekends. But the rules were not strictly enforced in Tire and not at all in the villages. I took the dogs for their daily walk at whatever time I chose. But otherwise I stuck pretty firmly to the rules on movement and wore a mask at all times.

I took on some extra students who wanted to learn English online. They included Lütfi's new wife Naime. Teaching her without charge would be a way of repaying him for all the kindnesses he had showed to Carolyn and me over the years.

The lessons helped to break up the solitude, which I learned to handle. Between August and December 2020, before travel restrictions between countries were imposed, I returned to the UK four times for work, to see family and, on the final trip, to celebrate Christmas. I had planned to fly back to Turkey on Boxing Day because I had an appointment early in January 2021 to renew my resident's permit. Missing the personal interview usually meant you had to begin the process all over again. My permit had actually expired on December 24th. But if you have already made an application to renew, have paid the relevant taxes and have all the paperwork you are normally allowed to travel for fifteen days with an out-of-date card. When I arrived at the check-in desk at Manchester airport, however, things quickly became awkward.

"Your resident's permit is out of date," said the Pegasus Airlines assistant.

"Yes, I know but look, here is the documentation to show I am due to have an interview at the immigration office next week," I replied.

"I'm sorry. But I don't think you can fly. We have just turned away an Iranian man in the same situation," she said. My heart sank. The prospect of the dogs staying in kennels and leaving the various properties unattended for an indefinite period, plus missing my permit interview filled me with dread.

"Look, let me photograph your documents and send them through for someone else to make a final decision," said the attendant. I had to stand at the side of the queue as happy travellers collected their boarding cards. After ten minutes the attendant called me over.

"I need to photograph them again. In Istanbul they say they can't read the papers," she said. Morosely, I resumed my vigil at the side of the desk. After a further ten minutes I saw the attendant speaking to a senior male colleague. He beckoned me over.

"Okay, you're good to go. Everything is in order." I could have kissed him. Direct flights to Izmir had been scrapped months earlier following the Covid 19 outbreak. So I had to dog-leg home via Istanbul. When I arrived at around 10pm at the city's Sabiha Gökçen airport, I followed a queue to have a polymerase chain reaction (PCR) test that determines if you are infected. I paid my two-hundred-and-fifty lira and was led to a booth where a white-coated man put his arm through a hole in a plastic window and inserted a long stick with a cotton bud on the end down my throat and then up my nose. I gagged both times and was glad I had not eaten on the flight. He gave me a piece of paper with a barcode on it.

"You can see your results in about three hours," he said, passing me a form with a list of instructions about pandemic precautions. Whatever the result of the PCR test I had to quarantine for seven days and then have a second test. So there was no way I could make my rendezvous at the immigration office. I would need to sort that out later. I had a nine-hour layover before the onward flight to Izmir so used my membership card for one of the airport lounges and tried to relax. Mine was one of the last flights before the airport closed for the night so the lounge was empty. Half a dozen cups of coffee and more than three hours later, I keyed in the barcode number on a Turkish website and received the news that my test was negative.

On landing in Izmir, I collected my car from the private car park just outside the airport, drove to the kennels to pick up the dogs and then headed home. When my second PCR test at the Tire hospital also came back negative, I made my way nervously to the immigration office in Izmir. They were quite entitled to make me start the permit application all over again. But a pleasant lady on the reception desk who spoke Turkish, English and Arabic took pity on me when I showed her my flight ticket from the UK and the negative test results.

"Here, take this number," she said, handing me a ticket from the machine. "You shouldn't have to wait long." The office was unusually quiet and there were plenty of spare seats in the waiting room as I looked anxiously for my number to light up on the screen. An hour later my application had been processed and sent to Ankara where the new card would be issued.

Levent had given me a lift to Izmir because he was visiting his mother Suzan, now in her mid-eighties, in hospital. A heavy smoker, her lungs were working at only twenty per cent and she also had trouble with her kidneys. After being admitted she then contracted Covid-19, although she appeared to have no symptoms. Doctors told Levent to prepare for bad news but Suzan seemed to rally and was allowed home. It was a false dawn. Three days later she was re-admitted to hospital in Tire and after a further few days she died. It was strange to experience, once more, the Turkish burial ritual I had endured with Carolyn. For reasons unclear Levent decided that Suzan would be buried in Tire's main cemetery, not in the village where Carolyn lay. With our mutual friend Lütfi, I helped him move Suzan from the mortuary to the funeral vehicle. When we arrived at the cemetery, where Suzan's body was to be washed, we discovered that the water had been cut off due to the ongoing installation of natural gas in the town. *Burası Türkiye.* The manager was apologetic.

"Why don't you go and have a tea while I call the regional manager of the water company," he said. Levent and I drove a few hundred yards to the shop/cafe where Lütfi had taken me in November 2019 to buy the paraphenalia for Carolyn's grave.

We sat on plastic chairs awaiting news. An hour later the water had been reconnected and the washing done. We returned to the cemetery where an elder from the mosque read prayers in front of a simple wooden coffin draped with an embroidered green cloth. I had brought flowers but they were the solitary bunch. It's not a tradition in Turkey, I was told. At the graveside I again helped to carry Suzan from the coffin in a white canvass bag to her last resting place. There were more prayers and then workers and a few people who had come to pay their respects took turns to shovel the heavy clay soil and rocks into the grave.

Suzan had been there at the start of my love affair with Turkey. It was sad to think she would no longer be a part of that. I thought back to the many times I had visited her and Levent over the years. After preparing tea she would always bring out the photograph albums and we would laugh and reminisce about previous times. One of my favourite memories was a visit to her relative in Gölcük about an hour's drive East from Istanbul. The roof of the family's wooden home was built out of flattened tin cans still displaying the companies' logos and the couple's seven children all had names beginning with the letter "E". My own mother died aged 53 when I was 23. Suzan had been like a surrogate mother to me, always checking on my welfare. And maybe I had been like a second son to her. Whenever we met after an absence, she would always hug me and call me *benim canım*, my dear.

A romance with a country is similar in many ways to a romance with a woman. There are highs and lows but always a mutual understanding, a feeling that you belong. Turkey has its idiosyncrasies, its volatile economy for example, always seemingly on the brink of collapse, its labyrinthine bureaucracy and the random electricity cuts. Like a partner's snoring you just get used to it. But it also has natural beauty and innate warmth, charm and friendliness, which never wanes. It had been quite an adventure, from the early wonderment of visiting sights like Nemrut, through the years of being part of the community in Şile to making a permanent home in Kaplan. I went to a local photographer's shop (Foto Tahsin) and asked him to take a photo of me to use on the back cover of this book.

"Don't print it just put it on a memory stick," I told him. He took a dozen shots and did as I requested.

"How much do I owe you," I said.

"Nothing," he replied. I urged him to take a fee but he refused. This is Turkey. Around the time of Suzan's death my youngest daughter Sophie announced she was pregnant with her first child. It was uplifting news and another reminder about the circle of life.

There are big plans for Kaplan. A national hiking association wants to include the village on its authorised list of walking routes. If that happens it will bring even more visitors and there is talk of more overnight accommodation opening and the possibility of the abandoned primary school being turned into a hotel. Some professional incomers are also lobbying Turkcell to erect a new telephone mast to improve the wifi. There's even talk of a village shop opening. If the march of progress continues at this pace, we might even get a minibus to go with the shiny but still unused bus stop.

Pic 1 Sue, George and Levent circa 1972

Pic 2 Danny, Gary and the viola da gamba

Pic 3 The derelict barn at Kaplan

Pic 4 The barn after renovation

Twelve Camels for Your Wife

Pic 5 House number two

Pic 6 Carolyn, George, Willow and Darcy.

Pic 7 George and Carolyn. Sultan and Sultana.

Printed in Great Britain
by Amazon